Developmental Evaluation of Children and Adolescents: A Psychodynamic Guide

Developmental Evaluation of Children and Adolescents: A Psychodynamic Guide offers an in-depth, multiperspective analysis of any delays, regressions, or aberrations in a child's developmental trajectory.

Blackman and Dring help the evaluator understand the child's internal conflicts, as well as the family/environmental context in which the child functions. Chapters move longitudinally through the developmental stages. In each chapter, there are several "key questions" for evaluators to ask parents, fulfilling the need for clinicians to quickly assess children, followed by a longer question sheet and explanation of various answers to the questions for a more thorough assessment. Each chapter also provides a discussion of the child's phase and a table listing the questions and answers for quick reference. Finally, brief case studies demonstrate how the developmental history and the initial session with the child should be integrated.

This book serves as an essential clinical guide to the developmental evaluation of children and will be suitable for all therapists working with children.

Jerome S. Blackman, MD, who has been in private practice of psychoanalysis and psychiatry for 47 years, is Professor of Clinical Psychiatry at Eastern Virginia Medical School and Training and Supervising Analyst with the Contemporary Freudian Society in Washington, DC.

Kathleen Dring, JD, PsyD is a licensed clinical psychologist and attorney, who has had a private clinical psychology practice for 26 years. She has focused on treating and evaluating children and adolescents.

Developmental Evaluation of Children and Adolescents: A Psychodynamic Guide

"This book is written by authors with extensive psychoanalytic knowledge of the developing mind and experience working with children and adolescents. I consider it a valuable handbook for mental health workers, parents, grandparents, child care workers, teachers, coaches and anyone involved with children and adolescents. They will find guidelines for understanding and dealing with the young ones and their families."

Vamık D. Volkan, MD, *Emeritus Professor of Psychiatry at the University of Virginia and Founder and Emeritus President of the International Dialogue Initiative*

"This is an up-to-date unique *synthesis* of all available developmental-dynamic and inter-disciplinary literature on the subject, brought together in a comprehensive, clinically applicable and reader-friendly illustrative form, to be used as a guide, a template, and a map.

A 'must read' for mental health clinicians working with children and adolescents (and their families), it can be immensely useful to parents, pediatricians and childcare workers in any field, and be a resource for any academic or clinical course on the dynamics of child development, psychopathology and psychotherapeutic intervention."

Eva D. Papiasvili, PhD, ABPP; *Chair, IPA Inter-Regional Encyclopedic Dictionary of Psychoanalysis (IRED)*

"Dring and Blackman are on a most laudable mission: to return long-established psychoanalytic developmental theory to wide use in evaluating mental health issues of children and adolescents. Their book is a comprehensive plain-English overview of theory along with a pragmatic step-wise guide to its implementation. It deserves wide readership among both clinicians and caregivers."

Jeffrey H. Golland, PhD, FAPA, FIPA; *Clinical Professor, Department of Psychiatry, Mount Sinai School of Medicine*

"With unabashed determination, the authors provide a relevant offering for evaluating children and adolescents, beginning with pregnancy. Their writing emanates from the explosion of developmental research since the 1970's. Clear descriptions of modernized psychoanalytic developmental theory, evaluation guidelines, assessment tools, and clinical examples afford the reader an organized way of understanding what children and parents need."

Janet Schiff, LCSW, FIPA, *Supervising and Training Analyst, Contemporary Freudian Society, Washington, DC*

"This is the book I wish I had available to read when I was a resident during my child psychiatry rotation. As mid-career adult psychiatrist, my practice is enriched by having read it. Drs. Blackman and Dring have created a concise, methodical primer filled with enlightening and practical guidance. I would recommend this book to anyone at any stage of their career who uses their specialized knowledge in caring for children, guiding parents, or is simply curious about the relevance of psychodynamic thinking in cultivation of adaptive family relationships."

Aileen Kim, MD; *President of Virginia Psychoanalytic Society, 2018–2022;*
Diplomate, American Board of Psychiatry and Neurology; President,
American Society of Psychoanalytic Physicians

"Developmental Evaluation of Children and Adolescents: A Psychodynamic Guide is a timely volume. It integrates psychodynamic and developmental principles which enable mental health practitioners to carefully evaluate the nature of children's problematic adaptations. I was particularly impressed with the list of simple questions for each phase, a wonderful guide for both the novice and the experienced."

Leon Hoffman, MD; *President, Center for Regulation*
Focused Psychotherapy; Chief Psychiatrist, West End Day School,
New York City; Codirector Pacella Research Center,
New York Psychoanalytic Society and Institute

"Through a skillful process of inquiry parents are helped in understanding their children's developmental status, including the need for treatment where indicated. Integrating psychoanalytic developmental knowledge, specific issues, such as autism and ADHD, and medical problems are addressed. The instructive interchange facilitates relationships between parents and therapists essential for treatment. This deeply thoughtful and comprehensive book is an invaluable resource for all mental health professionals who work with children and/or parents."

Harold P. Blum, MD; *Training and Supervising Analyst,*
Psychoanalytic Association of New York; former Editor-in-Chief
of the Journal of the American Psychoanalytic Association

Developmental Evaluation of Children and Adolescents
A Psychodynamic Guide

Jerome S. Blackman and Kathleen Dring

Routledge
Taylor & Francis Group

NEW YORK AND LONDON

Designed cover image: © Getty Images

First published 2023
by Routledge
605 Third Avenue, New York, NY 10158

and by Routledge
4 Park Square, Milton Park, Abingdon, Oxon, OX14 4RN

Routledge is an imprint of the Taylor & Francis Group, an informa business

ISBN: 978-1-032-18945-1 (hbk)
ISBN: 978-1-032-18944-4 (pbk)
ISBN: 978-1-003-25711-0 (ebk)

DOI: 10.4324/9781003257110

Typeset in Goudy
by SPi Technologies India Pvt Ltd (Straive)

Access the Support Material: www.routledge.com/9781032189444

Contents

Illustrations

Figures

Tables

About the Authors

Jerome S. Blackman, MD

Professor Blackman is a psychiatrist—certified by the American Board of Psychiatry and Neurology—and a psychoanalyst—certified by the American Psychoanalytic Association, the American Board of Psychoanalysis, the Council of Independent Psychoanalytic Societies, and the International Psychoanalytic Association.

He has been in private practice since 1975 and is currently a Full Professor of Clinical Psychiatry at Eastern Virginia Medical School in Norfolk, Virginia. Since 1996, he has also been an International Psychoanalytic Association (IPA) Training and Supervising Analyst with the Contemporary Freudian Society in Washington, DC.

Dr. Blackman was the 12th recipient of the *Akhtar-Brenner Lectureship* Award from Sidney Kimmel Medical College of Thomas Jefferson University in 2017. He was an invited lecturer at Mount Sinai Icahn School of Medicine Department of Psychotherapy in 2017.

The *Jerome S. Blackman, MD (yearly) Lectureship in Psychoanalysis* was established in his honor, in 2019, by the Virginia Psychoanalytic Society (an affiliate society of the American Psychoanalytic Association) and the Department of Psychiatry at Eastern Virginia Medical School.

For 30 years, he taught psychiatry residents and psychology interns at the Naval Medical Center Portsmouth (Virginia), where the *Jerome S. Blackman MD Teacher of the Year Award* was given to 25 different teachers from 1992–2016.

Dr. Blackman received the *Edith Sabshin MD Award for Teaching* from the American Psychoanalytic Association. He was awarded the *Gold Medal Award* from the American College of Psychoanalysts (honorary society of psychiatrist-psychoanalysts), of which he was President in 2015. *The Henry P. and M. Page Laughlin Distinguished Teacher Award* was granted him by the American Society of Psychoanalytic Physicians in Washington, DC.

Early in his career, while in child psychoanalytic training at the New Orleans Psychoanalytic Institute, he was a consultant to Child Protection Centers for the state of Louisiana. He was designated a Louisiana State Sexual Abuse Treatment Resource and evaluated over 5,000 cases of child abuse over a ten-year period. In 2016, he coauthored *Sexual Aggression against Children: Pedophiles' and Abusers' Development, Dynamics, Treatability, and the Law* (New York: Routledge) with Dr. Kathleen Dring.

In 2003, his paper on countertransference was published in the *Psychoanalytic Quarterly*. He later published several book chapters on topics including stepparenting, porn addiction, laziness, shame, philandering, fear of injury, and the death of the analyst.

After the publication of *101 Defenses* in Chinese in 2011, he was asked to teach in China. He has since lectured at many universities in China. He has also been an invited lecturer at psychoanalytic institutes and universities, in the United States and worldwide.

From 2018 to 2021, he was appointed *Distinguished Professor of Mental Health at* Shanxi Medical University in Taiyuan.

He was a keynote speaker at the sixth and seventh China Psychoanalytic Association Congresses in Shanghai (2019, 2021) and received the "High End Foreign Talent" Honor from Shanxi Province in 2018.

He has authored three books in English, which have been translated into Mandarin:

- *101 Defenses: How the Mind Shields Itself.* New York: Routledge, 2003; Shanghai: East China Normal University Press, 2011 (translated by Guo Wen Tao); 2nd ed., *101+ Defenses*, Shanghai: E. China Normal University Press, 2021 (translated by Wang Jing, Edited by Wu Chunyan).
- *Get the Diagnosis Right: Assessment and Treatment Selection for Mental Disorders* (New York: Routledge, 2010; Beijing: Capital Normal University Press, 2018, translated by Zhao Chengzhi).
- *The Therapist's Answer Book: Solutions to 101 Tricky Problems in Psychotherapy* (New York: Routledge, 2013. Beijing: Capital Normal University Press, 2016, translated by Zhao Chengzhi).

Kathleen Dring, JD, PsyD

Kathleen Dring, JD, PsyD is an attorney and a licensed clinical psychologist who has had a private clinical psychology practice for 26 years. Her private clinical practice has focused on providing psychodynamic psychotherapy for children and adolescents.

Dr. Dring has also specialized in evaluating children and adolescents for special education services and for federal disability benefits.

She coauthored, with Dr. Blackman (2016) *Sexual Aggression against Children: Pedophiles' and Abusers' Dynamics, Development, Treatability, & the Law.* New York: Routledge.

She is the past President of the Virginia Psychoanalytic Society and Past Chairperson of the Barry Robinson Local Human Rights Committee in Norfolk, Virginia. She has taught courses at Old Dominion University and at Eastern Virginia Medical School to mental health clinicians and trainees regarding child development and psychotherapy, and forensic issues in clinical psychology.

Dr. Dring has served as an expert witness in hundreds of cases involving parental capacity issues, child abuse cases, and child custody evaluations. She has also served as a mediator in divorce cases and has been court appointed to assist parents with coparenting their children after a divorce.

One-Page Developmental History Checklist of Questions for Quick Evaluations

Pregnancy and Immediate Post-partum Period
- ☐ Was the baby planned and wanted?
- ☐ Were there any complications of pregnancy or delivery?
- ☐ Did the baby ever sleep in a room alone, in the parents' bed or room? Where was feeding done?
- ☐ Breast or bottle? Any problems? Was weaning attempted at any time? Results?

Birth to 1 Year of Age Attachment and Normal Symbiosis
- ☐ What was the infant's temperament (Thomas & Chess, 1977)?
- ☐ Was the baby fed looking at the mother?
- ☐ Was the baby soothed when crying, or did the parents allow the baby to "cry it out"?
- ☐ Was weaning begun, and when?
- ☐ Was toilet training attempted?
- ☐ When did the baby smile specifically at mother?
- ☐ Was there stranger anxiety at 8 months of age?

1–3 Years of Age Separation-Individuation Phase
- ☐ Did the child dart off and run back? Does father engage in play with child?
- ☐ Did the child sleep alone in a crib?
- ☐ At what age was weaning completed?
- ☐ When was toilet training begun, and how did the child adapt to this?
- ☐ Have there been any separations from the parents for lengthy periods of time? How did the child tolerate them?
- ☐ How did the parents react to the child saying "no"?

2–7 Years First Genital Phase (Overlaps Separation-Individuation)
- ☐ Where did the child sleep most of the time?
- ☐ Did you bathe nude with the child, or did the child see the parents naked at any time?
- ☐ How did you manage the child's masturbatory play?
- ☐ Were corporal punishment or long time-outs used? When and details?
- ☐ What kinds of games, activities, and athletics did you allow the child?

6–11 Years Latency
- ☐ Where did the child sleep? What types of punishments were used? Any hitting? The child's response?
- ☐ Did the child have friends?
- ☐ What were the child's hobbies and participation in sports?
- ☐ School performance?
- ☐ Any interferences by TV, cellphone, computer?

12/13–18/25 Years Adolescence
- ☐ Is there evidence of maturation and autonomy?
- ☐ Can the teenager organize schedules and study independently?
- ☐ Has the teenager developed adequate social skills?
- ☐ Has the teenager had very unrealistic thoughts or hallucinations—serious mental illness?
- ☐ Are there any indications of body image disturbances, anorexia, or bulimia?
- ☐ Can the teenager verbalize disagreements without violence?
- ☐ Has the teenager become immersed in computer games, social media, or substance abuse?
- ☐ Can the teenager control emotions and impulses fairly well? Any self-destructive thoughts/behaviors?
- ☐ Does the teenager maintain close friendships? Is the teenager easily influenced?
- ☐ Is there evidence of ideals for a career or family in the future? Morality?
- ☐ Is the decrease in idealization of the parents proceeding without undo grief?
- ☐ Has the teenager become a daredevil?
- ☐ Has the teenager developed a sexual relationship with anyone?

⚷ All Key Questions to Be Answered by Parents about Each Developmental Phase

Summary

Pregnancy and the Immediate Post-partum Period

- **Was the Baby Planned?**
  - Were there parental wishes about the gender of the baby?
  - Did the parents have genetic counseling, and what effects did it have on them?
  - Did the parents use Assisted Reproductive Technology or other alternatives to pregnancy?

- **Were There Any Complications of Pregnancy or Delivery?**
  - Did the mother have any post-partum depressive symptoms?
  - Looking for interferences with the mother's ability to be responsive to infants' signals for feeding, soothing, changing, and any history of an unsupportive husband (Blackman & Kaplan, 1969).
  - Did the mother have any medical illnesses such as toxemia, hyperemesis gravidarum, diabetes, preeclampsia, abruptio placentae, placenta praevia, breech, C-section, or strangulation of the cord?
    - Looking for overprotectiveness in parents whose babies had health problems
    - Kernicterus, APGAR score, congenital anomalies, need for amniocenteses, hypospadias (urethral opening misplaced)
  - Were there any external stressors in the family: financial, health, employment?
  - Is there a history of prior miscarriages, stillbirths, or other child-related losses—looking for "replacement child?"

- **Did the Mother Take Any Prescribed Medication or Use Drugs or Alcohol While Pregnant?**
  - Looking for the mother's anxieties about motherhood.
  - Looking for any explanation of the child's later developmental delays.
  - Looking for preexisting mental disturbance in the mother and father.

- **What Happened to the Marital Relationship and Sexual Relationship?**

  - Looking for disturbances in emotional closeness and supportiveness toward one another.
  - Looking for conflicts regarding work and childcare.
  - Looking for interferences with sexual activity.
  - Looking for envy by either parent of the other.
  - Looking for interferences in tolerating fluctuations in dependency and independence.

- **Were Alternate Pathways to Pregnancy Utilized?**

  - Looking for parents' reactions to the process.

- **Did Baby Sleep in a Room Alone or in Parents' Bed or Room? Where Was Feeding Done?**

  - Looking for symbiotic wishes in the mother and anxiety about any separateness.
  - Looking for conflicts between parents regarding sleeping arrangements.

- **Breast or Bottle? Any Problems?**

  - Did the mother or baby have any trouble instituting nursing?
  - Looking for attachment problems.
  - Looking for failures to soothe the infant through oral gratification.
  - Looking for feeding disturbance in the infant (refusing nipple).
  - Looking for intellectually or neglectfully based failures by parents to soothe the child.

Birth to 1 Year of Age

- **Was the Temperament of the Baby "Easy to Soothe," "Slow to Warm Up," "Active," or "Difficult to Soothe"? How Did You Handle It?**

  - Looking the for degree of secure-organized attachment: i.e., baby feels relief on seeing parent (3–6 months of age).
  - Looking to see if the baby developed trust in parent's response to stress signals (crying).
  - Did the baby root (looking for attachment issues)?
  - Did the baby suck easily and seem to find pleasure in eating?

    - Looking for attachment and oral drive gratification (or not).

- **Was the Baby Fed on a Demand or Fixed Schedule? Response?**

  - Babies fed on a schedule may not have been adequately soothed.
  - Looking for subsequent problems with independence and autonomy.

- **Did You Let the Baby "Cry It Out" or Respond with Soothing/Feeding When the Infant Cried? How Successful Were You?**

  - Looking for the baby to show apathy or lack of interest in the parent after 3 months of age ("low-keyedness")—often the result of allowing infants left to "cry it out" without soothing.
  - Looking for the parent's self-esteem and pleasure in relation to the stresses of caring for an infant (mother's identity stabilization).

- **Did the Baby Look in Your Eyes while Nursing/Feeding? Was There a Specific Smile at Mother by 3 Months, Laugh at 4 Months?**

  - Looking for disturbances in pleasurable interactions (disturbed internalization, in the child, of self and mother images).
  - Looking for development of imitative play between infant and parent (mirroring as a precursor to empathy).

- **Were There Multiple Caretakers? Attachment to Any? Was the Baby in Day Care: At What Age? How Many Hours a Day?**

  - Looking for the baby's response to separations, leading to the baby feeling terror or low-keyed.
  - Looking for early interference with babies' knowing themselves as different from their parents (breakdown in the differentiation and early practicing subphases)—important for babies' developing a sense of their environment as separate from themselves ("reality testing").

- **Any Traumas (e.g., Parental Separation), Neglect, or Abuse?**

  - Looking for emotional disruptions that were overwhelming to parents and affected the child (death of grandparent, divorce, e.g.).
  - Looking for incidents that were overwhelming to the child (illness in the child, e.g.).
  - Looking for the impact on the child's attachment and social behaviors.

- **Did the Baby Ever Sleep in a Room Alone, in Parents' Bed or Room? Where Was Feeding Done, and Breast or Bottle? Any Problems? Was Weaning Attempted at Any Time? Results?**

  - Looking for evidence of persistent symbiosis (excessive clinging at a later age), or physical agitation with the mother—often due to co-sleeping.
  - Looking for attachment problems in stressful situations where the infant felt helpless or inadequate.

- **Was Toilet Training Attempted before the Child Could Walk?**

  - Since physiologically not possible, premature toilet training indicates the parents' obsession with cleanliness.

- Asking the child to perform a task that is impossible sets the stage for future pressures to perform.

- **Were There Indications of Social Connectedness and Attachment to Caregivers?**

  - Did the child show a social smile and cooing sounds by 2–3 months?
  - Did the infant develop stranger anxiety and preference for a selected caregiver?

1–3 Years of Age (Separation-Individuation Phases)

- **Did the Child Dart Away and Run Back to Explore the Surroundings? Did Father Engage in Play with Child?**

  - Looking for disturbances in separation-individuation.
  - Looking for disturbances in caretakers who did not allow enough independent curiosity in the child.

- **Did the Child Sleep in Their Own Crib?**

  - Looking for persistent symbiosis.
  - Looking for parental figures who abandon the child.

- **At What Age Was Weaning Completed?**

  - Looking for delayed weaning and persistent oral dependency.
  - Looking for premature weaning, with agitation and irritability.

- **When Was Toilet Training Begun, and How Did the Child Adapt to This?**

  - Could the child understand what was expected?
  - Was there rebellion?
  - Did parents become overly controlling, punish, or use schedules or enemas?

- **Were There Any Separations from Mother for Long Periods of Time? How Did the Child Tolerate Them?**

  - Looking for chronic anxiety and depression due to lengthy or multiple separations.
  - Looking for separation traumas, such as death or illness.
  - Looking for damage to object constancy (which should be reached between ages 2 and 3.5). During this time, the child should be able to tolerate short separations from parents.
  - Looking for splitting—seeing other people as all good or all evil.

- Looking for exaggerated separation anxiety and resulting clinging as a defense.

- **How Did the Parents React to the Child Saying "No"?**

  - Looking for parents not allowing reality testing to develop in the child.
  - Looking for overly controlling parents who allow no autonomy.
  - Looking for spoiling parents who allow infantile grandiosity to emerge.

- **Did the Parents Encourage Language Development?**

  - Looking for failures of girls to speak by age 18 months.
  - Looking for failures of boys to speak by age 24 months.

- **Was the Child Sent to Preschool or Day Care? What Was the Child's Reaction?**

  - Looking for disturbances in emotional stability.
  - Looking for disturbances in self and object constancy leading to

    - tantrums or
    - failures to emotionally attach to caregivers.

  - Looking for nightmares and fears of being alone due to insecure attachment.

3–6 First Genital Phase

- **Where Does the Child Sleep Most of the Time?**

  - Looking for persistent clinging (symbiosis) and troubles with separations (preschool, e.g.).
  - Looking for evidence of inadvertent sexual overstimulation (agitation, compulsive masturbation).

- **Did You Bathe Nude with the Child, or Did the Child See the Parents Naked at Any Time?**

  - Looking for evidence of inadvertent sexual overstimulation, agitation.
  - Looking to see if the child grabbed at the parents' bodies.

- **How Did You Handle the Child's Masturbatory Play?**

  - Looking for conflicts regarding obedience, excessive sexual curiosity, and self-image (autonomy).
  - Looking for parents' inhibitions or exhibitionism.

- **Did You Use Corporal Punishment or Long Time-Outs?**

    - Spankings lead to anger, negativism, inhibition, and refusal to obey.
    - Long time-outs lead to fears of abandonment, increased self-hatred, and emotional distance.
    - Look for in cases of children who are violent with other children, especially siblings.

- **What Kinds of Games, Activities, and Athletics Did You Allow the Child?**

    - Isolated children tend to be more inhibited, more irritable, depressed, and dependent.
    - Outlets for destructive feelings are very important for socialization and intellectual development.

Latency Ages 6½–10½/11½

- **Where Did the Child Sleep?**

    - Looking for persistent anxiety over night-time separation (persistent symbiosis).[1]
    - Looking for sexual overstimulation.
    - Nightmares exacerbated by co-sleeping.[2]

- **What Types of Punishments Were Used? Any Hitting? The Child's Response?**

    - Looking for the child's weakness in handling powerful emotions (overwhelmed affect tolerance).
    - Looking for misbehavior and malicious mischief (identification with the aggressor).

- **Did the Child Have Friends?**

    - Looking for empathic supportive relationships outside the family (vs. autism).
    - Looking for interference (too much anxiety) in interacting with other children.

        - Damaged social skill and judgment.
        - Excessive hostile aggression or paranoia.
        - Psychological testing, including Rorschach, may be helpful.

---

1 Mahler et al. (1975).
2 Blackman and Dring (2016).

- **What Are the Child's Hobbies and Participation in Sports?**

  - Looking for problems channeling aggression into productive pursuits (sublimation of aggression).
  - Looking for poor channeling of curiosity into intellectual activities (sublimation of sexual curiosity).
  - Looking for disturbance of developing morality.

    - Not following rules
    - No respect for authority: no humility, bullying

- **How Has the Child Performed Academically and Behaviorally at School?**

  - Looking for interferences with learning caused by emotional conflicts.
  - Looking for disruption in attention (caused by neurological factors, developmental delay, or overwhelming affect).
  - Psychological testing, including intelligence level, may be useful.

- **Does the Child Have Intact Reality Testing?**

  - Looking for odd behaviors, hallucinations.
  - Psychological testing, including intelligence, academic, and personality testing, may be useful.
  - Looking for failures to cooperate with time management.

- **Has There Been Interference by TV, Cellphone, Computer?**

  - What types of controls have parents instituted, if any?
  - Looking for poor social and family interactions, leading to withdrawn, egocentric children.
  - Looking for effects of corrupt moral values absorbed from TV programs or internet (e.g., video games about stealing or killing police officers).
  - Looking for interference with sleep-wake cycle.

Preadolescence: End of Latency (10½–11½) to Puberty (9–17)

- **Have You Noticed an Increase in Emotional Volatility?**

  - What behaviors have you noticed? Any antagonism?
  - How have you handled it?

- **Has There Been an Upsurge in Interest in the Other Sex (~95% of the Time in Boys, 85% of the Time in Girls)?**

  - Approach behavior in girls toward boys?
  - Curiosity in boys about girls, glancing interest in prurient visual materials?

- **Have You Witnessed Withdrawal in the Child?**

  - Has the preteen rejected being seen with you?
  - Is there an avalanche of interest in connection with friends or rejection of friendships and hiding?
  - Have social awkwardness, language difficulty, and impulsivity suggested an autistic pattern?

- **Has There Been Oral Symptom Development?**

  - Anorexia—conscious, willful food avoidance?
  - Bulimia—overeating followed by self-induced emesis?
  - Obesity—overeating for pleasure?

- **Has the Child Been Punished? How?**

  - Looking for escalation of autonomy matters.
  - Looking for runaway behavior.

- **Any Drug Abuse or Sexual Acting Out by the Preteen?**

  - Has menarche or spermarche been reached?
  - Is the preteen allowed to lock the bedroom door at night?

- **Has the Preteen Become a Bully or Been Bullied?**
  - Looking for management of upsurges of aggression and effects on the self-image.
  - Looking for passivity and inhibition of the self-preservation function.

- **Has the Preteen Dropped Any Favorite Activities?**

  - Looking for rebellion interfering with sublimatory channels.
  - Any family disturbances affecting the child?

Adolescence 13–Early 20s

- **Ego Functions of Language, Integration, and Reality Testing**
  - Is there evidence of maturation and autonomy?
  - Can the teen verbalize disagreements without violence?
  - Is the demoralization regarding the parents proceeding without severe depression?
  - In what areas has the teen developed mastery?
  - Can the Teenager Organize Schedules and Study Independently?
    - If the teenager cannot organize working and playing, this portends badly for the post-high school years, whether they be in college or work.

- Peer pressure and ostracism can lead to depression and misbehavior.
- Has the Teenager Developed Adequate Social Skills?
  - Needed for group functioning.
  - Needed for interacting with authorities.
- Has the Teenager Had Very Unrealistic Thoughts or Hallucinations—Serious Mental Illness?
  - Schizophrenia frequently arises during this stage, earlier in boys.
  - Looking for referential thinking, persecutory feelings, and hallucinations.
  - Looking for a history of suicide attempts and self-cutting.
  - Chaotic, abusive family history may predispose the teenager to develop a "psychotic core."
  - Ego Strengths
- Can the Teenager Verbalize Disagreements without Violence?
  - This is needed to contain the many frustrations of adolescence.
  - If parents limit their teens' verbalization (and/or do not model by engaging in discussion with their teens), this can lead to teens engaging in destructive actions.
- Has the Teen Become Lazy, Lost in Computer Games, or Engaged in Substance Abuse?
  - Teenagers need time for some laziness (Blackman, 2017) but may not move from play to work.
  - Addiction to games or substances *weakens impulse control.*
  - Has the teenager engaged in substance abuse? If so what substances, how long, and how much?
- Can the Teenager Control Emotions and Impulses Fairly Well?
  - Has the teenager become immersed in computer games or social media?
  - Does the teenager have a terrible temper?
  - Has the teenager become "addicted" to pornography and masturbation?

- **Object Relations**
  - Does the Teen Maintain Close Friendships?
    - Does the teen have any friend who can be trusted?
    - Has the teen become withdrawn from friends (schizoid)?
    - filial piety been kept in good balance with individual desires and identity?
  - Regarding Friendships, Can the Teen Maintain Individuality or Be Easily Influenced?
    - If the teen is not developing some identity stability, the teen will be vulnerable to gangs, cults, and cataclysmic fads.
    - Dedifferentiation from parents or friends (giving up identity and values to be accepted) is dangerous.

- Has the Teen Remained Emotionally Close to Family?
  - Looking for disturbances of separation, with teenager at home, failing in school.
  - Looking for running away behavior due to wish to avoid home.
  - All teenagers will rebel against a value of their parents—but is this rebellion self-destructive or illegal?
  - Is some rebellion allowed by the parents? If not, the teenager can become severely inhibited or potentially violent.

- **Superego and Ego Ideals**
  - Is There Evidence of Ideals for a Career in the Future?
    - If not any, this will decrease ambition.
    - If confused, the teenager should be testing reality to discover strengths:
      - E.g., if a teenager wants to be a professional baseball player but could not make the varsity baseball team in high school, this indicates divergence between the ego ideal and real abilities, leading to depression.
    - May indicate damage to self-esteem from many sources.
    - Depression over failures may also be due to inhibition of function conflicting with reasonable ego ideals.
  - What Kind of Morality Is the Teenager Developing?
    - Regarding sexual activity? Violence?
    - Is sex treated cavalierly?
      - If so, there is danger of sexually transmitted disease, lack of integration of sex and love.
    - Is there severe sexual inhibition?
      - Painfully shy teens may have difficulty establishing committed relationships later.
    - Regarding community activity:
      - Can the teenager help with projects?
  - Is the Teenager Concerned with the People in the Environment?
    - If not, narcissistic elements may pervade the character.
    - Spoiled teens will lack ambition and may have life failures.
  - Is There Evidence of Ideals regarding a Future Family? What Is the Evidence?
    - If the teen becomes demoralized about the value of a family, close and committed relationships can become inconsequential.
    - Lack of respect for the other sex may continue and interfere with later work and personal relationships.
  - Is the Decrease in Idealization of the Parents Proceeding without Undo Grief?
    - Reality of the parents' personalities needs to be clarified and accepted.

- Complete rejection of the parents is a sign of possible rejection of all authorities in the future.
- If the parents are too damaged, the teen may become suicidal to relieve their painful realizations (and guilt) about the parents.
- Regarding Helping in the House, Will the Teenager Pitch In?
  - Regarding school and other forms of work?
  - Movement from play to work.
  - Movement from laziness to work.
  - Conflicts, Defenses, and Compromise Formations
- Has the Teenager Become a Daredevil?
  - Counterphobic defenses can lead to injury and death
  - Thrill seeking can lead to injury to others or illegal behavior.
- Has the Teenager's "Adolescent Rebellion" Been Channeled in Positive Directions?
  - All teenagers will rebel against a value of their parents—but is this rebellion self-destructive or illegal?
  - Is some rebellion allowed by the parents? If not, the teenager will become severely inhibited or potentially violent.
- What Hobbies (Sublimations) Has the Teenager Developed?[3, 4]
  - Without some success in these "sublimated" areas, there is danger of developing destructive or sexual impulsivity, recklessness, or perverse activity, such as peeping, compulsive masturbation, fetishes,[5] and suicidal proclivities.
  - **Sports**—looking for sublimations of aggression.
  - **Dancing**—looking for sublimations of aggression and exhibitionistic wishes.
  - **Music, Art**—looking for sublimations of sexual curiosity.
  - **Math, Physics**—looking for inhibitions of special intellectual abilities.
  - **Other Clubs**—looking for inhibitions or delay of social skills.
- Sexual Matters
  - When did the teen reach puberty?
    - Looking for precocious or delayed puberty.
    - Looking for both parents' and teenager's responses to this.
  - Has the teenager experienced sexual intercourse? Has the teenager developed a sexual relationship with anyone?
    - If so, how have parents responded?

---

3 Hartmann, H. (1955). Notes on the theory of sublimation. Psychoanalytic Study of the Child, 10, 9–29.

4 Loewald, H. (1988). Sublimation: Inquiries into theoretical psychoanalysis. Yale University Press.

5 DeMijolla-Mellor, S. (2012). La Sublimation. QUE SAIS JE; PUF Press.

- According to the Centers for Disease Control and Prevention, "An estimated 55% of male and female teens have had sexual intercourse by age 18,"[6] and only 80% used contraception during the first sexual experience.
- Is the sexually active teenager using contraception?
- Has the teenager had a Human Papilloma Virus vaccine?
- Has the teenager expressed a gender identity?
- Is the teenager able to lock the bedroom door at night?
  - Looking for interference with autonomy, especially regarding masturbation.
  - Looking for persistent separation anxiety.

6 https://www.cdc.gov/nchs/pressroom/nchs_press_releases/2017/201706_NSFG.htm.

A Memo to Readers about Why We Decided to Write This Book

To our colleagues and students:

Both of us have been in practice for a long time and have evaluated, between the two of us, approximately 10,000 children and their families. We both have had many years of training and experience regarding the study, assessment, and treatment of children and their families. Those experiences included assessing allegedly abused children for child protective services, assessing parents, and consulting with school systems.

Over the past decade, we had become despondent and critical regarding the trend toward using the *DSM* to list a child's complaints and then prescribe a medication plus a "pat-on-the-head, kick-in-the-pants" type of therapeutic approach. We also think the behavioral approach of offering rewards and punishments to children is limited, at best, and destructive, at worst (e.g., using time-out for children under the age of 4 tends to exacerbate their separation anxiety!) for most children.

Our despondency and irritation were magnified because of the explosion of knowledge, since the 1970s, about the development of children. Fifty years' worth of valuable psychoanalytic child research seems not to have penetrated into most mental health training programs or made it to the general public! The internet can be a wonderful tool, but it contains tons of misinformation and propaganda—so it's hard to find the right data there.

Frankly, we were tired of seeing the wonderful research findings and knowledge restricted to a few thousand therapists in the country and decided that, instead of complaining to each other about the sad state of things, we should try to do something about it. So, integrating what is available from analytic child research and our own experience, we developed guidelines for gathering information that would lead to indications for different types of interventions for different children and their families. We have tried to do this in a constructive manner and apologize if our frustrations filter through from time to time.

But at least you're getting our unfiltered opinions and arguments, as clearly as we can present them. We hope that our intellectual honesty and emotionality about these opinions will make the book more utilitarian and more enjoyable to read. We have also endeavored to make the research knowledge understandable, so we have used as little jargon as possible and defined the terms we found needed.

We hope you find our labors worthwhile and useful.

Sincerely,
Dr. Dring and Professor Blackman

What This Book Is and What It Isn't

It is our intention, in this book, to help the clinician and the family assess children's problems at each stage of the child's development. You will find, at the beginning of each chapter, several "key questions" that should be answered (by parents or primary caretakers). Following that, we describe what the answers to the questions mean. For *very short evaluations* (e.g., 15–30 minutes), we have included a one-page checklist.

There are three main foci of full evaluation: (1) specific questions the therapist should ask the parents[7] about the child's current behavior, thoughts, and *living situation*; (2) specific questions the therapist should ask the parents about the child's **developmental history**; and (3) specific data to be gleaned from the therapist's interactions with the child and parents.

In favorable situations, we see important purposes in meeting with the parents:

- To obtain information about the child's *current state of functioning* in different spheres, with some attention to the *precipitating events* that led to the evaluation. To this end, we suggest the therapist ask certain specific questions. Then we explain why the therapist should ask those questions—what information is sought? We then outline how modern theories of child and adolescent development can be used to assess expectable functioning vs. that which is, well, abnormal at the child's age.
- To obtain a **Developmental History**. We recommend specific questions be answered by the parents about the child's functioning and interactions with parents at every developmental stage, up to and ending with the child's current stage of development. In our current mental health climate, we felt it was useful to outline what these developmental stages are. What is supposed to happen during each of those phases? What is within the range of normal vs. what is not, and how could those developmental factors contribute to the child's *current problems*? We offer an outline of

---

7 By convention, throughout this book, we will refer to the "parents" for simplicity, but this includes primary caretakers or "the psychological parents."

the questions that should be asked about each developmental phase—to figure out, as best as possible, what has been facilitative vs. what has been pathogenic.

The outline we suggest for asking questions of parents regarding the child's current functioning and developmental history serves as a guide to the first step in evaluation. As for the second step, we discuss how the therapist can go about obtaining diagnostic information from the initial interactions with children—of course, differently at different ages. Taken together, these data help the therapist make the best recommendations for the appropriate type of treatment for any given children and their families.

We have limited the purpose of our contribution to the evaluation process. We have not attempted to provide a textbook on how children's problems should be treated, either short or long term. Neither have we endeavored to provide in-depth discussions about conflicting theories of child development. We have used what is known from child psychoanalytic and other developmental research we consider germane and have tried to incorporate as much common sense as possible.

Although we list what psychological testing may be useful at different stages of child development, we have not entered into a lengthy theoretical discussion of the techniques for these. Other assessment modalities, such as school or nursery observation of children have also not been included, although these modalities can be particularly important in some cases. Finally, we have not attempted to address evidence-based studies that attempt to prove the veracity of any developmental theoretical schema.

Nota Bene

- A common complication in the evaluation of children is that some third party may wish to see a written assessment, which will be used for purposes other than designing an approach to resolving the presenting problems. For example, teachers, divorce courts, and child protective services might wish to obtain the material the therapist has gathered and organized. (This sometimes is an issue with adults, as well.)
- At the beginning of the assessment, therefore, it is recommended that the therapist clarify the immediate as well as the potential uses of the evaluation. Based on the risks of exposure of confidential material regarding the child and the parents, the therapist will need to decide whether to pursue evaluation—and if evaluation is done, the therapist may need to decide how to describe what is found that is relevant to the third party.
- We are aware of the reality that a diagnosis pursuant to the DSM (*Diagnostic and Statistical Manual of Mental Disorders*) or the ICD (*International Classification of Diseases*) is often necessary for families to file for insurance benefits. It is a shame the PDM-2 (*Psychodynamic Diagnostic*

Manual-Second Edition) was never accepted by insurance companies or many courts. We have not attempted to directly correlate our schema with either *DSM or ICD* (see Blackman, 2016). Instead, we hope our suggestions will allow you to assess the child with more clarity and accuracy (Frances, 2013, e.g., noted the *DSM* is so cumbersome that most clinicians don't read it). After formulating a case, the diagnosis can be easily correlated with symptom-oriented *DSM* categories.

- Throughout this book, we will define the following terms, or use simple English when possible. For those of you in the field, who are interested in the concepts we will be describing, here are the technical terms (and some references for them) for the mental factors that need to be assessed at each stage of the child's development. (You will find a more complete description of these theories in the chapter on that topic). These are collected during the taking of the Developmental History as well as the initial examination of the child:

  - Basic mental ("ego") functions, including intellect, integration, and cognition (Piaget, 1952; Hartmann, 1964; Blackman, 2010; Blackman & Dring, 2016)
  - Ego strengths (control and delay capacities, including sublimated activities) (Sarnoff, 1976; Kernberg, 1985; Blackman, 2010; deMijolla-Mellor, 2015)
  - Object relations development: reciprocity, empathy, trust, emotional closeness

    - Mahler et al.'s (1975) phases of development (including Erikson, 1950a 1980)
    - Blos's (1960) stages of adolescent development (Blackman, 2010)
  - Superego precursors and later development (Bornstein, 1951; Blos, 1970; Blum & Blum, 1990; Emde et al., 1991; Blackman, 2010)

    - Reciprocity
    - Empathy
    - Values
  - Temperament (Chess & Thomas, 1986)

    - Easy to soothe
    - Slow to warm up
    - Active

  - Physiological milestones and developmental lines: timing and reactions (Freud, 1956)
  - Drive derivatives: psychosexual and psycho-aggressive stages (reviewed in Blackman, 2010, Chapter 10)
  - Prominent affects (summarized in Blackman, 2010, Chapter 8)
  - Real interpersonal elements with caretakers

- Other realities of the child's environment (Kris, 1956; Meers, 1973)
- Traumata (Becker, 1974; Blum, 2005; Volkan, 2009;)
- Nature of attachment (Ainsworth, 1978; Bowlby, 1958) and detachment (Akhtar, 2020)
- Self-development and parental releasing factors (Kohut, 1971; Stern, 1985)
- Defensive operations and compromise formations (symptoms) (Blackman, 2003; Brenner, 2006)

1 The Theoretical Basis of This Book

We have attempted to make this book accessible to all people interested in evaluating children and therefore have tried to use standard English when possible. In some cases, when we use psychoanalytic or other psychological and psychiatric terms, we have defined them.

For psychoanalysts and others who are interested in the framework we are using to assess children, however, we have included this overview. The following is a technical description of the theories on which we are basing the history-taking and evaluation of children at each developmental stage.[1]

The ideas we are using derive from ego psychology, object relations and self-psychology, attachment theory, psychosexual development, superego formation, and conflict theory (drives, reality, superego, affects, defensive operations, and compromise formations). We are particularly interested in failure to develop in any of the following areas, as well as damage to those areas—causing deficits in functioning (#1–6). Then we add an assessment of conflicts, as described in #7.[2]

Autonomous Ego Functions (Sometimes Referred to as the Development of Cognitive Abilities)

Autonomous ego functions were so defined by Heinz Hartmann (1964) because they seem to be brain based functions which develop *on their own;* that is, they are not solutions to inner or external conflicts. There is a genetic factor in the development of some of these functions (such as psychomotor control in star athletes or fine motor control in grade school students).

In addition, all these functions are heavily affected by parents' encouragement or interference throughout development. The functions are also modified through identification with parents, teachers, and others. Finally, if a task

1 For more in-depth summary of these theories, see Blackman (2010) and Blackman and Dring (2016a). We do not significantly rely on the *Diagnostic and Statistical Manual of Mental Disorders* (see Blackman, 2016).
2 A potentially useful mnemonic device for recalling all the factors that need to be assessed might be 😲 CORA SEES: Conflicts, Object Relation, Attachment, Self, Ego functions, Ego strengths, Superego.

DOI: 10.4324/9781003257110-1

is presented to a child when the task can be accomplished, the child will be able to complete the task and then take pleasure in mastery. For example, asking a 4-year-old to read a clock will produce frustration; in contrast, most 8-year-olds will experience pleasure in learning to tell time. Complex abstract concepts cannot be understood, usually, until adolescence.

All these functions develop gradually. Some, such as perception, memory, and integration, seem to be present in nascent form at birth, whereas others, such as reality testing and social skill, develop during the school-age years. Adaptation, executive function, abstraction ability, judgment, and introspection are not fully operational until late adolescence. All these functions continue to develop throughout adulthood.

The "autonomous ego"[3] refers to basic mental functions (or "ego functions"), including

- perception (five senses);
- psychomotor control;
- memory (many types: affective, long term, short term);
- organization of thought ("integration");
- intellect;
- abstraction ability (understanding symbols and metaphors);
- relationship to reality;
- reality testing;
- self-care (hygiene);
- self-preservation;
- superficial social skills;
- concentration and attention;
- orientation to person, place, and time;
- secondary process (logical, time-oriented) thinking;
- primary process (symbolic) thinking;
- executive function (decisions regarding actions);
- ego interests (skills and hobbies);
- abilities to adapt to the environment (autoplasticity);
- abilities to make the environment adapt to you (alloplasticity);
- anticipation of consequences;
- judgment about danger;
- critical judgment about others' personality traits;
- clear sensorium (awakeness) (important in assessing substance abusers);
- sleep-wake cycle;
- moving from "play to work" (Freud, 1956);
- moving from "laziness to work" (Blackman, 2016b); and
- mentalization (or "observing ego")—the ability to introspect and to think about others.

3 A good compendium and discussion of these functions is found in Hartmann (1964), and Blackman (2010, 2018c) summarized and added some definitions.

Factors that may interfere with the development of these functions include, but are not limited to

- genetic endowment,
- parental support or discouragement,
- physical illnesses,
- traumatic experiences, and
- overwhelming affects.

Ego Strengths

These are control and delay capacities, which also develop over time. Specifically, they include

- impulse control (of wishes for soothing, control, love, sex, success in winning, obtaining acquisitions, ambition, and dominance),
- affect regulation (tolerating powerful emotions of joy, stimulation, anxieties, depressions, rages),
- frustration tolerance (waiting for external gratifications),
- tension tolerance (putting up with inner struggles until a solution can be found),
- containment of primary process (keeping symbolic, dreamlike fantasies mostly out of consciousness),
- ARISE (adaptive regression in the service of the ego) (Kris, 1956; Bellak, 1989) (allowing some fantasy into consciousness to play with children, to make jokes, and to create art),
- sublimatory channels (Kernberg, 1975) (channeling destructive fantasy and sexual curiosity into productive activities), and
- using fantasy as trial action (Hartmann, 1964) (the ability to imagine certain scenarios before testing their reality).

These capacities, first, seem to have a genetic basis: some children seem almost "immunized" (Kliman & Rosenfeld, 1980) to overwhelming urges and emotions, and develop normally even though they come from emotionally disruptive homes. Second, the environment in which the child grows up can have a steadying or a disruptive effect on these abilities; war zones (Freud & Burlingham, 1942) are particularly destructive to "internalized schemata" (Sandler, 1960). Third, a secure-organized attachment (Bretherton, 1992) to parents seems to facilitate the development of these regulatory structures. Finally, secure detachment (Akhtar, 2020) during preschool and school-age years contributes to the strength of all these. (Also see Blum, 2004.)

   In general, as children get older, they should be better able to tolerate impulses and emotions. Nevertheless, there does seem to be a diphasic quality: considerable strength usually develops from ages 6 to 10. But from 10 ½ through middle adolescence, there is a decrease in impulse control and some destabilization of affect regulation due to the power of sexual and aggressive wishes (Freud, 1956, "power of the drives"; Knight, 2005).

Sublimatory channels are critical to latency children. But an additional factor during adolescence is the experience of some hardship (and learning from impulsive mistakes). The experience of real frustrations tends to contribute to affect tolerance. Those adolescents who engage in heavy substance abuse, relieving affective overloads with those substances, will likely experience interference with the development of ego strengths.

Object Relations Theories

These clinically based theories arose to explain disturbances in relationships involving

- warmth – toward others,
- empathy – with others,
- trust – when judged safe,
- holding environment – internalized security,
- identity – maintaining views and attitudes even under pressure,
- closeness – to others when this is wanted, and
- stability – in maintaining love.

Blackman (2010) suggested a mnemonic device to remember these clinical factors: *Warm-ETHICS*. According to Emde (1991), early reciprocity evolves to empathy by age 3 or so, when self and object constancy make empathy possible. Early precursors of the conscience begin to form (Blum & Blum, 1990) during the toddler years and the first genital phase (3–6). By the age of 6 or 7 (Bornstein, 1951), in children within the normal developmental range, guilt and values form (e.g., if I love you, I feel guilty about hurting you).

The theory of object relations began early (Freud, 1914); was later codified by Mahler, Pine, and Bergman (1975); and has been further elaborated by Akhtar (1994).

Developmentally, we expect to see warmth and a "specific smiling response" in children by age 2–4 months (Spitz & Cobliner, 1966; Beebe & Lachmann, 2002b). "Basic trust" (Erikson, 1950a) develops out of predictable parental soothing during the first year of life (Spitz & Cobliner, 1966; Ainsworth, 1967; Blackman, 2018a). Emde discusses how reciprocity (between ages 1 and 2) leads to empathy between ages 2 and 3; this sequence is supported by Mahler et al.'s (1975) research findings about self and object constancy—meaning stable internal images of the self and of other important people—occurring at age 3.

A sense of internal safety (Sandler, 2003) derives from a stable, supportive "holding environment" (Winnicott, 1969) during childhood. Identity coalesces toward the end of adolescence (Blos, 1962; Erikson, 1994) so that dedication to a committed relationship is normally possible by early adulthood (closeness and stability).

Object relations theory also explains clinical presentations related to difficulty with Warm-ETHICS (Blackman, 2010). The theory posits the internal development of stable, realistic, and integrated pictures (also called mental representations, introjects, internal representations, and self and object images) in the child and adolescent. There is also a more or less biphasic quality to object relations development.

The first phase consists of several stages delineated by Mahler and others. It includes the following:

- Symbiotic attachment (0–7 months of age)
- Separation-individuation (7–36 months of age)

  - Hatching (7–10 months of age [Blum, 2004; Pine, 2004]) with differentiation crisis (9–12 months of age)
  - Practicing (10–16 months of age)
  - *Rapprochement* (16–25 months of age)
  - Unstable self and object constancy (25–36 months of age)

- Self and object constancy (36–42 months of age)

The second phase of object relations, as pioneered by Peter Blos (1970), includes

- 10½–11½ (preadolescence) beginning of the second individuation,
- early and middle adolescence ("recrudescence" of self and object differentiation), and
- late adolescence (about 16–21/25 years of age), where identity (clarity of self and object images) is intensified and stabilized.

Prior problems may be repaired or exacerbated during adolescence. Eventual consolidation of the self-image (personal identity) occurs in healthy individuals, as well as their perceptions of others and the outside world (Jacobson, 1964). Identity continues to be influenced by internal and external factors throughout life (Marcus, 1973).

Factors that interfere with or delay the separation-individuation process throughout life include, but are not limited to

- lengthy co-sleeping,
- neglect (emotional and/or physical),
- emotional abuse and witnessing domestic violence,
- physical abuse (spankings which are lengthy, utilize implements, break the skin, and/or cause emotional breakdown in the child),
- sexual abuse (accidental or inadvertent overstimulation, primal scene exposure, inappropriate touching, and penetration) (Blackman & Dring, 2016),

- traumatic losses of and/or separations from parents and other caretakers,
- blindness in the child (Fraiberg & Adelson, 1973),
- parental and peer pressures to conform during latency and adolescence, and
- identification with psychopathic group leaders (Freud, 1921), identification with a nation's chosen traumas or chosen glories during adulthood (Volkan, 2014).

Attachment Theory

In 1944, John Bowlby published his findings that 44 juvenile thieves in England had been severely deprived of maternal attachment from birth through the school-age years. He concluded, at the time, and this has been borne out since, that a child's empathy and conscience derive from sufficient attachment to a loving mothering figure. Almost simultaneously, Rene Spitz, a British pediatrician, noticed that orphan infants, victims of the Nazi blitzkrieg in London, were dying in the orphanages that had been set up to care for them. The reason: the infants were being fed, but not held! They thus were not forming the attachment to the mother, which, in humans, is necessary to promote the activity of the sucking reflex (Spitz & Wolf, 1946).

Since then, Mary Ainsworth and Mary Main further divided attachments from birth throughout childhood (and adulthood), demonstrating four types of interpersonal attachments, involving insecurity, disorganization, and anxiety. An adult attachment inventory was later added (George, Kaplan & Main, 1984).

A major contribution of attachment theory, aside from promoting empathy, has been the discovery that secure-organized attachments were needed for children to regulate (or tolerate) powerful feelings (analysts call feelings "affects").

Salman Akhtar (2020) has recently upgraded this theory, pointing out that "detachment" as the toddler reaches age 3, and later during adolescence, is of equal importance.

As Blum (2004) has astutely pointed out, attachment concepts are necessary but not sufficient to assess the nature of empathy, trust, and human closeness as they develop. Attachment is an empirical set of observations and conclusions (especially the "strange situation test" developed by Mary Ainsworth). The theory must be integrated with concepts about the self-image of the child at different phases, as well as how much autonomy has developed in age-appropriate ways at each stage of separation-individuation.

In taking a developmental history, parents should be asked about how attached their baby was, and at what age they witnessed the child becoming more individuated and detached. This gives us material that points to what has happened in the mind of the child (see Mahler et al. 1975). In particular, in examining children who get overwhelmed easily, cling to their parents, or have become bullies, we can find out if the child, from the outset, did not attach sufficiently—or did not separate and feel comfortable away from the parents as they got older.

Self-Psychology

Heinz Kohut (1971) made several important contributions to the analytic theory of child development. He figured out that children take in ("introject") their parents' attitudes about the child's self-worth. Parents can overdo this, praising the child inordinately, which causes the child to become self-centered and insufferable. On the other hand, parents can "emotionally abuse" children by communicating that the children are worthless, regardless of the children's age-appropriate proficiency in a subject, skill, or accomplishment.

His theory, technically, involved the idea that parents comingle their concept of their child with a concept of their own idealized self, forming what he called a "selfobject." When the parents communicate their opinions about the child's value, they project their comingled, somewhat distorted view onto the child. The child will then introject the parents' selfobject ideas, which affects the child's self-esteem regulation.

Kohut was one of the first to notice (although Maslow had discussed the same matter using the slightly different terminology of stages toward "self-actualization") that in favorable parent-child interactions, the child will develop what he called "normal narcissism." This concept has been exaggerated in some school systems, where "everyone gets a prize." The perversion of Kohut's concept, in these settings, tends to impair the ego ideal of the children and may easily cause the child to lose motivation toward competition.

Another major theoretical suggestion of Kohut's was the understanding that from early childhood through late adolescence, children's friendships involve what, years before, Freud had called "narcissistic attachment." In these situations, friendships are based heavily on similarities between the children. In late adolescence, if teenagers become involved in relationships that include penetrative sexual relations, they tend to make the image of the lover part of the selfobject concept they have of themselves. If and when those relationships break down, the adolescent feels as though he or she is worth "nothing," and there is commonly what Kohut called discharge of "aggressive breakdown products." This neatly accounts for the destructive rage often seen after sexual relationships during adolescence break down. The affected teenager can become destructive or use the defense of turning aggression against the self (Menninger, 1935; Blackman, 2003), resulting in a suicide attempt.

For major updates on these concepts and integration into other theories, see Lichtenberg (2019).

Otto Kernberg and his team at Cornell-Weill Medical Center have, for over four decades, put forth dozens of books and scores of articles regarding the development of the self. They integrated ideas from Melanie Klein regarding split objects, which are unrealistic perceptions of people as imbued with all loving or all destructive qualities. The same exaggerations, termed "splitting," can likewise apply to the self-image. Such children and adolescents often have internalized their parents' ideas or regressed to pre-whole object relations due to emotional conflicts (Kumin, 1995). The results of such mental mechanisms include but are not limited to grandiose self-concepts, self-hatred, damage to reality testing about others, pathological narcissism, and hollow feelings of emptiness alternating with piquant rage. In such cases, the narcissism relieves (defends against) dependency, selfobject annihilation, selfobject fusion, splitting, and violent rage.

Again, the first three years of life and the first several years of early adolescence are eras of risk for these pathological developments. However, scholars such as Ted Becker (1974) and Rona Knight (2005) have shown that disturbances of self-image and suicidal tendencies can be found in latency age children, as well.

Superego Development

As mentioned, a sense of internal guilt should be present by around age 6. Parental "reminders" from fourth through sixth grade are usually not as needed (for doing homework, using the restroom, e.g.) and may be counterproductive (producing irritation in the child, which causes the child to re-externalize values onto the parents—so the controlling function is only seen as external [Johnson & Szurek, 1952]).

The concept, "superego," today, encompasses about ten features that can be represented in the acronym, FIRE LIGHTS (Blackman, 2010, 2018c). The acronym stands for the mental elements that make up the superego: Fairness, Ideals, Reliability, Ethics, Lawfulness, Integrity, Guilt, Honesty, Trustworthiness, and Shame.

The first to develop is shame, usually centered around toilet training and cleanliness. Next, we see guilt over hurting someone's feelings (ages 4–7). Fairness becomes important during the school-age years ("latency," Sarnoff, 1976) when playing by the rules becomes associated with honesty. The concept of lawfulness also develops late in the school-age period. Ideals show a marked increase in importance during adolescence. Reliability becomes a prototypical conflictual matter between teenagers and parents. As teenagers move into early adulthood, trustworthiness and integrity become notable features. Finally, the more sophisticated notion of ethics appears during adulthood.

So, we do not expect 3-year-olds to feel guilty or to be honest. We do hope that latency children will feel guilty and play fairly. Reliability continues to be an issue throughout adolescence and adulthood.

Conflict Theory

In assessing children throughout childhood and adolescence, we must also consider the conflicts they are experiencing. These conflicts occur among their various wishes, the reality (and personal) impediments to gratifying those wishes, and how the wishes come into opposition to the child's values (after age 6). These predictable conflicts produce the emotions of anxiety, depression, and anger. Finally, the mind will institute mechanisms to shut some part of the conflict out of consciousness (defense mechanisms).

The five points of most conflicts include (1) a loving or hostile wish, (2) reality impediments, (3) clashes with values (superego—guilt and/or shame), (4) the affects generated by the conflicts, and (5) the defensive operations used to quell the unpleasurable affects (see the Compromise Formation Star, Figure 7.1, p. 102). All five factors together constitute what is known as a "compromise formation" (Freud, 1926; Brenner, 2006; Waelder, 2007; Blackman, 2010, 2018c). Compromise formations may be adaptive or maladaptive. When a child or teen is brought for evaluation, the compromise formations that occurred at each stage of psychosexual development (see p. 000) are superimposed on any developmental delay, including damaged ego functions, ego weaknesses, object relations impairments, and superego lacunae (Johnson & Szurek, 1952).

Conflict theory (Brenner, 2006) requires us to examine the "stages" each child has passed through and the normative and pathological solutions to the conflicts that occurred during each of those stages. Each stage is defined by the primary biological substrate that arose anew. The biological milestone becomes quickly associated with pleasurable gratifications. The perception of these gratifications is then integrated with pleasures associated with the memories of the people involved in providing the gratifications (or lack thereof).

The biological series of development was outlined, more or less correctly, by Freud (1905). The oral (symbiotic) phase: neurological reflexes of sucking and rooting become associated with pleasure, soothing, and memories of the experience with the soothing adult. Lack of soothing leads to many problems, including failure to thrive (Spitz & Wolf, 1946). The child enjoys "mirroring" the mother. Wishes to be taken care of, fed, soothed, and "supported" have their origins during the first year or year-and-a-half of life.

The anal (separation-individuation) phase begins with the myelinization of the nerves that control the anal and urogenital musculature—giving the child "control" between 18 months of age and about 3 years of age. The pleasure of withholding and expelling becomes associated with the pleasures of pleasing parents and of frustrating them.

The first genital phase overlaps with the anal phase, starting somewhere around age 2 (Roiphe & Galenson, 1972). During this stage, the child finds pleasure in voluntary touching of the genital organs, simply for pleasure. The child is surprised to find pleasure in this activity (Marcus & Francis, 1975), but the pleasure becomes associated with the people in the child's life. Freud called this the stage of "infantile sexuality." (For a dissertation about this topic, see IRED, 2022.)

During latency, there is repression of many pleasurable wishes, and the focus changes to the channeling of fantasies associated with the wishes—into productive curiosity and physical activity (sublimation).

Most of the time, orgasm becomes possible at puberty. Children experience secret pleasure in this activity. In some countries and in some cultures in the United States, children begin to have sexual intercourse right after puberty.

During these five stages, other matters also come into conflict. Children also have "wants" for things, feel competitive, and can become negative and even destructive. The destructive tendencies parallel the development of other wishes. Aggression has, no doubt, its origin in the grasp reflex, which becomes associated with pleasure and the people associated with those pleasures. The theory of the aggressive drive is more contentious (Parens, 1991; Blackman, 2010, Chapter 10). See the chart on page 000 for an outline that includes aggressive drive development

Conflicts begin in earnest as soon as the child "awakens" and has conscious volition. First, the child's wish may be thwarted by reality (e.g., the wish for soothing vs. parent unavailability).

By the end of the first genital phase (age 6–7), as the superego is forming (or not), wishes inevitably conflict with feelings of guilt and shame. By latency, full compromise formations, including all five variables, begin occurring. Affects are then generated not only by external dangers but also by internal conflicts of which the child is unaware. These affects are then managed by swaths of defense mechanisms, working together—and all of these factors contribute to the child's behavior, personality development, successes, and symptom formation (panic, phobia, obsession, compulsion, depression, conversion). The compromises in adolescence are more dramatic, as they involve all five features, but the actual pleasurable experiences of orgasm, love, competition, and winning are more powerful.

Throughout, the depressions, anxieties, and angers of children must be assessed by looking at how these are managed—by ego strengths and ego functions, and by defenses creating potentially maladaptive compromise formations at each stage of development. How these conflicts are managed has a bearing on the development of symptoms and personality functioning in adulthood.

Summary

Diagnosis of children and adolescents can then be recalled using a mnemonic device—namely,

- **CORA SEES** relating to
  - *Conflict theory*
  - *Object Relations*
  - *Attachment theory*
  - *Self-psychology*
  - *Ego functions (autonomous)*
  - *Ego strengths*
  - *Superego intactness*

The evaluator is always looking, throughout development, for

- results of deficits in development,
- results of conflicts, and
- interpersonal and environmental factors (culture).

We use all of the aforementioned concepts in this book to inform the developmental history we recommend and the approach to the initial evaluation of the child. Of course, we do not expect parents or children to be familiar with the theoretical bases of their problems. We must be aware of these and ask questions, in the vernacular, to obtain the information that will confirm or negate the utility of understanding the presenting disturbances using one or many of these theories.

Table 1.1 Libidinal and Aggressive Drives Throughout Development

Libidinal Drive	*Aggressive Drive*
Oral phase (0–3 years) **physiology:** sucking, rooting **added pleasures:** cuddling, dependency, basic trust, taking in **normal adult remnants:** eating, kissing, touch, oral foreplay, dependent trust **abnormal persistence:** eating disorders, oral sexual obsessions, alcoholism, severe dependency, mistrust	*Oral phase:* (0–3 years) **physiology:** grasping/holding, motor (muscle) activity **added pleasures:** moving, holding on, letting go, biting **normal adult remnants:** "holding on," "letting go," exercise, motion, acquisitiveness, biting wit **abnormal persistence:** restlessness, clinging, stealing, "the money disease" (hyperacquisitiveness, materialism), "Type A Personality"
Anal phase (1.5–5 years) **physiology:** excretion; myelinization of nerves to sphincters ➔ voluntary control **added pleasures:** teasing, messing, pleasing **normal adult remnants:** sexual teasing (foreplay); performing to please others **abnormal persistence:** messiness, scatology, procrastination	*Anal phase* (1.5–5 years) **physiology:** walking, hitting, speech **added pleasures:** stubbornness, saying "No!", breaking things, hurting others **normal adult remnants:** tolerating getting "hands dirty" to "clean up a mess," saying "No!" (self preservation), ability to hurt others when necessary **abnormal persistence:** demandingness, contentiousness, negativism, physical destructiveness, sycophantism
First genital phase (2–7 years) **physiology:** volitional self-stimulation, penile/clitoral *corpora cavernosa*	*First genital phase* (2–7 years) **physiology:** muscle development: rough-and-tumble play

(Continued)

Table 1.1 (Continued)

Libidinal Drive	Aggressive Drive
added pleasurable features: sexual curiosity/theories; genital masturbatory play; bisexual fantasies; primal scene and family romance fantasies; Oedipus complex, leading to *desexualization*; narcissism about gender	**added pleasurable features**: destructive fantasies about war; defiance; competition with parents, siblings: Oedipus complex, leading to *deaggressivization*; narcissism about strength or ability to attract attention
normal adult remnants: enjoyment of sexual fantasy, self-confidence, wishes for children and family, empathy for opposite sex, desexualized relationships	**normal adult remnants**: pursuit and securing of a special sexual partner; ability to compete, with pleasure in winning; deaggressivized relationships
abnormal persistence: severe sexual problems, nonintegration of sexual stimulation with object ties ➜ womanizer, man-eater	**abnormal persistence**: severe problems with competition in games and in life, untamed hostile aggression/destructiveness
Latency phase (6–10 years.)	*Latency phase* (6–10 years)
physiology: growth, improved coordination	**physiology**: growth, improved coordination
drive accretions: sublimation of sexual curiosity and fantasies into hobbies, interests, and intellectual pursuits; deinstinctualization ➜ fond friendships (avoidance of sexual stimulation; ipsisexual socialization)	**drive accretions**: sublimation of violence or competition into sports, arts, and schoolwork; deinstinctualization ➜ friendly competition; ipsisexual (same-sex) socialization
normal adult remnants: continued sublimations (become ego interests), control of sexual stimulation, ipsisexual friends	**normal adult remnants**: continued sublimations (become ego interests, especially games and sports); control of ambition, competition, attacks
abnormal persistence: failed sublimations ➜ promiscuity; decreased ego interests; sexual inhibition, avoidance of the opposite sex, neurosis	**abnormal persistence**: failure of sublimations ➜ violence, greed; competitive inhibitions, neurosis
Preadolescence (10–12 years)	*Preadolescence* (10–12 years)
physiology: growth of sex-oriented organs; capacity for sexual excitement; +/− masturbation	**physiology**: growth of muscles, bones
added pleasures: improved ego functions: better reality testing, motor, integration, intellect; teasing re: body	**added pleasures**: improved ego functions: reality testing, motor, integration, intellect; independence; friendly competition: sports, school, games
normal adult remnants: independence of object choice; teasing; tolerance for sexual excitement	**normal adult remnants**: friendly competition; control through intellect
abnormal persistence: perverse teasing; inappropriate sexual comments/behavior	**abnormal persistence**: preference for games over competitive work: e.g., fishing, golf, bingo

(Continued)

Table 1.1 (Continued)

Libidinal Drive	Aggressive Drive
Second (mature) genital phase (puberty onward)	*Second (mature) genital phase* (puberty onward)
Adolescence (13–18 years) **physiology**: intensification of sexual wishes and fantasies; capacity for orgasm; fertility; menstrual cycle	*Adolescence* (13–18 years) **physiology**: intensification of wishes (purposive intentionality), pursuit, destructiveness in response to threat, motor strengthening, coordination
drive accretions: sublimation ➜ heightened interest in arts, creativity; increased sexual impulsivity; integration of fantasies from prior phases and from environment; quick shifts in "objects"; withdrawal or group formation for avoidance and control; masturbation to orgasm; eventual sexual activity with intercourse; narcissism	**drive accretions**: sublimation ➜ career choice and avocations; capacity to "fight back," defend self; pleasure in succeeding: capacity to reject what is not wanted; group formation with direction of hostility toward other groups; pleasurable discharge phenomena in sports and achievements
normal adult remnants: intense sexual desire, with focus on one object; developed interest in artistic pursuits; spontaneity; humor; pleasure with sexual intercourse and procreation	**normal adult remnants**: pursuit of interests, career, and competition; rejection of what is not wanted; identification with groups ➜ productive activity; excelling in work
questionably abnormal persistence: continuing shift in object; excess need for group functioning at expense of intimacy; preference for masturbation and equivalents; continuing narcissism	**abnormal persistence**: identification with hate groups; failed sublimations ➜ violence, poor frustration tolerance; passivity; nonintegration of hostile-destructive aggression with self-preservation
Adulthood (+/− 18years ➜) **physiology**: pressure for drive expression (sexual gratification and orgasm); stable love objects	*Adulthood* (+/− 18 years ➜) **physiology**: pursuit, holding onto things, using muscle strength
drive accretions: capacity for sublimation, work; desexualized relationships: spontaneity; humor; *integration with autonomous ego functions and object relations*	**drive accretions**: +/− stable preferences, ability for group identification, excelling/winning at work and love, making things go one's way, friendly competition, *integration with self-preservation and executive function*

2 Structure for Evaluation

Meet with the Parents

Overview

We believe it is best, in most situations, to meet with the parents first. The child-therapist interaction and interview can be done at a separate appointment. Finally, a third feedback session can be held with the parents to discuss the evaluation results and recommendations.[1] If the evaluation involves an adolescent, it is often advisable to include the adolescent in a feedback session. The third feedback session may include the following:

- A formulation about the child's emotional problems and diagnoses;
- Recommendations for further evaluations, such as medical evaluations or psychological testing; and
- Recommendations for treatment options, the focus of the treatment, and referrals if appropriate.

Before parents contact a mental health clinician for an evaluation of their child/adolescent, the parents have likely consulted other professionals (pediatricians, psychotherapists, teachers, school counselors) about their child's problems. It is helpful if parents bring with them to the initial session a list of names and contact information for these professionals (or better yet, reports of their findings) so collateral information about the child can be accessed after the appropriate release forms are signed by the parents. It is also advisable to request that the parents provide current report cards, notices of disciplinary actions by the schools, or court referral documents.

At the outset, practical matters regarding parental responsibilities for the evaluation should be established and clarified. This includes the fee, how the

---

1 In difficult practical situations, all three sessions (meeting with parents, child evaluation, and interpretive session with parents) can be done in one day. Leaving a child alone in the waiting room presents multiple problems, however. Children under the age of 6 are well nigh impossible to evaluate over the internet since play materials are not present. The initial parent interview may be held online, but it is harder to assess the parents' resistances and personalities.

DOI: 10.4324/9781003257110-2

parents will pay for the evaluation, and setting appointment times. These details should not be arranged through the child or adolescent. Some parents, especially of teenagers, will want to "send" a check for the fee with the child.[2] This needs to be discouraged with empathic understanding expressed about the parents' frustration with these limits. Fees and appointment times are adult ("secondary process" [Freud, 1900]) concerns and are always irrelevant to children. These contractual elements, even of the evaluation process, must be arranged with the parents.

Initial Session

At the initial session, it is important to review with the parents issues surrounding confidentiality and exceptions to confidentiality, such as mandatory reporting laws regarding child and elder abuse. This discussion often includes how the information from the evaluation will be used and who may have an interest in the information.

During the initial meeting with the parents, the therapist should direct the order of material as follows:

- Their major worries about their child (sometimes called the "chief complaint")
- How long the problem has existed ("present illness")
- What the parents (and others) have already tried to do to resolve the problems
- What other problems are present in the family
- The *developmental history*:
  - "Key Questions" that should be answered by the parents regarding each stage of development.
  - Parents often give material about these matters anyway, so the questions need not be literally asked. But if the parents do not offer material, they should be asked.

Dealing with Resistances in the Parents

Most parents find it difficult to consult with a psychotherapist for an evaluation of their child. They consult the psychotherapist as a last resort, after having little to no success in solving the child's issues on their own or with other professionals. When the parents have decided to consult with a psychotherapist for the evaluation, they may find the task depressing, time-consuming, stressful, anxiety-provoking, and embarrassing. These feelings can lead to parental resistance to the process, both conscious and unconscious.

---

2 Often, such parents wish to send a message to their teenager about how much trouble the parents are going through to be of help. They think seeing the fee will motivate the teenager to work harder at therapy. (This predictably will be counterproductive.)

When the evaluator notices parental resistance, it is useful to discuss this empathically and to immediately address the parents' concerns and anxieties. Parental resistance may be manifested by hesitation and/or forgetfulness about important matters. They also may seem suspicious about the necessity for openness about the child's problems and their thoughts about the problems.

Parents often respond positively to discussions about how their guardedness stems from their self-criticism and shame that their child has emotional or behavioral problems. Also, some parents who may be involved in forensic parenting matters are cautious about how the information may be used in the future. This needs to be addressed directly and completely.

The discussion with the parents about their defensiveness regarding the evaluation provides the evaluator with valuable information about the parents and the child. This discussion also helps the therapist assess the potential for future treatment of the child, with the parents as allies. The child will predictably become resistant to seeing the therapist, and the parents will be a needed source of support.

Some issues related to resistance and anxiety about the evaluation we have commonly heard mentioned by parents are as follows:

- Fears of being blamed for the child's problems;
- Anxiety about the possibility of being informed that their child is seriously emotionally disturbed;
- Finding the process intrusive, as it involves parental family history, which may arouse pain about the parents' own childhood or marital difficulties. In many evaluations, parents eventually discuss how their child's problems remind them of similar problems they had as a child; and
- Frustration and anger about feeling ordered or coerced (by schools or courts) to have the evaluation completed.

Finally, during the initial meeting with the parents, parents often manifest their own emotional problems. Often, though not always, the parents are contributing to the child's problems in some way. To the extent that this is the case, the parents will no doubt need to be flexible and self-critical to modify any interactions the therapist feels are pathogenic. Most children are more or less treatable in direct relation to the parents' openness to considering their own contributions to the family problems. Some parents will need their own individual treatment, of course. Other parents present severe mental illness or are so suspicious, and mistrustful of any therapist that the child may not be treatable.

Psychotherapist-Child Interaction (with Parent Present if Needed) or Interview with an Adolescent

With children under age 3, often a parent's presence will be needed for part or all of the child-therapist interactions. This interaction is generally done in the therapist's playroom equipped for engaging with the child in therapeutic play. Children 3–6 years of age can sometimes be seen alone. Those who have not developed self and object constancy will still have separation anxiety and should be seen with their parents in the room. The parents' presence also provides information about attachment and parent/child relationship issues.

Children from 6 to 9 years of age may need drawing materials to facilitate communication, a playhouse with dolls and animals, and some games. Interactions with the therapist revolve around the therapist expressing interest in the drawing and the play in which the child may include the therapist. The therapist's counterprojections (Havens, 1980) can be verbalized in relation to the child's projections onto the play material.

Children from 9 to 11 years of age may or may not want to draw or play. If the child has reached puberty, verbalization is often preferred. Most children over 11 or 12 years of age should be encouraged to verbalize their thoughts about themselves and their families. The therapist notes the child's descriptions, expresses interest, and may give a few instructions—such as "maybe you can tell me what's bothering you about school." Children this age may feel more comfortable in a play therapy office setting, even if they do not access the play materials. Some children this age feel more comfortable in the adult-oriented therapy office.

The approach to adolescents, in general, should encourage teenagers to discuss their problems openly. Resistance can be gently interpreted along the lines usually recommended for adults: mentioning the reluctance of teenagers to come to the evaluation, their reluctance to talk, and the reasons for this: to avoid embarrassment, to avoid mistrust, and to avoid discomfort about revealing anything personal to an adult. In many situations, the evaluator should clarify with the adolescent how the information gathered will be used and who will have access to the information. This will include matters of confidentiality. Also, issues of mandatory legal reporting of child abuse should be explained at the outset.

Interpretive and diagnostic detail regarding the material gathered from the child/adolescent interactions is provided in the chapters of this book. The developmental history can be obtained for each developmental stage.

Meet with the Parents Again for an Interpretive and Planning Discussion

The combination of understanding the parents' worries, taking a developmental history, and evaluating the child should lead to localizing when, during development, conflicts and delays in development appeared. These findings should now be discussed with the parents.

If there is confusion about the diagnostic formulation or inadequate data, psychological testing or a medical evaluation may be needed to supplement what material has already been obtained. In cases of severe developmental delays, neurological, endocrinological, and other medical specialists may be needed to give their opinion. Also, medical evaluations may be recommended if the child's emotional problems appear to have impacted their physiological functioning (e.g., gastrointestinal symptoms, headaches, tremors, dermatological conditions, and sensory issues).

The decision about what kind of treatment is needed rests largely on the following:

- Ego function status (such as integration, concentration, motor control, abstraction ability, intellectual status);
- Control and delay functions (such as impulse control, affect regulation);
- Attachment type (such as secure-organized or disorganized);
- Capacities for empathy, trust, and emotional closeness;
- Superego development (guilt and shame); and
- Defensive operations handling the major emotional components (such as provoking punishment to relieve guilt).

In the feedback session, the therapist can review the significant answers to the key questions and the results from the child interaction/interview, and then correlate these with the recommendations for further testing and treatment recommendations.

Therapists must decide whether their therapeutic orientation and skill set are sufficiently matched with the psychopathology and indicated treatment for the child. The therapist can discuss with the parents the following possible recommendations:

- If children need medication

    - In rare cases of psychotic adolescents (2%–4% of the population), referral for a psychiatric evaluation may be warranted;

- If the child needs supportive therapy;
- If the recommended treatment involves seeing the child alone, and/or periodically with either or both parents;
- If the child needs interpretive therapy, either using play materials or not, and how frequently the child needs to be seen psychotherapeutically;
- If self-destructiveness or suicidality is a concern, immediate interventions may be required;
- If the family needs child-centered counseling; and
- If one or both parents needs individual or marital therapy.

During the feedback session, a discussion of the parents' reactions to the recommendations, diagnosis, and formulations is vital. If a parent has objections to the recommendations or diagnosis, these should be discussed fully. The therapist is also advised to continue establishing mutual empathy with the parents. The parents are legally the child's guardians, so without mutual trust and understanding, the parents will usually not initiate or will prematurely stop the child's treatment.

3 Pregnancy and the Immediate Post-partum Period

Key Questions Regarding Pregnancy and the Immediate Post-partum Period

- **Was the Pregnancy Planned**
    - What were the parents' thoughts and feelings regarding hearing of the pregnancy that the infant may later internalize?
    - Were there parental wishes about the gender of the baby?
    - Did the parents have genetic counseling, and what effects did it have on them?
    - Did the parents use Assisted Reproductive Technology or other alternatives to pregnancy?

- **Were There any Complications of Pregnancy or Delivery?**
    - Did the mother have any symptoms of post-partum depression?
    - Looking for interferences with the mother's ability to be responsive to the infants' signals for feeding, soothing, changing.
    - Looking for history of an unsupportive husband or partner.
    - Did the mother have any medical illnesses such as toxemia, hyperemesis gravidarum, diabetes, preeclampsia, abruptio placentae, placenta praevia, breech, C-section, or strangulation of the cord?
        - Looking for overprotectiveness in parents whose babies had health problems
        - Kernicterus, APGAR score, congenital anomalies, need for amniocenteses, hypospadias (urethral opening misplaced)
    - Were there any external stressors in the family: financial, health, employment?
    - Is there a history of prior miscarriages, stillbirths, or other child-related losses—looking for "replacement child"

DOI: 10.4324/9781003257110-3

- **Did the Mother Take any Prescribed Medication or Use Drugs or Alcohol while Pregnant**

  - Looking for the mother's anxieties about motherhood.
  - Looking for explanations of the child's later developmental delays.
  - Looking for preexisting mental disturbance in the mother and father.

- **What Happened to the Marital Relationship and Sexual Relationship?**

  - Looking for disturbances in emotional closeness and supportiveness toward one another.
  - Looking for conflicts regarding work and childcare.
  - Looking for interferences with sexual activity.
  - Looking for envy by either parent of the other.
  - Looking for interferences in tolerating fluctuations in dependency and independence.

- **Were Alternate Pathways to Pregnancy Utilized?**

  - Looking for parents' reactions to the process.

- **Did the Baby Sleep in a Room Alone or in the Parents' Bed or Room? Where Was Feeding Done?**

  - Looking for symbiotic wishes in the parent and anxiety about any separateness.
  - Looking for conflicts between parents regarding sleeping arrangements.

- **Breast or Bottle? Any Problems?**

  - Did the mother or baby have any trouble instituting nursing?
  - Looking for attachment problems.
  - Looking for failures to soothe the infant through oral gratification.
  - Looking for feeding disturbance in the infant (refusing the nipple).
  - Looking for intellectually or neglectfully based failures by parents to soothe the child.

Answers to the Key Questions

Was the Pregnancy Planned?

In pathological situations, unplanned pregnancies can cause severe ambivalence toward the child during pregnancy and afterward. In such situations, neglect of the child is more likely, as is post-partum depression. If the pregnancy was a surprise that induced the parents to marry, either parent may feel trapped and controlled by the baby, and then defensively argue or avoid contact with the spouse/partner. When an unwanted surprise pregnancy occurs during middle age, this can interfere with the parents' wishes for freedom from childcare, and thereby cause depression and irritability between the parents (Kliman & Rosenfeld, 1980).

Were There any Complications of Pregnancy or Delivery?

First, there are myriad medical problems that may occur. Some are treatable—such as placenta praevia, abruptio placentae, strangulation of the cord—in a hospital setting. Some are reversible, such as neonatal jaundice. Some are life-threatening, such as cephalopelvic disproportion, severe hemorrhaging, and severe infection. Some are potentially irreversible, such as kernicterus, chromosomal syndromes, and congenital anomalies. In such cases, emotional disruption to the parents is inevitable. What exact emotional impact these may have depends on the parents' personalities, but severe anxiety about the safety of the mother or infant is predictable.

Secondly, external factors may interfere with the parents' attitude toward the pregnancy. Financial problems, intrafamily arguments, and decisions about when the mother (or father) returns to work will result in stress. The resolution (or not) of these dilemmas impacts the "feeling of safety" (Sandler & Joffe, 1966; Joffe & Sandler, 1968) in the child immediately after birth. Unresolved practical problems may also lead to unworkable marital incompatibility.

Thirdly, we must consider the phenomenon of post-partum depression in the mother. The depression is often caused by unconscious guilt over rage toward an unsupportive (or sadistic) husband (Blackman & Kaplan, 1969). Many other conflicts can cause the mother the identical depressive symptoms, including identifications with her own neglectful mother and/or insufficient affect tolerance to manage the demands of a neonate.

In women who suffer from narcissistic personality disorder (Kernberg, 2004), self-esteem is often based on the woman's idea of "perfection" in the shape of her body. The alteration of body shape during pregnancy in such cases causes a feeling of loss and narcissistic injury. The primary importance of the newborn, who receives so much attention, may cause these women to feel a loss of self-esteem or to experience competitive feelings with the baby conflicting with guilt.

In parents with "borderline" features, who are overwhelmed by the burden of caring for someone other than themselves, depression may occur due to emotional depletion. In severe cases, the depressive affect overwhelms the new mother's reality testing, resulting in post-partum psychosis. This is often the case in mothers who have conscious wishes (or hallucinations telling her) to kill the child.

Did the Mother Take any Prescribed Medication or Use Drugs or Alcohol While Pregnant?

Some pregnant women, for many reasons (see the "Essay" later in this chapter), develop undue anxiety during pregnancy and take psychotropic medicine for it. Although these medications do not usually affect the fetus, this history suggests the mother had conflicts regarding the pregnancy that may have interfered with her tending to the child. Two percent of parents are likely to have suffered with a psychotic illness before the pregnancy (meaning their view of the child or themselves may be disorganized or delusional).

Of course, several drugs (legal and illegal), as well as alcohol, have a negative effect on the fetus (e.g., "fetal alcohol syndrome"). This may be a suspected etiology in children who later develop a variety of serious anomalies (especially developmental delays in walking, talking, or verbalizing, as well as unusual disturbances in body habitus[1]).

What Happened to the Marital Relationship and Sexual Relationship?
Except in high-risk pregnancies, sexual relations during pregnancy are not contraindicated. Some couples may avoid sex due to symbolically based anxieties (such as guilt over fantasies of harming the fetus or the mother). Complete avoidance of sex may lead to marital problems, including defensive emotional distancing. If either spouse causes emotional distance to occur, the marriage may suffer, and the environment for the new baby may be problematic.

During the pregnancy, parents start considering what changes will be needed regarding childcare and work responsibilities. This may be difficult. Many parents make initial plans, then change their minds after the child is about 3–4 months old.

The male's envy of the female's procreative function has been described in both children and adults (Lax, 1997). On the other hand, the stresses of pregnancy may cause a woman to envy the freedom of men who do not have to bear children. If either type of envy arises during pregnancy, this will affect the parents' attitudes toward each other as well as the child.

Increased dependency is a reality for many women during pregnancy, especially during the third trimester, when sitting, walking, and sleeping often become difficult. The woman's need to focus on herself may cause a reaction of deprivation in the partner. Both future parents must tolerate fluctuations in their own dependency needs, or the neonate will be experienced by both parents as a further deprivation.

Were Alternative Pathways to Pregnancy Utilized?
Parents who have chosen "alternative pathways" to parenthood—e.g., adoption, *in vitro* fertilization (IVF), or surrogacy (Samish, 2006)—face unique developmental tasks, which may include grief over infertility. The parents' experiences with those methods of conception invariably influence their perceptions and fantasies about the child and about themselves as future parents.

The process of IVF is physically painful to the future mother (injecting herself). The irritability produced in both parents can lead to arguments and sometimes divorce. Surrogacy has been studied psychoanalytically for the past

---

1 For a listing of all the many features of fetal alcohol syndrome, see https://www.mayoclinic.org/diseases-conditions/fetal-alcohol-syndrome/symptoms-causes/syc-20352901.

several years. The child may have problems later, especially during the first genital phase, when the child predictably will ask ("family romance") questions, such as "Where do babies come from?" And, "Am I adopted?" (Casey, 2017).

Did the Baby Sleep in a Room Alone or in the Parents' Bed or Room? Where Was Feeding Done?

Paul et al. (2017) reviewed the many reasons babies should not sleep in the parents' bed, focusing on the danger of unwitting asphyxiation of the baby. Emotional developmental concerns are also raised by co-sleeping. Even if the baby survived co-sleeping in the immediate post-partum period (most do), commonly symbiotic conflicts (merger of the baby's own images of self and mother) will be aggravated. Settlage (1964) points to the potential psychotogenic effects of persistent symbiosis when early separation-individuation is stunted.

Information regarding sleeping arrangements in the immediate post-partum period, as well as later, is therefore quite useful in formulating the etiology of severe disturbances in children at any age (and in adulthood—see Akhtar, 1994). Another potential problem of co-sleeping is the interference with the resumption of the parents' normal sexual activity.[2] The results of this omission in the new parents' life can lead to multiple problems (Levin, 1969).

Breast or Bottle? Any Problems?

The neonate comes replete with its own set of neurological reflexes. Sucking and the cephalogyric reflex—rooting—are connected to viability (Spitz, 1957). Anxious mothers sometimes cannot help the baby find the nipple. This is important because the newborn does not actually hunt for the nipple (or root); the baby simply moves the head back and forth; when the mouth encounters the nipple, the mouth automatically clamps down.

Children must also be held for the suck reflex to continue (Spitz & Wolf, 1946). Failure to soothe through the oral gratification of sucking *and being held* leads to a refusal to suck ("anaclitic depression" Spitz & Wolf, 1946). Later, these early difficulties may give rise to older children and adults who refuse help of any kind. Secure-organized attachments may not form. Parents who do not soothe the newborn (but who let the child "cry it out") are doing the child a grave injustice. Myriad diagnoses appear in children with this history (Blackman, 2018a).

Essay

Upon learning of a pregnancy, parents process a series of emotions relating to how the newborn will impact their lives (Lester & Notman, 1986; Diamond, 1998; Slade et al., 2009). Many expectant parents rework issues related to their own childhood experiences and how the birth of the infant may change

---

2 After 6–8 weeks post-partum, after the mother has healed from childbirth.

their family dynamics (Benedek, 1959; Pines, 1982; Apprey, 1987; Blum, 2017). These parents also (often without knowing it) reorganize their internal representations of self and others, and experience changes in the attachment patterns they had with their own caregivers.

During pregnancy, women experience expectable stress related to the changes in their bodies. The increased anxiety surrounding the upcoming birth of a child often causes an increase in the parents' own dependency needs (Lester & Notman, 1986; Pines, 1990; Trad, 1990).

The parents' feelings, thoughts, and fantasies about their unborn child influence the child's future attachment patterns and trust levels. Attachment research indicates that the parents' attachment to their infant begins during the pregnancy, and this impacts the parental attachment to the infant after birth (Bowlby, 1969; Frank et al., 1994; Condon & Corklindale, 1997).

Pregnancy as a Developmental Phase or Process

The emerging role of "mother" and the challenges of motherhood present women with new developmental conflicts, as well as opportunities for change (Slade et al., 2009). Mothers who experience serious conflict regarding pregnancy's emotional and physical changes are at risk to be inconsistent in the way they relate to their newborn infant—they view the neonate as both a blessing and a curse (Pines 1972, 1982; Trad, 1990).

The ability of parents to progress effectively through this developmental phase depends on many internal psychological and external factors, including the following (Bibring et al., 1961; Ammaniti & Trentini, 2009):

- their emotional health prior to pregnancy, including any history of abuse and trauma (DiPietro et al., 2006; Huth-Bocks et al., 2013);
- their physical health, age (adolescent mothers may be particularly vulnerable), and access to healthcare during pregnancy;
- their internal representations of themselves and others (Pines, 1972; Frank et al., 1994; Blum, 2017);
- the attachment style they developed in childhood (Benoit et al., 1997; Condon & Corklindale, 1997; Siddiqui & Hagglof, 2000); and
- the mother's relationship with the father of the child and the support she receives from others in her life (Liebman & Abell, 2000).

As the infant's birth becomes imminent and during the immediate post-partum period, the mother will at times (especially when the fetus kicks) perceive the child as emotionally and physically separate from herself. At other times, she will experience the infant as part of herself (Benedek, 1959; Bibring et al., 1961 Pines, 1972; Fonagy & Target, 1996; Ammaniti & Trentini, 2009). These oscillations in the parents' perceptions and identifications influence the parents' relationship with the child after birth.

Winnicott (1975) describes how the mother's "primary maternal preoccupation," before the infant is born, sensitizes her to the baby's later emotional and physical needs. As she is preoccupied with her role and identity as a good mother, her emotional responses influence the infant's "vital affects" (Stern, 1985). Stern (1995) describes a "motherhood constellation" that includes (1) concern for the growth and development of her baby, (2) emotional engagement with the baby, (3) promotion of support systems for the baby, and (4) transformation of her own identity to facilitate the prior three areas (see also Hoffman, 2013).

Colarusso (1990) extends Mahler's (1974) theory of the toddler's separation-individuation and Blos' (1967, 1983) ideas regarding adolescents' "second individuation" by describing a "third individuation" phase in adulthood. During this later phase, adults experience further separation of their internal images from those of their parents. In this process, there is a focus on greater independence, new identity formation, and a readiness for "a family of procreation."

Conception begins the process of the third individuation phase, which, in turn, is necessary for parents to be psychologically ready to nurture, love, and care for their baby. Parents' new sense of identity, separate from their own parents, lessens their narcissistic focus on themselves while promoting their prioritization of the infant's emotional needs.

Attachment and the Prenatal Period

Attachment theory, as developed by Bowlby (1944a & b, 1969a & b, 1973, 1980), posits that an infant's secure bond with the mother is necessary for the baby's survival as well as cognitive and social adjustment. If infants are deprived of a secure attachment to an *available* caregiver, they will likely experience depressive affect. Mary Ainsworth (Ainsworth et al., 1978) described three attachment styles in infants, in order to identify their *internal working models* (Levy & Blatt, 1999; Fonagy & Target, 2007a & b). See Chapter 4 ("Birth to 1 Year of Age") for a description of these attachment styles.

A fourth group, *disorganized/disoriented*, was later identified (Main & Hesse, 1990; Main, 2000). These children showed inconsistent, disorganized strategies for managing stress in the playroom. They had little capacity or inclination to use their mothers as a secure base for exploration of the world.

Consistent with Bowlby's theories, numerous studies using the strange situation paradigm have shown that children with secure attachments are more resilient, self-reliant, socially oriented, empathic, and self-confident (Fonagy, 1996; Sroufe, 2002; Fonagy & Target, 2007a & b). Attachment style has also been linked with the ability to engage in reflective functioning, which is the ability to think about one's own as well as others' thoughts. Reflective functioning is a foundation for significant relationships and identity formation (Fonagy et al., 2002).

Brazelton and Cramer (1990) described pregnancy as the "dawning of attachment." Secure infant attachment can be predicted, within limits, by the parents' attachment style and by examining how the parents understand their childhood relationship with their own parents (Fonagy et al. 1991). Steele et al. (1991) concluded that expectant parents' narrative accounts of their developmental history provide important clues concerning the "likely adaptation they make to the parental role, and the observed quality of the subsequent parent-child relationship" (p. 111).

The *Adult-Attachment Interview (AAI)* (Main, 2000) classifies adult attachment styles in a manner similar to the three categories developed by Ainsworth et al. (1978): (1) secure-autonomous, (2) dismissive (similar to avoidant children), and (3) preoccupied/ambivalent. Research has indicated a connection between an infant's attachment classification and the classification later received by these individuals as adults on the AAI (Alfonso, 2009). Adults' attachment style impacts the quality of their interactions with their infants, which also affects the infant's attachment style (Meissner, 2009).

Alternative Pathways to Parenthood

Parents who have used Assisted Reproductive Technology (ART) experience unique emotional and physical challenges. The process of preparing for ovulation and later the implantation of selected embryos often causes emotional upheaval in both parents. In addition to the usual lengthy gestation, these parents must cope with the increased danger of miscarriage or stillbirth. Worries that accompany reproductive endocrinological approaches can later result in disturbances of attachment between parents and child, particularly overprotection of the child (Samish, 2006). Parents may differ regarding whether to keep the ART a secret from the child, although later research on therapy in these families has revealed that by age 9 or so, most children have figured out that something unusual surrounded their conception. Some couples suffer narcissistic injury because of their initial infertility.

Adoptions pose multiple difficulties, one of which is the lack of a pregnancy "history" for either the child or the parents.[3] Brinich (1990) identified the following developmental and psychological problems often seen with adopted children: insecure attachments, narcissistic injury due to being given up by their biological parents, fusing the images of the two sets of parents, and greater difficulty resolving family romance issues.

---

3 When an adopted child has been traumatized by previous parenting and separation, that child's adjustment to a new family is in jeopardy. Many adoptive parents undergo costly, emotionally wrenching legal procedures during the adoption process. If the adopted child has been previously abused or neglected, the child is likely to use the defense of "turning passive to active." The child thereby provokes abuse by the new parent as a way of mastering fully expected abuse (transference) (Fleming, 2015). The enormous number of complex issues surrounding adoptions is beyond this summary (se Schechter, 1967; Blum, 1983; Brinich, 1990; Brabender & Fallon, 2013; Fleming, 2015).

Adopted children generally have two fundamental questions: "Who are my biological parents?" and "Why did they give me up for adoption?" (Hodges, 1989). The adoptive parents' responses to these questions and the adopted child's fantasies regarding the answers to these questions are important. The child's identity, self-esteem, trust of others, and feelings of security are impacted. The fantasies and experiences surrounding these two questions become part of children's view of themselves and how they believe others see them (Berger, 1981). So, for example, if the child's fantasy is that the biological mother gave him/her away because the child was unwanted, the child may develop a self-view as being damaged or of low value.

Pregnancy after Prior Loss

Parents who experienced a prior miscarriage, stillbirth, or induced abortion may have recovered. But some still experience unresolved grief (Leon, 1996; Bennett et al., 2005; Côté-Arsenault & O'Leary, 2015) over the demise of the fetus (*"fetal death" refers to death from 20 weeks gestation through one month post-partum* [Slade et al., 2009]). If this is the case, both parents may feel disrupted in their developing attachment to the subsequent (as yet unborn) child (Bennett et al., 2005; O'Leary & Thorwich, 2008).

Sequelae from such a painful experience include long-term depression and lowered self-esteem. For many parents, the loss of a fetus triggers unresolved feelings and memories regarding other losses (Côté-Arsenault & Mahlangu, 1999; Grout & Romanoff, 2000; O'Leary & Thorwich, 2008). A child born after the loss of a prior child may become a "replacement child" or a "vulnerable child" (Kokotos, 2009; Wiener & Schellinski, 2020). Later in development, these children often develop undue guilt. Parents' unresolved mourning increases the chance that the later child will have emotional problems (Green & Solnit, 1964; Stern, 1991; Slade et al., 2009) or that the parents will become overprotective.

Unfortunately, parents who have gone through a pregnancy following the loss of a prior infant often suffer delay in the process of attachment to the new baby—for fear of yet another loss (O'Leary & Thorwich, 2008; Slade et al., 2009). Anna Freud (1936) called this defensive operation "identification with the aggressor before the fact," meaning, in this situation, something like "before you abandon me (as my prior child did), I'll abandon you first."

Pines (1990) advocated a multidimensional psychoanalytic view of the loss of a fetus: developmental interferences, revival of earlier conflicts, complicated grief, defenses against guilt and helplessness, and narcissistic injury.

Case History

Angie, a 35-year-old-woman, was referred by her attorney for a competency evaluation. She had given birth to a son one month previously. The son, upon routine testing, had been found to have a common inborn error of metabolism called phenylketonuria (PKU). PKU causes severe intellectual development delays if the child is fed anything that contains phenylalanine (Phe).[4] Unfortunately, milk (even breast milk) contains high levels of Phe, and most authorities recommend against any breastfeeding at all for safety.

Angie's mother, who was living with Angie, had reported Angie to child protection services because Angie paid no regard to the warnings of the doctors and was arguing with her mother to bottle-feed the child with regular milk. Angie's mother was afraid Angie was not heeding the doctors' warnings when the mother was out of the house.

At the age of 32, Angie married a man who did not want children because he was already paying child support to his ex-wife. Angie had agreed not to become pregnant and had used birth control pills for contraception. Angie and her husband overused alcohol regularly on weekends. When Angie was 34, she forgot to take her birth control pills; she became pregnant. Angie and her husband argued about whether to terminate the pregnancy. Angie realized she wanted to have a child, and she decided to carry the baby to term.

During the entire pregnancy, Angie experienced chronic vomiting (*hyperemesis gravidarum*). She could not have sex with her husband because of her nausea and was often bedridden for hours from exhaustion. She could no longer drink alcohol with him. This exacerbated an already seriously conflicted marital relationship. Angie's husband continued to be angry about the pregnancy and began to drink more alcohol. He stayed late at work or stopped with friends after work for a drink. He routinely got home after dinner.

He spent almost every weekend fishing with friends. He paid little attention to Angie. When Angie was three months pregnant, she asked her mother to move in with her. Angie was not only sick but also lonely and unhappy. Angie's mother had always been critical of her and now continued that pattern, often calling Angie "lazy," even though Angie was ill. This criticism, and Angie's resentment at having to depend upon her mother while she was pregnant, interfered with Angie developing her own identity as a mother. Angie could not resolve her residual separation-individuation conflicts with her own mother.

After the birth of the child, Angie's husband left her for another woman. Angie found out he had been cheating during the pregnancy. He "gaslighted" Angie by blaming her for being unavailable to him sexually for nine months (Calef & Weinshel, 1981). She internalized his criticism and her mother's, causing her to develop guilt-based post-partum depression. The depression

4 For a good review of the problems of breastfeeding children with PKU, see https://blog. pregistry.com/phenylketonuria-breastfeeding/. It is tedious and difficult for most mothers to breastfeed these infants because there is a "Goldilocks Window" regarding the level of phenylalanine that must be consumed by the child: this window is difficult to ascertain. For safety, most mothers simply use a special formula that has the tiny amount of phenylalanine needed by way of a bottle. There is some controversy about how much breastfeeding can be safely allowed, but any breastfeeding increases the risk of PKU causing severe intellectual and physical dysfunction in the child.

was so severe that it had overwhelmed her sleep-wake cycle, her appetite, and her interest in activities outside of her home. She became isolated and mistrustful of others.

Angie was determined to raise the baby in her own way, refusing to listen to doctors, her mother, or her husband's admonitions about breastfeeding the baby. She disidentified from her mother and rebelled against all authority figures she irrationally believed were controlling her and her infant. Angie's mother had then called child protection because of fear that the baby would develop brain damage. At that point, Angie had been referred for evaluation.

When seen, Angie was quiet but argumentative. She did not believe the doctors about PKU causing damage to her baby. She believed they were in cahoots with her mother and her husband, and everyone was trying to make her depressed.

Because of her concreteness and delusional thinking, which complicated her depression, it was felt that she was not competent, at that time, to parent the child. Angie's mother did not want to care for the child, which further complicated Angie's feeling of being abandoned by her own mother.

Fortunately, Angie's brother, Steve, and Steve's wife, Shirley, offered to assist with raising the baby until Angie was emotionally stable enough to parent her infant. The court awarded temporary custody of the baby to Steve and Shirley. Angie was allowed to visit the baby daily and even feed her with a special bottle made up by her brother and sister-in-law. Angie reluctantly agreed with the evaluating psychiatrist to obtain psychotherapy from a social worker and medication from a different psychiatrist.

During treatment, Angie lived with her mother and obtained alimony from her husband. Child support went to her brother. The new psychiatrist prescribed a low dose of risperidone, an antipsychotic medication, to relieve Angie's delusional anxieties. The analytic social worker was able to show Angie that Angie had incorporated the criticism from her husband as a way of punishing herself—in order to relieve guilt over wanting to kill her husband—because he had rejected the baby, abandoned her, and was verbally sadistic toward her.

Because her husband's attitude echoed the miserable treatment she had always gotten from her mother, Angie had condensed the two, thus imagining they were conspiring against her. Angie eventually understood the therapist's explanation that Angie's feeling that her husband and mother were working together against her came only partly from the reality that each of them rejected her. In addition, the therapist explained, Angie was projecting: Angie, herself, wanted revenge on each of them but felt too guilty and desperate to allow herself to think that. So, she saw her own rage coming toward her from them. This aggravated their real neglect of her. She also responded well to the interpretation that she had taken all that anger and turned it on herself. The resulting depression inflamed the misery she had experienced from the hyperemesis during pregnancy and magnified the pain of the situation in which she found herself.

Medication was tapered off after about three months of treatment, and Angie was able to understand the need to avoid milk and (later) any Phe-containing food. She eventually moved in with her brother and sister-in-law, who helped her find a good divorce attorney. She gradually could see the baby as separate from herself.

After the baby was 3 years old, Angie moved to an apartment with a female friend. She was able to sustain herself on alimony and child support. On follow-up two years later, she was living alone, and the child was doing well in kindergarten. Because her brother and sister-in-law had encouraged her to have regular visits with her baby, the baby had developed a secure attachment to her mother, despite the difficult circumstances. Angie was shy about admitting that she had been dating a new man.

In this case, the pregnancy had been a surprise. Although wanted by the mother, the child was not wanted by the father. Medical problems during the pregnancy made sex unworkable, but the husband had emotional problems, particularly with empathy, and cheated on Angie with another woman. Because of his neglect, she was forced to turn to her mother during pregnancy, although she and her mother had not been on good terms.

Both Angie's mother and husband blamed Angie for many unreasonable things, and she used the defenses of introjection and turning on the self, which made her depressed. In addition, her unconscious murderous rage against both her husband and mother caused her guilt, especially since the mother helped her during pregnancy. That guilt, in turn, led Angie unconsciously to turn her rage against herself, making her severely depressed.

Angie's depression and anger were so intense that she used projection, but that wasn't enough to protect her reality testing. In addition, because of splitting of object images, she not only disbelieved the doctors regarding PKU but she developed a delusion that her mother and the baby's father were colluding against her. Interestingly, she did not attempt suicide, and when presented with the opportunity for help, she voluntarily accepted it. This indicated that she was probably not schizophrenic before the pregnancy but that the psychotic symptoms (breakdown in reality testing and trust) were the result of overwhelming rage and depression.

Reasonable, humane approaches to her problems were able to protect the neonate as well as the attachment between the mother and her baby. Fortunately, she had a compassionate brother and sister-in-law who helped out.

4 Birth to 1 Year of Age

Key Questions

- **Was the Temperament of the Baby "Easy To Soothe," "Slow To Warm Up," "Active," or "Difficult To Soothe"? How Did You Handle It?**
    - Looking for the degree of secure-organized attachment: i.e., the baby feels relief on seeing the mother (3–6 months of age).
    - Looking to see if the baby developed trust in the parents' response to stress signals (crying).
    - Did the baby root (looking for attachment issues)?
    - Did the baby suck easily and seem to find pleasure in eating?
        - Looking for attachment and oral drive gratification (or not).

- **Was the Baby Fed on a Demand or Fixed Schedule? Response?**
    - Babies fed on a schedule may not have been adequately soothed.
    - Looking for subsequent problems with independence and autonomy.

- **Did You Let the Baby "Cry It Out" or Respond with Soothing/Feeding When the Infant Cried? How Successful Were You?**
    - Looking to see if the baby developed apathy or lack of interest in the parents after 3 months of age ("low-keyedness")—often the result of allowing infants to "cry it out" without soothing.
    - Looking for the parent's self-esteem and pleasure in caring for an infant (mother's identity stabilization).

- **Did the Baby Look in Your Eyes While Nursing/Feeding? Was There a Specific Smile at the Mothering Figure by 3 Months, Laugh at 4 Months?**
    - Looking for disturbances in pleasurable interactions (disturbed internalization, in the child, of self and mother images).

DOI: 10.4324/9781003257110-4

- Looking for the development of imitative play between infant and mothering figure (mirroring as a precursor to empathy).

- **Were There Multiple Caretakers? Attachment to any? Was the Baby in Day Care: At What Age? How Many Hours a Day?**

  - Looking for the baby's response to separations, leading to the baby feeling terror or low-keyed.
  - Looking for early interference with babies knowing themselves as distinct from their mothers (break in the differentiation and early practicing subphases)—important for babies to develop a sense of their environment as separate from themselves ("reality testing").

- **Any Traumas (Parental Separation, Neglect, or Abuse)?**

  - Looking for emotional disruptions that were overwhelming to the parents and affected the child (death of a grandparent, divorce, e.g.).
  - Looking for incidents that were overwhelming to the child (illness in the child, e.g.).
  - Looking for the impact on the child's attachment and social behaviors.

- **Did the Baby Ever Sleep in a Room alone, in the Parents' Bed or Room? Where Was Feeding Done? Breast or Bottle? Any Problems? Was Weaning Attempted at any Time? Results?**

  - Looking for evidence of persistent symbiosis (excessive clinging at a later age), or physical agitation—often due to co-sleeping.
  - Looking for attachment problems in stressful situations where the infant felt helpless or inadequate.

- **Was Toilet Training Attempted before the Child Could Walk?**

  - Since physiologically not possible, premature toilet training indicates parents' obsession with cleanliness.
  - Asking the child to perform a task that is impossible sets the stage for future pressures to perform.

- **Were There Indications of Social Connectedness and Attachment to Caregivers?**

  - Did the child show a social smile and make cooing sounds by 2–3 months?
  - Did the infant develop stranger anxiety and preference for a selected caregiver?

Answers to the Questions

What Was the Infant's Temperament (Thomas & Chess, 1977)?

Although parental activity with infants and children has an enormous effect, children are not born with a blank slate. Infants immediately manifest different inborn "temperaments," which vary among warm and engaging, difficult to soothe, slow to warm up, difficult to engage, "active" (muscularly), inhibited, and uninhibited (Kagan, 1994). Each child, therefore, requires different amounts of parental effort and responds differently to soothing.

The most difficult-to-soothe neonates actually arch their backs away from their parents (opisthotonus). This type of child requires much more patience from the parents than an infant who is "warm and engaging."

Parents often can relate their memories of the soothing problems from the first year of life. The evaluator can then assess whether the parents' approaches were attuned, neglectful, or aggravating to the child's affect regulation.

Since attachment begins with the first sucking experience, the parents' approaches may have set the stage for a lifetime of other difficulties in subsequent stages.

Spitz (1957) described the cephalogyric reflex, meaning the baby instinctively turns its head back and forth, sideways. The mother must help the neonate find the nipple; as soon as the nipple is encountered, the baby should have begun sucking. If the mother did not hold and guide the child, this may have caused "failure to thrive" and other feeding problems. Children with this kind of history often have difficulty gaining weight, enjoying close contacts, and later making close friends, as well as other attachment problems.

Was the Baby Fed on a Demand or Fixed Schedule? Response?

In most cases, neonates need their "mothers" to be flexible regarding nursing. Newborns have a relatively unstable neurological makeup and do not soothe themselves for quite a while. So, mothers who followed some advice to put the baby on a schedule of feeding, say every four hours, will have exposed their infants to long periods of unsoothed frustration mixed with "nonspecific" emotional overload (crying). So-called colic is defined as "crying for three or more hours a day, three or more days a week, for three or more weeks" (Mayo Clinic, accessed March 2022). Scheduled children may or may not respond to the mother's schedule, which will cause the mother to feel self-critical or frustrated—both factors in post-partum depression.

If children were kept on a strict feeding schedule, they are highly likely to develop an attachment that is insecure. They are more likely to have poor frustration tolerance later. And their "sense of safety" (Sandler, 2003) and trust may not have developed properly.

Did You Let the Baby "Cry It Out" or Respond with Soothing and Feeding When the Infant Cried? How Successful Were You?

Children 0–1 year of age will eventually stop crying out of exhaustion, but *not due to dependency gratification* from the mothering figure; they are at risk of becoming apathetic, incurious children that Mahler et al. (1975) called "low-keyed." A subject of controversy, some research has shown that a woman's voice may be more soothing than a man's voice in soothing an infant (Fifer & Moon, 1994). The verbalizations of the mother, though not literally understood by the infant, set the stage for the child to be soothed through talking later. The baby's nascent identity, including self-esteem in being able to obtain help, starts here, as well.

Parents who let the child "cry it out" actually put the infant at high risk for many later developmental problems (Blackman, 2018a).

Did the Baby Look in Your Eyes While Nursing? Was There a Specific Smile Response by 3 Months, Laugh at 4 Months?

The eye-to-eye contact during nursing is key to the development of pleasurable interactions. If the infant's smile did not develop specific to the person nursing the baby, this would indicate disturbed internalization of soothing sources, and may be a precursor to difficulties in the development of self and mother images. Later sequelae of these problems include disturbances of object relations, i.e., developmentally based psychosis, borderline personality organization, and masochism (Novick & Novick, 2016).

Laughing at 4 months of age has been extensively studied (Beebe, 2005). If mutual glee between parent and infant did not develop (disturbed mutual cuing and mirroring, or reciprocity [Emde, 1991]), empathy often does not develop in later phases of development.

Were There Multiple Caretakers? Attachment to Any? Was the Baby in Day Care: At What Age? How Many Hours a Day?

During the first year of life, the more caretakers there are, the greater the risk that the child will not develop self and object constancy by age 3. This is not axiomatic, since a consistent stay-at-home parent with a difficult-to-soothe child may still encounter difficulties. Usually, a consistent, loving nanny (or grandparent), if available until the child is 3 years old, will similarly reduce the risk of the child having severe separation anxiety after age 3.

"Impersonal"[1] day care during this stage is the riskiest to the child. The warmth of the symbiotic phase, as well as the early separation of the babies' self-image from images of others, are more likely to be delayed. McDevitt (1975) opined that parents probably needed to spend about two hours a day with the infant for the infant to develop self and object constancy.

---

1 By this we refer to large, institutional-style, day care centers. These places may hold dozens of children, with a small staff/child ratio. In such settings, the child rarely obtains sufficient soothing and attachment.

Interpersonally, the baby's response to actual separations that may have occurred, for any number of reasons, may give useful evidence of an early delay in secure attachment. Problematic reactions in the infant include terror and low-keyedness.

The earliest elements of reality testing occur during months 6–12. Interference with attachment and soothing often disrupts babies' knowing themselves as distinct from their mothers (break in the differentiation and early practicing subphases)—important for babies' developing sense of their environment as separate from themselves ("reality testing").

Did the Baby Ever Sleep in the Parents' Bed or Room? Was Feeding by Breast or Bottle? Any Problems? Was Weaning Attempted at Any Time? Results?

The highly contentious issue of babies who sleep with parents comes up in every phase of development and has different consequences at different phases.

During the first 6 months of life, the baby is vulnerable to being accidentally smothered and to SIDS. After that, co-sleeping tends to interfere with the beginnings of separation-individuation. The separation "crisis" (McDevitt, 1985) at 9–12 months of age, where the child wakes up crying in the middle of the night, is likely to be exacerbated when there is co-sleeping.

The child who co-sleeps is also likely to have difficulty with weaning, basic trust, and perhaps more importantly, "basic mistrust" (Erikson, 1950a). Basic mistrust means that children know they are alone, and realize the parent may not come (although the child is relieved when the parent arrives). The little time it takes parents to respond to a crying baby in the next room actually fosters the notion that the parent is not always available and is believed to be one basis of later reality testing (Schur, 1966). If the parents respond to the babies' distress consistently, within a reasonable time frame, the babies' reality testing and trust in others will be enhanced.

Certain medical problems may require the infant's hospitalization. Ear infections, if gone untreated, may result in serious febrile illnesses,[2] all of which can interfere with feeding, smiling, and attachment.

Toward the end of the first year, if the baby cannot focus on eating (problems with self-image and eating regulation), the baby may refuse to eat, not have gained weight, or become unsoothable. How did the parents respond to these difficulties?

Also, near age 1, many babies show some sign of reciprocity toward the mother and father. Babies who pick up a spoon and feed themselves are imitating the gestures of the parents. Sometimes the baby will grab the spoon and attempt to feed the feeder—early reciprocity.

---

2 Such as streptococcal pharyngitis, scarlet fever, and later, rheumatic fever.

Elements of developing assertiveness begin to show when the baby pushes away food or throws it. This is distressing to parents but demonstrates early attempts at independence. How parents handled this may have ramifications later.

Was Toilet Training Attempted?
The nerves serving the anal and urogenital sphincter muscles do not become myelinated until the child is 18 months old. Therefore, attempting to toilet train a child during the first year of life is practically and realistically not possible. Clinically, it is not uncommon to find instances where premature toilet training has been attempted.[3] If parents are attempting to toilet train the child before age 1, they should be advised to desist from doing so. This is the reason parents must be asked a question about toilet training during this phase of life. *Premature attempts to toilet train a child can lead to problems with a child's self-esteem and often herald the beginning of power struggles to come, especially over food and toileting (e.g., encopresis).*

Clinically, bizarre toilet training practices (such as strapping a 12-month-old's legs to the toilet seat, or using enemas) should alert the clinician that a serious disturbance may be present in one or both parents. If that is the case, a few questions to the parents about their sexual involvement with the child should also be asked. Frank sexual abuse of children under the age of 1 is fairly rare, but not unheard of (see Blackman & Dring, 2016, for examples).

Was There Stranger Anxiety at 8 Months of Age?
When a secure attachment has developed between parent and child, the child will become afraid of strangers. This is seen when the parent gives the child to another adult to hold. The baby may first be curious, but after a period of time, will usually start crying. The ability to differentiate the parent from others will show up in stranger anxiety as well as distress ("separation protest") when separated from the parent. During this time, even other familiar people, such as grandparents and day care providers, may cause the infant distress.

More serious is the way the parent handles the predicable stranger anxiety. Does the parent make it worse by criticizing the baby or becoming overly ashamed in front of others? Could the parent soothe the baby?

Evaluation of the Child

The first observations made by the therapist concern the parent-child interaction in the waiting room. Especially at this age, when the child is preverbal,

---

3 In China, one old school method of toilet training involved holding infants, before they could walk, over the opening in the floor. A second common method for children between 1 and 3 was to put children in crotch-less pants, which allowed them to defecate *ad libitum* on the floor, or outside on the ground. The mother's job was simply to clean up the mess. This latter culturally based technique has faded out in the major cities of China in the past ten years.

the child can only be evaluated together with the caregiver. Subsequently, in your treatment room, the baby can be observed with the caregiver while the therapist and the caregiver interact. Does the caregiver never put the infant down? Or does the caregiver put the child down and then ignore the child?

The therapist observes the caregiver, the infant, and the reciprocity between them in order to evaluate whether the caregiver/infant relationship seems to enhance the infant's stability.

Does the caregiver demonstrate, by verbal response, facial expression, movement, and vocalization, awareness of and responsiveness to the infant's behaviors, facial expressions, and emotional needs? Useful observations also include how the infant responds to the caregivers' behaviors, how attentive the infant is to the caregiver, and how engaged the infant is with the caregiver (Masling & Bornstein, 1996).

Finally, behaviors observed during the evaluation give the evaluator a window into the infant's internal structure, conflicts, and self-development (A. Freud, 1965).

Here are some suggestions for what the therapist should observe and the type of information that can be obtained through such observation:

- **Is the baby alert?**
  - Looking for healthy curiosity—Is the child looking around, actively attentive, interested in play with the caregiver? These are indications of relatedness.
  - Looking to see if the child laughs with the parent—indicates parent's playfulness.
  - Looking for low-keyedness—(being ignored)—child seems fatigued and disengaged from the caregiver.
  - Does the infant initiate any play or activity, and how does the caregiver respond?
    - Examine (1) the mother's ability to pick up cues from the infant, (2) the infant's development of self, and (3) the child's expectations that the caregiver will respond.
    - If the infant is fussy, how does the caregiver respond to this? And how does the infant respond to the caregiver's attempts at soothing?

- **How do parents respond to the baby's crying or agitation?**
  - Some parents don't soothe—they allow the baby to cry; some babies seem not to respond to the parent's soothing efforts.
  - Some parents become overwhelmed—and may look to the therapist for help.
  - What is the intensity, duration, and volume of the baby's fussiness?
  - Does the parent increase vocal timbre to stop the baby's crying, only to exacerbate the crying?

- Looking for the infant's development of an *internal working model* of the caregiver based on the caregiver's nurturing responses to signals of distress from the early infant (Bowlby, 1969, 1973).
- How do the parents talk to the child, especially when the infant is distressed?
- Does the parent touch the child—gently or with anger?

- **What did the parents bring to the office?**

  - Are parents overprotective? Did they bring a suitcase full of materials?
  - Adequate supplies to care for the baby? (Or not?) Diapers, bottles. Were toys and other items age-appropriate? These factors relate to the caregiver's attunement to the cues, needs, interests, and abilities of the infant.
  - Did mistrustful parents bring you written materials regarding children this age, or an internet search result about their child's condition?

- **Are the parents holding the child?**

  - Some parents feed the baby facing away from them—which would facilitate object relations pathology in the child.
  - How is the father: engaged or distant? Disengaged fathers often increase the likelihood of post-partum depression in mothers, causing some mothers to have difficulty tending to their child.
  - Does the infant look away from the parent or an object of their joint attention?

    - Looking for the infant's development of relatedness and trust in others (Gilmore & Meersand, 2014).
    - Looking for reciprocity between the infant and caregiver. Is there give and take in their interactions; Do they both seem to enjoy the interaction, and if not, what seems to interfere with the enjoyment?

- **Do parents seem relaxed or tense?**

  - Possibly competitive with the therapist? Parents who see the therapist as a "better parent" will need clarification and reassurance from the therapist to reduce resistance to the therapist's interventions.
  - Are parents afraid they have done something wrong?

    - The inadvertent mistakes of parents (due usually to a lack of knowledge of the first year of life) can be corrected gently by the therapist after discussing the anxiety of the parents.

- If the child is walking, do the parents allow the child to explore the waiting room?

  - Parents who can't set limits will allow the child to crawl or walk into dangerous situations (such as behind a door that is frequently opened).

- Parents who are overly restrictive will not let the child explore at all, and may restrain the child (who can crawl or walk) from any independent activity. The child usually manifests hypercompliance or high levels of frustrated whining.

- How does the baby (between 8 and 12 months) react when the therapist enters the waiting room?

    - Any stranger anxiety? Indicating healthy attachment to the mother.
    - Has the baby been sleeping with the parents? Co-sleeping exaggerates the symbiotic tie, interfering with the development of "vital affects" (Stern, 1985) and the modulation of separation anxiety.
    - Does the child hide behind the parents or run away from them? Hiding behind them suggests high levels of stranger anxiety; running away from them may indicate a delay in the development of trust; running to a stranger may indicate severe attachment problems (technically termed "reactive attachment disorder").

- Was there the appearance of "social referencing"—meaning infants looking to a parent's emotional signals in order to gauge their own affective reactions (Emde, 1983; Stern, 1985)?

At the end of the interaction, evaluators should ask themselves how they felt watching the interaction. Did they want to intervene or make suggestions? Did they experience tension/frustration/sadness more in regard to the infant or the caregivers? Were the infant's behaviors distracting to the interactions between the caregiver and the evaluator?

Essay

Introduction

The Latin word *infans* means "not able to speak." While the infant may not be speaking with words, the infant is not silent. Infants' crying, cooing, gazing, smiling, and motoric activity speaks volumes about their biological, emotional, attachment, and physical needs. Like any communication process, it is multidirectional, with each participant influencing the other. The parents'/caregivers' response and attunement to the infant's communication create the foundation for the infant's emotional, interpersonal, defensive, and ego development.

What is it like to be a newborn? We really do not know. None of us remember our first year of life. The capacity for evocative memory (Blum & Blum, 1990; Meltzoff, 1995) does not begin until about 18–24 months. We must rely on the parents' perspectives/memories when assessing infant development. If we are assessing older children/adolescents, they often have heard "stories" about themselves from family members.

Psychoanalytic child research has found that warm, consistent, and predictable parental soothing is necessary for an infant to develop a self-image, reality testing, affect control, and basic trust (and mistrust) (Erikson, 1950a; Blackman, 2018a). As Spitz (1945) and Anna Freud (1956) discovered, babies must be held as well as fed. Otherwise, they can become hopeless, stop sucking, and may die of starvation.

Nota Bene

1) Many parents will not ask for an in-person evaluation of their infant, though there are specialists who perform such evaluations (Anzieu-Premmereur, 2017).
2) For evaluation of children at any age, parents should be asked to describe their interactions with their infants from birth to one year of life. That way, the evaluator can gather information about any problems that may have set the stage for later difficulties during development.
3) Psychoanalysts initially understood infant conflicts by reconstructing these through the conscious recollections and dreams of adult patients. While these data were not considered factual recreations of the infant experience, theories about infant development were initially drawn from such patients (Tyson, 1990).

Child psychoanalysis began with Freud's understanding that childhood experiences could be the genesis of adult psychological symptoms. Using reconstruction, Freud could see patterns and then formulate regular maturational stages in a child's life (Kris, 1956a). Anna Freud considered the infant's development as a prototype for adult development (Freud, 1965).

While the precursors of psychological disorders may lie in infancy, there is an ongoing debate about whether psychopathology can even be present in the first year of life (Zeanah & Zeanah, 2019). In our view, the assessment of the infant is vital to understand later evolving mental disturbances. Evaluation should include assessment of the caregivers and the relationship between the caregivers and the infant (Sroufe, 1989). The deprivation of attuned and nurturing relationships with infants has been found to adversely impact neurodevelopment (Green, 2003; Berens & Nelson, 2019).

Diagnostic Classification Systems

Rene Spitz (1951) devised one of the earliest classification systems of infant "psychogenic diseases." His schema suggested that the main etiology of infant emotional distress was to be found in a disturbance of the mother toward the infant: overt rejection, overpermissiveness, hostility related to anxiety, inconsistent care, mood lability in the mother, and narcissistic use of the child. He related a child's specific psychological illness (coma, colic, dermatitis, hypermotility, fecal play, aggression, and depression) to the degree of dysfunction in the mother's relationship with the child.

Subsequent classification systems have maintained Spitz's emphasis on the first year of life: the quality and character of the caregiver-infant relationship continue to be regarded as primary elements in the development of infant mental health.

The early days of life have also been considered crucial in understanding the development of autonomous ego functions. Brazelton (1973, 1980) devised a classification system to detect neurobehavioral deviations in infants that require early interventions to optimize an infant's developmental potential (Neonatal Behavioral Assessment Scale or NBAS). Broadly, this system evaluates the infant's response to stimulation and consciousness, specifically, the infant's: (1) response to sensory stimuli, (2) muscle tone, (3) alertness, (4) responses to cuddling, (5) trajectory of crying responses, (6) startle reactions, (7) tremulousness, (8) autonomic lability, and (9) motor activity. This neonatal classification system emphasized the importance of the parent-infant relationship.

Anna Freud's concepts of "Developmental Lines" in the *Diagnostic Profile* (Freud, 1963, 2018) involve gauging children based on developmental norms in the areas of inner conflicts, sexual and aggressive drives, ego and superego functions, psychosocial stages of development, attitudes, and achievements. The *Diagnostic Profile* was not limited to infants; it covered all of the stages of childhood. The profile was aimed at learning about the child's internal functioning and comparing this to the child's manifest behavior. The diagnosis of a child was based on what was interfering with the child's developmental progress.

In *Normality and Pathology* (2018), Anna Freud suggested that "infantile neurosis" was prototypical of adult psychopathology. Revisions of Anna Freud's *Profile* have moved away from diagnosing psychopathology; now, the total personality is examined (Malberg & Pretorius, 2017). Anna Freud's *Diagnostic Profile* was revised in 2001 and 2016 to include attachment and developmental research (Green & Joyce, 2017).

Despite reluctance to view infants as having psychopathology, Wieder et al. (1987) devised a psychoanalytic and developmentally based classification system of infant psychopathology. A stated goal of this system was to refute the idea of many physicians and mental health providers that the first year of life was devoid of serious, life-endangering emotional problems. Wieder's classification system identified six syndromes:

1) Disorder of homeostasis
2) Disorder of human attachment
3) Disorder of somatopsychic differentiation
4) Disorder of internalization
5) Disorder of psychological differentiation
6) Disorder of consolidation of basic personality functions (failures connected to the development of object constancy)

In the *Clinical Interview of the Child*, Greenspan, and Greenspan (2003) use a developmental approach to study and evaluate children of all ages. They note the importance of assessing an infant's ability in the following areas: to achieve homeostasis, to develop initial capacity for human attachment, to differentiate self from others (emotional differentiation and reality testing), and to internalize, initiate, and integrate behavior.

Greenspan (2003) emphasized clinically observing a child when making a thorough assessment. He divided clinical observations into seven categories:

1) physical integrity;
2) emotional tone;
3) child's ability to relate to the clinician;
4) the specific affects and anxieties elaborated during the clinical interview;
5) how the child uses the environment in the waiting room and the playroom;
6) thematic development – how the child develops themes in terms of depth and organization of experience; and
7) the feelings the child evokes in the clinician.

Greenspan also developed the *Functional Emotional Assessment Scale (FEAS)* to assess the functioning of children from 7 months to 4 years of age (Greenspan S. & DeGangi, 2001).

The *DSMs* and *ICDs* have dominated psychiatric classification systems, but they do not adequately address infant mental health issues. The *DSM-5* is atheoretical and symptom-focused (Blackman, 2016a). Most of the criteria in *DSM-5-TR* only apply to children 2 years of age or older. What is clearly lacking in the *DSM-5-TR* is consistent recognition that the relationship between infant and caregiver may produce problems—thus omitting a crucial focus when addressing problems in newborns.

The *Research Diagnostic Criteria-Preschool Age—RDC-PA* (Scheeringa, 2003) is a diagnostic system sponsored by the American Academy of Child and Adolescent Psychiatry. It addresses diagnostic criteria of children 2 years and older, but it does not address infancy.

The Diagnostic Classifications—The Zero to Three Project (2005, 2016) focuses on the classification of disorders in infants and toddlers that were not covered by the *DSM*. Unlike the *DSM-IV* or *DSM-5-TR*, it uses a classification system that considers the quality of the parent-child relationship and recognizes that disturbances in that relationship impact the infant's development.

The latest version of the diagnostic system, *DC:0–5*, covers the following categories: Neurodevelopmental Disorders; Sensory Processing Disorders; Anxiety Disorders; Mood Disorders; Obsessive Compulsive and Related Disorders; Sleep, Eating, and Crying Disorders; Trauma, Stress, and Deprivation Disorders; and Relationship Disorders. It uses a multiaxial system with provisions for *DSM/ICD* diagnoses. One of the assumptions of this system is that it is important to identify problems as early as possible to decrease the potential negative impact on the child's future emotional and developmental health.

The *Psychodynamic Diagnostic Manual–Second Edition or PDM-2* (Lingiardi & McWilliams, 2017) is an encyclopedic textbook that offers the scholar a vast bibliography regarding emotional problems in infancy (*see* Speranza et al., 2018). The nosology in the *PDM-2* is based on classic psychoanalytic theory, object relations considerations, and psychoanalytic research,[4] making it more accurate than the phenomenologically based *DSMs*.

The *PDM-2* (p. 626) uses a five-axis system, similar to the *DSM-III and DSM-IV*. Infancy is viewed from the biopsychosocial perspective suggested by Greenspan (1992, 1996). The *PDM-2* also recognizes how attachment patterns and other aspects of relationships are connected to an infant's normal and pathological development.[5]

Theories for Assessing the Infant-Caregiver Relationship

Evaluation and intervention during the first year of life always involve both the infant and caregivers. This total assessment involves the bidirectional nature of the relationship, as well as each individual's contributions. The characteristics of this relationship are crucial to the infant's survival and development. *Ghosts in the Nursery* (Fraiberg et al., 1975) demonstrates how parents' own unresolved early psychological conflicts can affect their infants.

Beatrice Beebe's microanalysis of mother-infant interactions further substantiates the significant impact of the parent-infant dyad on the infant's development, especially interactions of which parents may be completely unaware. Beebe (2005) also described interventions that help the parents become aware of how the infant and mother impact each other. Specifically, the mutual social exchanges between mother and infant are crucial to the infant's development of object and self-representations (*see also* Beebe, 2000).

Another important indicator of social reciprocity during the first year is "joint attention" between mother and infant when the infant shifts gaze between the mother's face and an object of mutual interest (Gilmore & Meersand, 2014).

---

4 The *PDM-2* was influenced by a manual put out by the Interdisciplinary Council on Developmental and Learning Disorders (ICDL), *Diagnostic Manual for Infants and Young Children* (ICDL-DMIC; ICDL, 2005), as well as the *Diagnostic Classification of Mental Health and Developmental Disorders of Infancy and Early Childhood, Revised Edition* (DC: 0-3R: Zero to three, 2005). In 2005, these were considered the best classification systems for infancy and early childhood.

5 "Notwithstanding the advantages of the DSM and International Classification of Diseases (ICD) systems, often their classifications do not meet the needs of clinicians. ... In focusing on the full range of mental functioning PDM-2 aspires to be a 'taxonomy of people' rather than a 'taxonomy of disorders', and it highlights the importance of considering who one is rather than what one has" (PDM-2, p. 2).

Margaret Mahler also recognized that the early months of an infant's life are crucial to the establishment of a firm attachment to the mother, although her group focused on the infant's intrapsychic development. In her theory about separation-individuation, the infant at 4 to 6 months of age begins to show interest in the world beyond the caregiver (1971, 1972, 1975). This interest coincides with the infant's improved motor ability—especially the ability to crawl away from the mother. Mahler called this stage "hatching." The infant explores the world, using the mother as a "secure base." This combination—exploration and a home-base mother—signals that trust in the mother's presence and nurturance is being established.

Pine (2004) refined Mahler's stages (Symbiosis, Hatching, Practicing, Rapprochement, and Libidinal Object Constancy) from birth until age 3–4 years. The completion of individuation is accomplished when internalized mental representations of mother and self are stable, so that the child can function securely without the mother's presence ("self and object constancy").

The adaptive qualities of the "infant attachment system" were described by Bowlby (1969, 1973). He theorizes that infants have an innate, adaptive, biologically based attachment system that becomes activated when the infant experiences distress. The infant maintains the mother's attention through crying, smiling, and crawling. During the early months of life, if the mother is responsive to the infant's distress, the infant develops an *internal working model* (mental representations of self and others in a social relationship). This internal working model is the foundation for the child's future relationships.

Attachment Disorders may result from social deprivation, neglect, or abuse. These are described in the *PDM-2, DSM-5-TR*, and *ICD-10*. Two types of attachment disorders listed are Reactive Attachment Disorder (RAD) and Disinhibited Social Engagement Disorder (DSED). Most children diagnosed with these disorders have been raised in institutions or have been abused (Spitz, 1945; Main & George, 1979; Finelli et al., 2019). RAD is characterized by withdrawn and inhibited behaviors; DSED references indiscriminate social behavior associated with social boundary violations.

The previously described attachment disorders are distinguishable *from attachment styles* noted by Ainsworth et al. (2015) in the Strange Situation Paradigm. These attachment styles include the following:

- *Secure* – Baby seeks the mother when distressed and is distressed when separated from the mother. The baby eagerly greets the mother when she returns. The baby is comforted when the mother returns.
- *Insecurely attached-avoidant* – The baby continues to explore the playroom when the mother leaves but shows no interest in her when she returns;
- *Insecurely attached-ambivalent* – The baby is upset when the mother leaves but is not comforted when the mother returns. These babies may demand to be picked up but then insist on being set down. (For a review of all attachment styles see Masling & Bornstein, 1996.)

Children with RAD show few selective or organized attachments to any person. Children with RAD and DSES also demonstrate, across most relationships and situations, more affective disturbances, emotional regulation problems, and lack of responsiveness.

Specific Symptom Complexes

Sleep Disorders

Putting oneself to sleep is a developmental task normally accomplished during the first three years of life. In psychiatry clinics, 10%–47% of parents of children report sleep problems. The affective and social environment in the family impacts the sleep patterns of the infant. Sleep difficulties in infancy are associated with anxious/insecure attachments. Children who are anxious about losing their mothers have more difficulty separating, and therefore may develop patterns of light sleep to be aware of her presence (Moore, 1989). The parent-infant relationship impacts the organization of the infant's sleep-wake cycle (Harrison, 2017) and the ability of the infant to regulate their sleep states (Hofer, 2014).

At birth, most infants sleep more than they are awake. They also sleep as much during the day as the night. During the first year of life, infants gradually sleep more at night than during the day. From age 3 months until age 2 years, infants tend to sleep 12–14 hours per day. From 2 to 3 years of age, many children wake up during the night, but because they can self-soothe, they should be able to get themselves back to sleep (Anders & Dahl, 2007).

Infants who sleep in their parents' room during the first year of life have more nighttime awakenings (Goodlin-Jones & Anders, 2005). Sleeping in the parent's room at 12 months of age was predictive of night waking at 2 years of age. A concern is that many parents do not believe co-sleeping is problematic (Goodlin-Jones et al., 2001; Goodlin-Jones & Anders, 2005). Research also indicates that children who have early sleep problems will likely continue to have sleep problems later unless there is intervention (Gaylor et al., 2005, p. 635).

Feeding and Eating Disorders

During the first 12 months of life, the infant should develop autonomous internal regulation of feeding. Feeding and eating disorders (as well as sleep disorders) are the most common problems seen by pediatricians and mental health practitioners. About 25% of normally developing infants and up to 80% of infants with developmental disabilities will have feeding issues.

While there may be biological, sensory, or medical reasons for some infant feeding disorders, a problematic infant-caregiver relationship, trauma, or attachment problem is often the culprit. Spitz (1945) recognized the connection between food refusal and anaclitic depression.

Anna Freud (1965) felt the process of being able to independently regulate food intake was vital to the infant's development. The process of being weaned from the bottle/breast is also significant because

> For the first time, [the infant is] leaning toward either progression and adventurousness (when new experiences are welcomed) [vs.]a tenacious clinging to existing pleasures…every change [may be] experienced as threat and deprivation. It is to be expected that, whichever attitude dominates the feeding process will also become important in other developmental areas.
>
> (p. 71)

From this perspective, food refusal expresses the infant's rejection of maternal care and attention. Traumatic separation from the mother or mother-substitute may result in either food refusal or "greed": overeating and treating food as a substitute for mother's love (A. Freud, 1965).

There is evidence that the parents of children who have eating disorders also experienced an eating disorder such as anorexia, bulimia, or binge eating (Sherkow et al., 2009). These mothers tend to be controlling with their children during meals and playtime (Cooper et al., 2004). They also tend to miss their infant's cues regarding readiness for self-feeding. Parents' controlling or inconsistent feeding behavior can result in the infant having difficulty recognizing internal states of hunger and satiation (Chatoor, 1989).

Caccia (2009) views eating disorders (vomiting, diarrhea, food refusal, and food intolerance) as the infant's concrete rejection of the caregiver's pathology, specifically anxiety. For a complete review of feeding and eating disorders in infants, see Keren (2019) and the *PDM-2* (2017).[6]

---

6 There are six subtypes of feeding disorders listed in the *PDM-2*:
- *Feeding disorder of caregiver-infant reciprocity* – Lack of engagement between mother and infant leads to poor food intake and growth failure.
- *Infantile anorexia* – Evident before 3 years of age. Transition to self-feeding involves issues of autonomy and dependency, but in these cases, the child eats little, throws food and utensils, and shows little interest in eating.
- *Sensory food aversions* – The infant's refusal of food is related to the taste, texture, temperature, or smell of the food. The infants grimace, spit food out, wipe their tongues, gag, or vomit.
- *Feeding disorder associated with a concurrent medical condition* – A combination of organic and psychological features. The infant associates eating with pain and may cry in anticipation of feeding.
- *Feeding disorder associated with insults to the gastrointestinal tract (also termed post-traumatic feeding disorder of infancy)* – Food refusal follows a traumatic experience to the orpharynx or gastrointestinal tract (after choking, gagging, vomiting).

Temperament

Chess and Thomas (1986) recognized that the infant's inborn tendencies influence the mother's interaction with her baby, and described "temperament" as a relatively stable personality characteristic present at birth (also see Kagan, 1994). A *goodness of fit* between the caregiver, infant, and the social and physical environment promotes healthy child development.

In other words, temperament is not solely dispositive of the future mental health of children. Later experiences, interventions, developmental changes, and the environment are also vital in shaping the psychological welfare of the individual (Brim & Kagan, 1980). Even problematic temperaments, such as inhibition/shyness, can be altered by interactions with a caregiver and/or an environment that is responsive to the infants' distress (Appelman, 2001).

In a longitudinal study, Chess and Thomas (1986) identified nine categories of temperament: (1) activity level, (2) rhythmicity of biological functions, (3) predominant tendency to approach or withdraw from new stimuli, (4) ease of adaptability to new situations, (5) threshold of responsiveness, (6) predominant quality of mood, (7) distractibility, (8) attention span, and (9) persistence. They further defined three broad categories of infant temperament:

- *Easy:* Infants who have regular sleep and feeding schedules, positive responses to most new stimuli, easy adaptability to change, and mild or moderately intense positive mood. About 40% of infants have an easy temperament.
- *Slow to warm up:* About 15% of infants, often called "shy," generally have a mixed response to new situations. They are slow to adapt to new situations.
- *Difficult:* About 10% of infants have irregular biological functions, negative responses to new stimuli, are slow to adapt to change, and show intense mood expressions.
- Mixtures of the three types account for 35% of infants.

Depressive Disorders in Infants and Mothers

Parents may not label their infants as depressed, but it is important to ask if the child had difficulty feeding, eating, and being soothed in the first year of life. Such symptoms occurring in association with a separation from caretakers suggest depressive affect in infancy. Sad facial expressions have been clearly established in infants as young as 2 months old. By 6 months of age, sad facial expressions are associated with sad external events (Izard et al., 1995).

Post-partum depression occurs in about 13% of mothers. It can impact the attachment style and emotional development of the infant. A mother's postnatal depression should be distinguished from a simple low mood (50%–80% of new mothers) and from post-partum psychoses (0.1%–0.2% of mothers). Parents who have a neonate in the NICU show high rates of distress and depression, which can negatively impact their child's subsequent development. The

National Perinatal Association (NPA) has recommended that a psychologist be embedded in NICUs (Steinberg & Patterson, 2017).[7]

Lawrence Blum (2007) provides a psychoanalytic perspective on post-partum depression. He categorizes mothers with post-partum depression as manifesting one of three problem areas: (1) conflicts about dependency, (2) difficulty expressing anger, and (3) unresolved issues with their own mothers. Blum provides a history of early psychoanalytic perspectives of post-partum depression, including S. Freud's description of an intervention with a mother who suffered with it—Freud addressed the mother's dependency conflicts and inhibitions about expressing anger.

Given the psychological conflicts facing mothers with post-partum depression it becomes easier to understand how these internal conflicts can impact the emotional functioning of infants (Beebe et al., 2002). Infants of mothers with post-partum depression have been found to be more likely to have anxious/avoidant attachment styles (Beebe, 2000; Toth et al., 2009). Also, depressed mothers are more likely to have difficulty focusing on the infant's signals and interests, resulting in the mothers being too withdrawn or too intrusive (Field, 2010) and having more difficulty regulating their infants' emotions.

Papiasvili and Mayers (2017) present a psychodynamic developmental review of post-partum depression and a clinical case highlighting the intergenerational impact maternal depression has upon infant attachment and adult functioning. Schechter (2017) identified that intergenerational transmission of maternal trauma can impact the mother-infant relationship outside the awareness of the mother and the developing child. This dyadic process can create unintegrated depressive aspects in the child's identity.

Assessment Measures for Use with Infants

Bayley Scales of Infant and Toddler Development-Fourth Edition (Bayley & Aylward, 2019).

This is an individually administered instrument that measures the developmental functioning of infants and children between the ages of 1 and 42 months of age. It can be used to identify intellectual delays and learning needs of children. It is the most widely used instrument in infant developmental assessment.

The Infant Behavior Questionnaire-Revised (Garstein & Rothbart, 2003)

This is a measure of temperament in infants 3–12 months of age. It assesses the following dimensions of temperament: activity level, distress following limitations, approach, fear, duration of orienting, smiling and laughter, vocal reactivity, sadness, perceptual sensitivity, high-intensity pleasure,

---

7 For a full review of the numerous studies of the impact of postnatal depression on infants and child development, see Murray, Halligan, and Cooper (2019).

low-intensity pleasure, cuddliness, soothability, and falling reactivity/rate of recovery from distress. It is available in multiple languages.

Greenspan Social-Emotional Growth Chart: A Screening Questionnaire for Infants and Young Children (Greenspan, 2004)

This questionnaire is completed by the parents or other caregivers. It is a screening measure to detect problems in social and emotional milestones. It is appropriate to use from birth to 42 months.

Infant-Toddler Sensory Profile (Dunn, 2002)

This provides a standard method for professionals to measure a child's sensory processing abilities and to profile the effect of sensory processing on functional performance in the child's daily life. This profile is designed for children from birth to 36 months. It is a caregiver questionnaire, and each item describes children's responses to various sensory experiences.

The First-Year Inventory (FYI) (Baranek et al., 2006)

The Inventory is a parent-report screening tool to identify 12-month-old infants who might be at risk for autism spectrum disorder (ASD) or a related developmental disorder. The instrument covers two broad developmental domains: social communication and sensory regulatory functions. The two domains are further defined by eight specific constructs: social orienting and receptive communication, social-affective engagement, imitation, expressive communication, sensory processing, regulatory patterns, reactivity, and repetitive behavior.

Ainsworth Maternal Sensitivity Scale (AMSS) (Ainsworth, Bell & Stayton, 1974)

This measure rates maternal sensitivity (accuracy in perceiving and interpreting an infant's cues and the ability to react in a timely and appropriate manner). It differentiates mothers of insecure-avoidant from those of insecure-ambivalent infants.

Case Example

Jane, a 37-year-old never-married woman, who had a total of four children, presented herself for consultation because her 11-month-old daughter, Tina, would not eat food. Tina would only nurse; Jane admitted that her milk supply had dwindled during the past few months. The pediatrician, Dr. Paul, had ruled out any physiological problem in either mother or baby. Dr. Paul recommended that Jane begin supplementing the breast milk with formula from a bottle and gradually introduce baby food because Tina was not gaining weight as expected.

Tina had been born at term. She had been healthy at birth and initially had gained weight. She had no medical problems, and her language development was within normal limits. At about 8 months of age, she stopped gaining weight, and her mother had difficulty producing enough breast milk to meet her dietary needs.

Currently, Tina refused to accept bottle feeding or any nutritional baby food. Anytime the mother attempted to feed the child, Tina would throw the spoon down and close her mouth tightly. Tina only wanted Jane to breast-feed her. Jane was frustrated, and she admitted, with significant guilt, that she would yell at Tina at these times.

Jane's mother, Betsy, was staying with her to help with the other children but argued with Jane over the feeding schedule for Tina. Jane wanted a rigid feeding schedule, every four hours, but Tina would scream until Jane breastfed her.

Tina's father, Will, a plastic surgeon, gave financial support but was inconsistent in his emotional attitude; he was angry that Jane had gotten pregnant. He left Jane when she was three months pregnant in order to go to Bolivia with a charity group that performed surgery on children in poverty-stricken countries. Jane was upset because Will had talked about marrying her before she got pregnant. But when he left, she kept herself busy with a part-time job and the children to distract her.

Jane was incensed about her mother's attitude, especially after Will left. Betsy had been critical of Jane all of her life, frequently yelling at Jane as a child—much as Jane now yelled at Tina.

Will returned to the United States and reconnected with Jane when Tina was 6 months old. Jane allowed him to live in the house but insisted that he sleep in a separate bedroom. Jane was still co-sleeping with Tina, reasoning that it was easier to handle Tina's erratic nursing needs with Tina lying beside her. In addition, Tina seemed to have a difficult temperament; Tina would scream endlessly if (1) Jane tried to feed her baby food or (2) Jane would not breastfeed Tina on demand.

Jane was tense because of her mother's criticisms of Will. It was also difficult for Jane to go to work because Tina was unhappy staying with Betsy.

Evaluation of Parent-Infant Interaction

To evaluate the parent-child interaction, Jane and Tina were seen together in the playroom. The playroom contained blocks and stuffed animals, as well as toys appropriate for older children.

Jane arrived 15 minutes early for the appointment. She had a large bag full of bottles containing formula to show the problem, plus peach baby food, and the child's soft toys from home.

Tina was whimpering loudly in the waiting room, although only Tina and her mother were present. When I (KD) walked in, the baby was sitting on the floor. Tina became startled, cried loudly, stopped playing with blocks, and looked at her mother. Jane raised her voice in frustration, "Stop crying! She's a nice friendly lady!" Tina cried more loudly. Tina was underweight and small.

Here, the pattern between mother and child could be seen. The mother could not soothe the child and did not seem aware that a stranger in the room might frighten the child. Jane made no effort to pick the child up and did not use a calming voice.

Jane's agitation appeared to be internalized by the child, who became more strident. Jane was prepared for the child's physical needs, but not the child's needs for soothing. "Goodness of fit" was not present.

I suggested to Jane that we should go to the playroom, where she could interact with Tina as she did at home. Jane said sarcastically that Tina was actually getting more attention in my office than she ever got at home. As we entered the playroom, I asked Jane if Tina's expressions were similar to the problems at home. Jane agreed they were.

Soon after entering the playroom, Jane put the baby on the floor. Tina cried loudly but was looking around the room. The mother talked to me about the feeding issues and seemed inattentive to Tina's distress. I wondered aloud if picking up the child to soothe her might help. Jane seemed surprised. She asked me, "Won't that reinforce the crying behavior?" I explained that, actually, holding Tina would probably help her calm down. After a brief delay, Jane picked up the baby, but did not rock her, look in her eyes, or calmly call Tina by name.

It was remarkable that Jane did not respond adequately to her frightened baby. She intellectualized (she told me later that she had read on the internet that picking up a crying infant would reinforce the "crying behavior"). When Jane did not look in her baby's eyes and did not immediately speak to Tina or rock her, I wondered to myself if these attitudes were caused by Jane being depressed. She had ample reason for depression: criticism from her mother, and the combination of feelings about Tina's father—anger, despair, self-loathing, and ungratified wishes for support. Jane's noted perfectionism seemed to cause her self-conscious, inhibited behavior in front of the therapist. She seemed more worried about my not criticizing her, also no doubt due to her internalized criticisms (from her mother) externalized onto me.

Tina gradually calmed down, began to crawl around the playroom, and explored the toys. At times, Tina also pulled herself up on a bench and was able to stand briefly. Tina would periodically turn to see if her mother was present and try to make eye contact, but Jane seemed preoccupied with speaking with me. I commented to Jane about Tina's smooth motor abilities. Jane responded that this was a recent development, and now that Tina could move away quickly by crawling, she was worried Tina might start to break things.

It sounded like Jane had not removed items in her home that would either be dangerous or breakable as Tina became more mobile. As the conversation proceeded, it appeared that Jane's neglect of this simple preparation was due to her depression and overwhelming stress in her relationships. Jane mentioned, in passing, all the things she had done with her previous children to "babyproof" the home. Jane now thought her mother or Will should babyproof the home. Jane expressed anger that Will was not helping more with the care of Tina.

At one point, Tina loudly banged two blocks together and laughed. When she looked over at her mother, apparently wanting Jane to laugh as well, Jane said, "SHHH, we need to be quiet." Tina immediately stopped laughing, gazed downward, and crawled away from the blocks.

Here, Jane had difficulty picking up on Tina's signals to play or share an enjoyable moment together. Jane's problem with this had an immediate impact on Tina's affect, as well as Tina's interest in the toy. Jane did not seem to notice the effect of her unresponsiveness on her daughter. Instead, Jane remarked that Tina was good because she stopped making noise with the blocks.

Tina was alert and motorically within normal limits, but Jane, due to depression, was having difficulty adjusting to this "practicing" aspect of the separation-individuation phase. While Tina would attempt to use eye contact to connect with her mother, she rarely crawled back to Jane for affection or reassurance. Jane did not use her voice to let Tina know she was paying attention to her and was physically present. Tina explored the room but seemed tentative and did not seem to enjoy playing with one particular toy.

Tina, therefore, seemed to be having difficulty proceeding through the practicing phase of separation-individuation; Tina was anxious about the safety of exploring the environment because of her mother's inattentiveness and depression. Tina's insecurity also was related to her resistance to receive food from sources other than the breast.

I formulated that Tina's resistance was part of a developmentally based attachment problem in which Tina was anxious about her mother providing a secure base. By taking in only mother's milk, Tina was internalizing aspects of her mother, but this was insufficient to provide her with sufficient nourishment for growth.

After about 30 minutes in the playroom, Tina began to whine and cry; she crawled onto her mother's lap and attempted to open her mother's blouse. Jane sighed and remarked, "Ugh, Tina wants to breastfeed." Jane took out the prepared bottles from her bag, but Tina cried louder when she saw the bottle. Her mother sat her on the floor and tried to put the bottle in her mouth. Tina would have none of it and angrily threw the bottle on the floor. Jane was tense and frustrated. In order to get Tina to stop crying, she began to breastfeed her. Jane did not look at Tina while nursing her. Jane had an angry look on her face. Tina initially looked at her mother but quickly looked away and began twirling her hair.

Jane remarked that she is very worried that her breast milk is "insufficient," that Tina needs more nutrition, and that she wants Tina to gain weight. Jane was tearful when she stated this and expressed guilt over not being the "mother to Tina that I was to my other children." She further noted that she had wanted to be different from her own mother, who was critical and at times neglectful with her. Jane ruefully expressed regret about having a child with Will. She knew Will would likely not be consistent as a father. After sharing these introspections, Jane felt exhausted, depressed, and ashamed.

Interpretive Meeting and Recommendations to Jane

Tina's feeding disorder seemed related to problems in the relationship between her and her mother. I recommended that Jane obtain immediate individual psychotherapy to address her depression, her relationship difficulties with

Will, and her defense of keeping Tina in the same bed with her (to relieve anxiety). Jane was receptive to my point that she needed more understanding of her own experiences of neglect and criticism as a child since we could see, already, that those impacted her parenting of Tina.

The internal problems of the child seemed to suggest persistent symbiosis (some failure to separate her own image from that of her mother). That was caused, in part, by Jane keeping Tina in the master bedroom bed with her, which delayed Tina from entering the "practicing" subphase of separation-individuation (Pines, 1982). Tina cried bitterly if left in her own crib. One remedy for this was to suggest to Jane that she rock Tina, then put Tina in the crib, then soothe her as needed, and stay in the child's room until the child was sleeping. A predictable bedtime would be forthcoming later.

I also recommended that Tina and Jane be seen in infant-mother counseling to help Jane become more attuned to Tina's cues (to form a more secure-organized attachment), more emotionally available to Tina, and more immediately sensitive to Tina's needs.

Importantly, Jane needed help in gradually shifting Tina to more formula and baby food to prevent Tina from experiencing malnutrition. Jane appeared willing to acknowledge the impact of her emotions on Tina.

Jane was motivated to help her daughter gain weight. After the evaluation, she realized that Tina's "eating disorder" was related to the child/parent relationship. She was hopeful that, with my help, she could effectuate significant improvement in Tina's feeding habits by changing the patterns in their relationship. I set up regular appointments for Jane with Tina and referred Jane to a colleague for her own confidential individual dynamic psychotherapy.

Follow-Up

After several weeks, Jane's depression and low self-esteem decreased. She began looking at Tina and responding to her. Jane realized, when I pointed out several of her problems to her and suggested different ways of managing Tina, that even what she felt were "minor" interactions with her daughter were important.

After several weeks of us working together, Jane was gradually able to get Tina to accept baby food.

5 Ages 1–3 Separation-Individuation

Key Questions to Be Answered by Parents

- **Did the Child Dart Away and Run Back, to Explore the Surroundings? Did Father Engage in Play with Child?**
  - Looking for disturbances in separation-individuation.
  - Looking for disturbances in caretakers who did not allow enough independent curiosity in the child.

- **Did the Child Sleep in a Crib?**
  - Looking for persistent symbiosis.
  - Looking for parental figures who abandon the child by leaving the child in the crib.

- **At What Age Was Weaning Completed?**
  - Looking for delayed weaning, and persistent oral dependency.
  - Looking for premature weaning, with agitation and irritability.

- **When Was Toilet Training Begun, and How Did the Child Adapt to This?**
  - Could the child understand what was expected?
  - Was there rebellion?
  - Did parents become overly controlling (for example, use enemas)?

- **Were There any Separations from Parents for Long Periods of Time? How Did the Child Tolerate Them?**
  - Looking for chronic anxiety and depression due to lengthy or multiple separations.
  - Looking for separation traumas, such as death or illness.

DOI: 10.4324/9781003257110-5

- Looking for damage to object constancy (which should be reached between ages 2 and 3.5). During this time, the child can tolerate short separations from parents.

- **How Did the Parents React to the Child Saying "No"?**

  - Looking for parents not allowing reality testing to develop in the child.
  - Looking for overly controlling parents who allow no autonomy.
  - Looking for spoiling parents who allow infantile grandiosity to emerge.

- **Did the Parents Encourage Language Development?**

  - Looking for failures of girls to speak by age 18 months.
  - Looking for failures of boys to speak by age 24 months.

- **Was the Child Sent to Preschool or Day Care? What Was the Child's Reaction?**

  - Looking for disturbances in emotional stability.
  - Looking for disturbances in self and object constancy leading to

    - tantrums and
    - failure to emotionally attach to caregivers.

  - Looking for nightmares and fears of being alone due to insecure attachment.

Answers to Key Questions and What They Mean

Did the Child Dart Away and Run Back to Explore the Surroundings? Did Father Engage in Play with the Child?

- Looking for disturbances in separation-individuation.
- Looking for disturbances in caretakers who did not allow enough independent curiosity in the child.

Children between 1 and 3 years of age are attempting to establish a sense of autonomy – where they know they are separate people, and not somehow psychological extensions of their caretakers. They do this by running away, exploring the environment, and provoking their parents to anger.

Parents can interact with children in ways that interfere with this important development. On the one hand, parents can infantilize children by not allowing them independent play or expression of any assertiveness or frustrated anger. Finding toys and activities that allow the child to channel aggression (building and then breaking down block towers or sandcastles, for example) is useful. If parents do not allow some of this, children are not likely to separate their own self-image from their images of their parents. They will likely have continuing conflicts about clinging and running away which may persist into adolescence.

On the other hand, if parents let children cry for inordinate periods of time without soothing intervention, or leave the child alone without interaction (such as in an "impersonal," sterile daycare situation, or alone in a house locked from the outside while the parents are away), the child is destined to become apathetic and uninterested in other people. These children may seem obedient and "easy," but are actually what Mahler et al. (1975) called "low-keyed." They are likely to have continuing lack of enthusiasm or excitement about anything, especially learning and friendships, later.

Finally, the father plays a particularly significant role at this stage. When the main attachment has been to the mother (due to breastfeeding and the mother's particular vocal characteristics), children usually need a father figure to attach to as they are feeling more independent from their mothers. The father, usually somewhat later than the mother, becomes a target for intense attachment ("symbiosis"—see "Essay" in this chapter). Children then engage in the same separation behaviors with their fathers as they had with their mothers.

As children go through the individuation process, they of course do not become autonomous human beings—they are still toddlers who need their parents. But internally, the sense of self will become separated so that by the time children are 2–3 years old, peekaboo is no longer fun: the images of the parents do not disappear when a hand is placed over the child's eyes.

In other words, peekaboo loses its interest as a game once the child has established self and object constancy. The hiding of the eyes does not result in loss of the parental images. More seriously, the children can handle a pre-school environment without fears of parents or themselves disappearing (usually verbalized as a fear that someone will die when the children are separated from their parents).

Did the Child Sleep in a Crib?

- Looking for persistent symbiosis.
- Looking for parental figures who abandon the child.

The American Academy of Pediatrics (AAP), for various reasons, approves of children sleeping in a crib in the parents' bedroom until age 6–12 months. The statistics are conflicting; some show that co-sleeping with the child (in the parental bed) increases the risks of accidental suffocation of the child or sudden infant death syndrome (SIDS). Some studies find no correlation with SIDS. After 12 months, the AAP has no advice regarding co-sleeping.

If the child has continued sleeping in the parents' (or someone's) bed from ages 1–3, there is physically less danger (of suffocation), but the psychopathology stemming from this can be quite profound (Settlage, 1964).

Some parents misinterpret the advice not to co-sleep. They put the child in a separate room and then do not make any attempt to soothe the child when the child cries or has nightmares. The result of this mistake is that the child *does* feel "abandoned" (a commonly used phrase). That is, the child can lose confidence that the parents will be available for soothing. That experience, in turn, leads to major interference with the development of trust. The child can also become pessimistic about ever turning to another human being when in need of emotional support; instead, later in life, the individual may turn to alcohol or drugs. In other words, the same problems that occur from birth to 1 year of age recur during this phase of development.

In another twist, some parents think that after rocking or singing to a child until the child is sleeping, letting the child sleep in his or her own room will cause the child to feel "abandoned." To relieve their guilt about committing such an imagined transgression, the parents allow the child to sleep in their bed. This has the untoward effect, from ages 1–3, of perpetuating the child's idea of not having a separate sense of self. Instead, the child will predictably suffer severe "separation" anxiety. To relieve the anxiety, the child may become a clinger, and not traverse the separation-individuation phase on time (see p. 000).

Alternatively, persistent merger sensations (technically referred to as self-object fusion) often lead the child to become more rambunctious, or even violent toward the parents (or others) in order to feel separate. If parents are quickly responsive to the child's predictable nighttime distress (anxiety or nightmares) by entering the child's room within minutes to soothe the child, that usually helps the child develop a sense of self without feeling abandoned or mistrustful.

How parents handled this situation with their toddlers gives much information not just about this stage, but about the origins of separation or low-keyed problems later, such as school reluctance (refusing to go to school) or adolescent delinquency.

At What Age Was Weaning Begun and Completed?

- Looking for delayed weaning, and persistent oral dependency.
- Looking for premature weaning, with agitation and irritability.

At this point in history, the timing of weaning is a hotly controversial topic which has even become political. A recent *Time Magazine* cover had a photo of a mother nursing a boy of at least 5 years of age while they are both standing.[1]

---

1 https://duckduckgo.com/?t=ffab&q=time+magazine+cover+child+standing+nursing&iax=images&ia=images&iai=https%3A%2F%2Fi.pinimg.com%2Foriginals%2F42%2F0a%2F7b%2F420a7b4287b4e8332b5ab4bf11fb0020.jpg.

On the other hand, brusque or even traumatic weaning during the first year of life can have a traumatic effect.[2]

There is little definitive research about weaning. As a matter of developmental sense, it is no doubt advisable that weaning be instituted before toilet training is attempted. Toilet training requires the child to "give up" something else that was pleasurable. It would be humane to allow the child to grieve over the lost nipple (bottle or breast) before demanding the child go through another loss. Toilet training can usually be started between 18 months of age and about 3 years of age, depending on the child's capacity for comprehension of language.

For generations, mothers have naturally wanted to wean infants once the infants developed teeth (9–12 months of age). The teeth could cause the mother pain if the infant bit the mother during nursing. In addition, the sucking on a nipple after teething is underway tends to cause problems with the child's dentition—overbites and other issues for the child. So, weaning just after the development of teeth still seems like a reasonable approach. Most children resist weaning because nursing is so pleasurable. Some infants reject all other food at 1 year of age and insist on the breast, but will start losing weight and develop malnutrition if this continues. Moving the child from the nipple to a "sippy cup" (a cup with a lid on it to minimize spills) takes considerable effort on the part of the parent, and involves some nondestructive aggression toward the child.

Persistent nursing after age 2 is usually problematic because the child is crossing over into the early phase of the first genital stage (Galenson & Roiphe, 1980). Persistent nursing after that often produces sexual overstimulation in children of any gender; overstimulation interferes with concentration and later may be misdiagnosed as ADHD.

The answer to these questions about weaning can indicate how delayed weaning (based on the aforementioned criteria) can also result in the child having developed *persistent oral dependency*. That is, the child may develop eating conflicts (obesity or anorexia). Hunger and clinging are more likely in

2 During Q&A after a lecture at Shanxi Medical University, Dr. Blackman was told by a student that in the village where she lived, there was an odd practice with infants. At 8 months of age, an infant was, as a custom, removed from the home by other neighborhood women and taken to the home of another. The mother was not allowed to see the child for two weeks. After the two-week hiatus, the child was returned to the mother; at that point, the other women put a foul tasting, sticky substance on the mother's nipples to cause the baby to pull away. The purpose of this cultural activity was to aid in weaning. The participant asked Dr. Blackman his opinion, which he furnished: that precipitous weaning at that age was no doubt inadvisable. The method also was likely to have untoward effects on the infant, which would be so numerous that they would be difficult to predict. The participant expressed gratitude since she had secretly, for years, objected to this aspect of her village culture, and she and several other mothers were trying to stop it. Unfortunately, no further information regarding that situation is available.

premature weaning; narcissism and a sense of entitlement (and oedipal victory dynamics—see chapter on the first genital phase) may also be produced, leading the child to become grandiose, haughty, and entitled.

When Was Toilet Training Begun, and How Did the Child Adapt to This?

- Could the child understand what was expected?
- Was there rebellion?
- Did parents become overly controlling?

First, a biological fact: the nerves that control the urogenital and anal sphincter muscles do not come under any conscious control until the child is 18 months old (Brazelton et al., 1999). The reason for this is that the nerves need to be myelinated, and myelinization does not occur until that age. Toilet training, where the child controls the elimination, is not physically possible before 18 months of age.

Brazelton recommends that children start toilet training once they have enough language capacity to understand what the parents want. It is common knowledge that girls, in general, can speak many sentences between 18 months and 2 years of age, whereas many boys often don't start using words in sentences until several months later. Therefore, most parents find that girls, in general, are trainable during the second half of the second year of life, whereas many boys often cannot be trained until well after age 2. At the time of this writing, research into this matter is controversial, clouded, for example, by debates over whether the factors that cause this difference are innate or not.[3]

Premature training usually winds up with the child becoming what is later called "oppositional." A history of mothers (and/or grandmothers, often) who became insistent, used belts to strap the child to the potty, or even use enemas to force the child to eliminate, is often found in later cases of encopresis (child's refusal to use the toilet, while insisting on moving the bowels in his or her clothing).

Delayed training, however, can lead to the child being rejected from certain preschools at age 3. In addition, the child's self-esteem may suffer if training is not completed by age 4 or 5 before kindergarten begins.

Parents can be asked at what age toilet training began and how successful it was. Was there persistent bed-wetting (nocturnal enuresis)? This may be genetically based, cause the child embarrassment, or may be based on wishes to stay an infant. Rebelliousness can also be a factor.

---

3 https://files.eric.ed.gov/fulltext/EJ1145869.pdf.

Parents can also describe whether the child understood what was expected. Was there rebellion? How did the parent handle it? What techniques were used?[4]

In American slang, calling someone "anal" refers to compulsive orderliness, overcleanliness, or perfectionism. Obsessive-compulsive traits are expectable during the school-age years (6–10) when a certain amount of perfectionism, fairness, and ritual formation are age appropriate.

On a final note, Moisy Shopper (1989) suggests that, for boys, urine training standing should precede bowel training (sitting). He recommends that fathers demonstrate, on one occasion, how to do this for the boy, so the boy can imitate it. This is very important for the boy's self-esteem and helps the boy "aim" accurately, so as not to make a mess.[5]

Were There any Separations from Parents for Long Periods of Time? How Did the Child Tolerate Them?

- Looking for chronic anxiety and depression due to lengthy or multiple separations.
- Looking for separation traumas, such as death or illness.

The studies of Mahler et al. (1975), refined by Pine (2004), emphasize the importance of the stability, consistency, and availability of the mothering figure from age 1 to 3: during the *practicing, rapprochement,* and *early self and object constancy* subphases, lengthy separations from the child will predictably cause a spike in separation anxiety. Separation anxiety refers to the disappearance of the image of the mother when she is not visible. This leads the child to wonder if the mother has disappeared or has died.

In conjunction with separation anxiety, its opposite, self-disintegration (or "annihilation anxiety") typically also occurs when toddlers are alone. This manifests itself in a child's continuous crying, inconsolability, and thrashing

---

4 In China, the ancient tradition of *kaidangku* involved putting infants and toddlers in crotchless clothing and letting them defecate wherever. Often, the mothers tried to anticipate, starting during the first year of life, when the child appeared to need to eliminate. They would then rush the child to the floor potty (often a hole in the floor), hold the child (sometimes balancing on the mother's knees), and hope the child would go. In the past decade in China, this arduous and bacterially risky type of training has become rarer in large cities; in the countryside, it seems to have persisted. Psychoanalytic observational studies on the effects of this type of training do not seem to be available in English at the time of this writing. There are many anecdotal posts on the internet, however, either touting or decrying the practice.

5 Kaplan (accessed 2022), a female family practitioner, agrees with Shopper about the technique of the father demonstrating urination for the boy, but opines that this should be done after bowel training and urine training have been completed sitting down. In our opinion, Shopper is no doubt correct from a psychological developmental standpoint, as far as the development of confidence in male identity formation.

about. Sometimes the child defends against these anxieties by becoming withdrawn and uncommunicative.

What is too long a separation? This question has befuddled all child researchers since the 1960s. John McDevitt (personal communication, 1979) reported Margaret Mahler's opinion that two hours of "quality time" was probably necessary daily between the primary maternal figure and the child in order for the child to develop self and object constancy. But there are no studies that indicate exactly how much time the mother/parent should have with the child for self and object constancy to develop.

Selma Fraiberg (1977), in her study of blind children, found that self and object constancy were delayed by several years because congenitally blind children cannot see their mothers. They can develop an image of the mother as separate from themselves, but it takes a lot of effort and many years. So, the corollary of the difficulties with the development of self and object constancy is that children seem to be resilient, and reparative interventions by the mother or a skilled therapist/clinic can help.

An example of a "lengthy separation" would be several weeks at a time. Whether for work, illness, or just other activities, this length of the physical separation can lead the child to develop an early depression that might be characterized as separation-depressive affect. The child becomes convinced that the mother has already died; grieving about this (even if the mother is alive) can interfere with many of the child's developing functions. Internet communication, while a mother is gone, may mitigate the problems.

Of course, the most serious of all difficult separations for a child of this age is the death of the mother or father. The painful grief about such a loss often cannot be "metabolized." Thereafter, the depression may carry over into later stages and produce untoward affects, defenses, and behaviors.

The key question to ask parents regarding any separations is how the child handled it. Did the parents notice any change in the child when the parent returned in the case of long separations? Or, if there has been a death, how did the parents handle this and how did the child respond?

How Did the Parents React to the Child Saying "No"?

- Looking for parents not allowing reality testing to develop in the child.
- Looking for overly controlling parents who allow no autonomy.
- Looking for spoiling parents who allow infantile grandiosity to emerge.

As children begin to speak, between 15 months and 24 months of age, one of their favorite words is "no." Interestingly, this is true cross-culturally, in any country and in any language. The verbal expression of negation reflects the developing nonhostile, nondestructive aggression in the child, where the child resists the parent and thereby relieves anxiety about self-object fusion. If the parents are rigid and do not allow the child to negate anything, or if they punish the child for saying no, this can result in disturbances in reality testing, and more commonly, very severe passivity in the child. This passivity is reflected in a fear of expressing any emotion in any circumstance, which may follow the child through other stages of development and into school.

Autonomy at this age is not about the child leaving home and developing a career! (That's of course toward the end of adolescence.) Autonomy is an internal factor during ages 1–3 and is centered around children feeling some confidence in their ability to have their own thoughts. The child can also accomplish certain simple tasks, alone, without the parents infantilizing or "helicoptering" the child. In fact, parents who are constantly hovering, spoiling the child, may interfere with the development of autonomy. On the other hand, parents who allow the child to say no to everything may wind up with a negativistic child, who shows grandiose entitlement, pays attention to no rules, and develops no respect for the parents.

Did the Parents Encourage Language Development?

- Looking for failures of girls to speak by age 18 months.
- Looking for failures of boys to speak by age 24 months.

The appearance of speech is genetically based. Language development generally appears in girls between 16 and 18 months of age and in boys about four to six months after that. There is quite a bit of variation, but there is a definite gender difference. What the parents do as the children begin to speak will affect the child's use of speech for expression of affect, desire, opinion, and autonomy.

Perhaps even more importantly, verbalization by the parents, and encouraging the child to use words, furthers the control of affect. Failure by caretakers to do so may cause a delay in speaking, damage to the child's impulse control, and an inability to tolerate powerful feelings.

This is therefore a quick, but highly important question to parents of children who are uncommunicative or overemotional.

Was the Child Sent to Preschool or Day Care? What Was the Child's Reaction?

- Looking for disturbances in emotional stability.
- Looking for disturbances in self and object constancy leading to

  - tantrums and
  - failures to emotionally attach to caregivers.

- Looking for nightmares and fears of being alone due to insecure attachment.

Children placed in impersonal and/or crowded day care–type environments before the age of 2 are at greater risk in the realms of attachment and inner stability. This is because self and object constancy are just developing at that age. Dangers can be mitigated by engaging a responsive person to care for the child on a consistent basis (such as a "nanny").

Different children respond to lengthy separations differently. The assessment of the child's actual development is no doubt more complex. The factors not only include time with the parents but also how the child reacts to the separations from the parents, the attachment and trust in the childcare situation, and the child's innate capacities for emotional regulation. (For a more thorough disquisition on the controversial matters surrounding daycare before 1½ years vs. 1½ to 3 years of age, see Nagera, 1975).

Tantrums are more common in children with externally imposed developmental delays. Severely neglected toddlers often need a reparative relationship with a therapist (Alpert, 1959) or even a therapeutic nursery for treatment. Milder problems can be handled by parents at home, with input from a developmentally-oriented therapist.

Whether at home with parents, staying with a grandparent, or at day care, supplemental questions concern to whom the child turns for safety. This can be investigated during history taking or during the evaluation session with the child. Nightmares often reveal, in their manifest content (the conscious content of the dream), people of whom the child is afraid.

The Child Evaluation Interview

The evaluation of a toddler begins when you first observe the child in the waiting room: what the child is doing, how the parent is interacting with the child, and how they all respond to the therapist's greeting. Having toys or child-friendly materials in the waiting room helps the child feel more comfortable. Children's use of the toys is also meaningful. Do they engage the parent while using them?

The therapist's interaction with children in the playroom symbolically reveals their unconscious thoughts and the way they master passively experienced events. In play, children reenact events, real or fantasy, that have important meaning to them. In a young child, the play interaction may also involve the parent, especially when the child is unable to separate from the parent to interact with the therapist. The parent and child together in the playroom give the therapist information about their relationship and their attachment.

Symbolic play is introduced by the parents during infancy (e.g., peekaboo). Interestingly, toddlers often realize this is pretend play, yet find significant pleasure in the interaction. As toddlers, children also engage in pretend play by themselves. As children reach latency, they focus more on reality and less on pretend play (fantasy).

When the child is seen alone (or with a parent in the room if needed), the child will choose toys and creative materials to use while in the playroom. The therapist "seeds" the play with a statement about why the child was brought for evaluation. The rest of the play can be seen as the child's answer to what the problems seem to be. Through metaphorical play, the therapist comments and, if the child is verbal, may ask the child to explain their play activities. Through this process, both conscious and unconscious conflicts can be discerned.

A playhouse with figures of different sexes, ages, and ethnicity is useful. A playhouse allows children, unprompted, to express and demonstrate what goes on in their minds (and in their homes). During children's play, the therapist can observe manifestations of internal representations elaborated in their fantasy play. Also, transference- and countertransference-related material can be obtained for the case formulation.

It is important to have play materials for a wide range of ages, genders, and interests. To enhance the understanding of children's unconscious conflicts, it is advisable to encourage them to choose what they want to play with and how they want to play with the various materials. The therapist should note whether the child involves the therapist in the play and the nature of this involvement. This technique helps the evaluator assess the child in the least intrusive way possible.

Creative materials, soft stuffed animals, toys to express aggression (such as action figures and nerf balls), games, puzzles, and sand trays/boxes are useful objects. A "feeling chart" or pictures of children with different facial expressions can also be helpful for children who are verbally inhibited.

Play observed by the therapist can later be integrated with other sources of information. Any differences between parental descriptions and the therapist's observations may be of great significance.

In the playroom, things can transpire quickly. Some children want to actively engage the therapist in play. Notetaking becomes impossible and can create inhibitions in the child. A good rule for playroom observations is not to stop or disrupt the flow of the play. For diagnostic reasons, the therapist will keep key areas in mind while interacting with the child. Greenspan (2003) identified areas of development that can be elucidated through the child-therapist playroom interaction. As the child matures, the following specific changes are predictable:

- *physical function* – neurological, sensory, motor, integrative;
- *pattern of relationship and characteristic style of relating* – i.e., withdrawn or autistic;
- *overall mood or emotional tone* – as seen in themes of play, specific emotions expressed, and whether they change during the interaction; and
- *affects* – consider the range, depth, appropriateness, and capacity for regulation, including

    - *anxiety*-observed in play or as expressed directly by the child.

We also would add assessment of children's defenses, as they arise during play—such as refusing to play, hiding, moving around, and avoiding certain topics and toys purposely.

Psychodynamic play therapy assessment measures have been developed to assist with diagnosis and recommendations for treatment interventions. These include the following:

The Play Therapy Observation Instrument (PTOI; Howe & Silvern, 1981)
The NOVA Assessment of Psychotherapy (NAP; Faust & Burns, 1991)
The Children's Play Therapy Instrument (CPTI; Kernberg et al. 1998)

Halfon (2017) discussed these instruments and presents empirical support for the CPTI to categorize four types of children's play:

The Adaptive Play Profile – Forward moving play where the child shows the ability to represent disturbing experiences and fantasy.
Inhibited Conflicted Play Profile – The child is conflicted about needs and emotions. The child shows a narrow range of affect and usually plays in isolation.
Impulsive/Aggressive Play Profile – Play does not flow due to outbursts and abrupt interruptions of play. These children cope with disturbing feelings through motion and activity.
Disorganized Play Profile – Anxiety is extreme in the play of these children. They may demonstrate activity below their developmental age. The themes of their play may be bizarre, inappropriate, or aggressive.

These styles of play are complementary to the areas of development described by Greenspan (2003).

Essay

Five elements of development can be assessed during the phases of separation-individuation between the ages of 1 and 3. They are (1) experience of a secure-organized attachment to a mother figure; (2) relative ability to function detached from the mother; (3) development of steady, whole internal images of themselves and others; (4) the ability to control waste elimination; and (5) early pleasures from masturbatory play.

These five factors influence the developing "ego" functions of speech and language, organization of thought, and early reality testing. Self-preservation and management of affects with verbalization are healthy signs. All of these developments can be impaired by persistent co-sleeping, neglect of requisite soothing, spoiling, beatings, and sexual abuse.

Galenson and Roiphe (1980) reported on a ten-year study of girls during this phase that indicated "protogenital" fantasies already developing between 1 and 3 years of age. They elaborate on and clarify Nagera's (1975) descriptions of the six possible permutations of the female oedipal situation (First Stage: Phallic-Oedipal; Second Stage: Oedipal [Krohn, 1978]). Parens et al. (1976) describe a "protogenital" phase between 18 and 36 months of age. This protogenital phase includes fantasies during infantile masturbatory play accompanied by anxieties about the safety of the genitals.

Ainsworth's studies of children 12–18 months of age resulted in categorization of attachment as follows:

a)   *Securely attached*
b)   *Insecurely attached-avoidant*, and
c)   *Insecurely attached-ambivalent*.

Hesse and Main (2000) identified another category of attachment:

d)   *Disorganized/disoriented*. This last category describes how children seek proximity to their caregiver—sometimes in strange and disoriented ways (approaches mother backward, stares into space, suddenly freezes). Disturbed toddlers perceive their own caregivers as frightening; this severe category is found only in about 10%–15% of toddlers.

Studies have shown that attachment styles can have a long-term impact on personality development. Individuals who have secure working models of early attachment are more likely, as adults, to perform caregiver functions with less feeling of burden, are less likely to experience prolonged grief after a loss, and are more likely to report positively on their own well-being (Fonagy & Target, 1998; Fonagy, 2000; Cassidy & Shaver, 2016).

An outgrowth of secure attachment is the infant's ability to form thoughts and expectations about the caregiver's response. Erikson (1950a) referred to this as *basic trust and basic mistrust. Mentalization* (Fonagy et al., 2005) is a multilayered, developmental process that promotes the child's ability to understand people's actions as meaningful, to distinguish outer and inner reality, and to communicate while keeping others' perspectives in mind (Akhtar, 2009). Basic trust and mentalization enhance a child's ability to self-regulate (Fonagy & Target, 1998).

Parents who possesses a good capacity for mentalization regarding their own and their infant's mind will have better empathy for the infant. Internally, the parents will retain a stable, "post-ambivalent" internal representation of their child. This in turn enhances their own child's developing empathy. This mutually reinforcing process supports the child's ability to see the caregiver as a separate person and adds to the developing child's individuation and autonomy.

Internal autonomy is the focus of the research done by Mahler and her group, the modifications of which were set out by Pine (2004). The process of developing individual, stable, whole images of self and others requires a separation-individuation process that is successful. The stages of symbiosis, separation-individuation (and its substages), and, finally, self and object constancy seem to take about 3–3½ years.

The initial image the child develops is fused between mother and self. This "symbiosis" lasts until approximately 5–6 months of age.

At about 4–6 months of age, signs develop that the child is attempting to separate images of self and parent. For the next three years, the process of separation-individuation proceeds and is repeated in preadolescence—the two years before puberty—and during adolescence (post-puberty). The four subphases of individuation include

> *the differentiation phase* (6–12 months),
> *practicing* (12–16 months) with walking,
> *rapprochement* (16–25 months)—intensified clinging and aggression, and
> *unstable object constancy* (25–36 months), where refusion and splitting may
> still predominate.

A final note on splitting (Kernberg, 1975): during this phase, reality testing is developing along with the path to object constancy. Between 1 and 3, children develop a slightly more realistic picture of their parents. For example, healthy children realize mommy has a temper but is also loving, similar to daddy. If this integration of potential loving and potential aggressive images does not occur, the child may wind up using the mechanism called "splitting." In this situation, one parent is seen as an angel and the other as a devil. Later, the world is often split into good and evil people, and the child has difficulty recognizing that all normal human beings have foibles.

The answers the parents give to the key questions will aid greatly in pinpointing where any trouble occurred, which may underlie the surface behavioral problems that worry the parents, teachers, pediatricians, or others who recommend the child be evaluated.

Case Example

John, a 32-year-old married man, sought help for depression; He asked for antidepressant medication. Instead, he was asked to discuss his current life situation. He responded,

> There's not much to talk about. I have a wonderful wife. We have a beautiful 2-year-old daughter, although she's anxious—but our pediatrician said that's normal. I like my job. I read depression is caused by serotonin deficiency or something like that.

After discussing his way of avoiding things—by using intellectualization (reading up on it), concretization (believing depression is caused by brain chemicals), and normalization (daughter's anxiety is normal), I (JSB) noted that he hadn't said anything about his sex life. He responded, laughing, "What sex life? You can't have sex with a 2-year-old in the bed!"

He explained that his daughter could not sleep in her crib in her room. She got too scared and screamed. He and his wife comforted her by allowing her to sleep between them. I wondered to myself if John might feel guilty about unconscious hostility toward a loved daughter, so I asked John if he would prefer the child sleep in her own room. John became defensive and asserted that he did not want any harm to come to his daughter. He was also concerned about his wife's anxiety should he "demand" that the child should feel "abandoned."

I was able to clarify with him that he was avoiding guilt over being "self-ish" and (passively) avoiding fear of his wife's reaction. I then told him that, according to Margaret Mahler, the child was a little behind schedule for handling separations—that Mahler and her group had found that "rapprochement" should be ending around 25 months of age; his daughter still had severe separation anxiety. This explanation successfully undid the normalization suggested by his pediatrician. But John did not know what to do.

I suggested to him (as I have suggested to many patients and therapists I supervise) that he discuss his wish for sex with his wife. Then, they could soothe the child by rocking her. They could then put the child in her crib in her room, and one of them could sit in a chair in the room, or stroke her body to soothe her, if needed, until she fell asleep. After she was asleep, the parent in the daughter's room should return to the master bedroom. If the child awakened crying, one parent could put on a robe and return to her room and go through the soothing and sitting with her again, until she got back to sleep. I used a supportive technique I sometimes ironically refer to "low-balling," by setting the expectations low. I told him this process might take many months since his daughter was a bit delayed in handling nighttime separation. He responded that he would try it.

John returned to see me the following week. He reported he had spoken to his wife about sex, and that she expressed her own wish to get back to their previous level of intimacy. She was apprehensive about my suggestions, but after getting a baby monitor, she agreed to try it. The first night, the baby fell asleep in her crib while he and his wife sat with her, and then they both returned to the master bedroom. For the first time in two years, they had sexual intercourse. His depression went away. He commented to me, "You know, my father would never have done such a thing. He was always a wimp when it came to my mother. Maybe I had taken on some of his attitude, or something. I'm glad it's fixed."

He thanked me. Therapy ended after two sessions. Not only had he relieved an identification with his passive father, but he had also relieved his conflicts about his wife and his daughter. He no longer felt frustrated, guilty, and defensive. And he avoided taking an SSRI antidepressant medicine, which has a notorious side effect of interfering with sexual performance (which, I thought, would have made him more depressed).

As importantly, he and his wife had prevented further inflammation of their daughter's separation anxiety by helping her gradually sleep by herself. She could restore the separation-individuation process and move to the stage of "on the way to object constancy" (approximately 24–36 months of age).

6 Ages 2–7 First Genital Phase

🔑 Key Questions for Parents

- **Where Does the Child Sleep Most of the Time?**
  - Looking for persistent clinging (symbiosis) and troubles with separations (preschool, e.g.).
  - Looking for evidence of inadvertent sexual overstimulation (agitation, compulsive masturbation).

- **Do You Bathe Nude with the Child, or Does the Child See the Parents Naked at any Time?**
  - Looking for evidence of inadvertent sexual overstimulation, agitation.
  - Looking to see if the child grabbed at the parents' bodies.

- **How Do You Handle the Child's Masturbatory Play?**
  - Looking for conflicts regarding obedience, sexual curiosity, and self-image (autonomy).
  - Looking for parents' inhibition or exhibitionism.

- **Do You Use Corporal Punishment or Long Time-Outs?**
  - Spankings lead to anger, negativism, inhibition, and refusal to obey.
  - Long time-outs lead to fears of abandonment, increased self-hatred, and emotional distance.
  - Look for this history in cases of children who are violent with other children, especially siblings.

DOI: 10.4324/9781003257110-6

- **What Kinds of Games, Activities, and Athletics Do You Allow the Child?**

  - Isolated children tend to be more inhibited, irritable, depressed, and more dependent.
  - Outlets for destructive feelings are very important for socialization and intellectual development.

Answers to Key Questions and What They Mean

Where Does the Child Sleep Most of the Time?

- Looking for persistent clinging (symbiosis) and trouble with separations (preschool, e.g.).

  - Signs of persistent symbiosis (failure to develop object constancy) include

    - fears of being separated from the home,
    - fears of going to preschool,
    - fears of sleeping alone,
    - exaggerated fears of thunder, and
    - temper tantrums regarding the parents leaving.

  - Excess hostility toward the parents requiring more discipline because the child's aggression (naughtiness, disobedience) is used to further the internal separation of the self-image from images of the parents.

- Looking for evidence of inadvertent sexual overstimulation.

  - Agitation and inability to sit still
  - Compulsive masturbation
  - Excessive curiosity about parents' and other children's genitalia
  - Problems with understanding reality
  - Children misbehave to draw attention to the fact that there is a problem that makes them uncomfortable

Do You Bathe Nude with the Child, or Does the Child See the Parents Naked at any Time?

- Looking for evidence of inadvertent sexual overstimulation, agitation

  - (See p. 000).
  - Parents often don't think of the effects of allowing the child with them in the restroom.
  - In public restrooms, the parent may stand in the stall with the child, instead of outside the stall.
  - Child may be overly exhibitionistic, often poorly controlled.

- Looking to see if the child grabs at the bodies of others.

  - Child may grab at genital areas of other children or parents.
  - Sexualized play with animals or toys.
  - Simulating coitus.
  - Excessive "playing doctor."
  - Excessive masturbatory activity.

How Do You Manage the Child's Inevitable Masturbatory Play?

- Looking for conflicts regarding

  - disobedience and
    sexual curiosity and self-image (autonomy).

- Looking for parents' inhibitions or exhibitionism that will exacerbate the child's behavior.
- Do you spank, discipline, or humiliate the child over masturbatory play?

  - With boys, do you threaten to "cut it off."
  - With girls, do you caution them, "That's what bad girls do," shaming.

- Do you allow the child to watch PG-13 or R-rated movies with you?

Do You Use Corporal Punishment or Long Time-Outs?

- Spankings lead to anger, negativism, inhibition, and refusal to obey.
- Corporal punishment can lead to deficits in basic functions. Areas of inquiry include the following:

  - Was an implement used?
  - Where on the body was the child hit?
  - How long did the spanking take?
  - How often was the child hit?
  - At what ages was the child hit?
  - Was the child made part of the punishment (forced to pick his own switch from the backyard or choose the belt to be used)?
  - Look for face-slapping creating inordinate shame in the child.
  - Was the pain so great that the child cried (breakdown in controls) and could not think straight (damage to integrative, intellectual, and concentration functions)?

- Long time-outs lead to fears of abandonment, increased self-hatred, and emotional distance.

  - How long was the time-out?
  - Where was it done?
  - How often were time-outs used?
  - For which transgressions was the child punished?

- Look for these causes in cases of children who are violent with other children, especially siblings.

  - Increased hostility, identification with the aggressor.

What Kinds of Games, Activities, and Athletics Do You Allow the Child?

- Isolated children tend to be more

  - inhibited,
  - irritable,
  - depressed, and
  - dependent.

- Outlets for destructive feelings are very important for socialization and intellectual development.

  - Games involving competition:

    - Board games
    - Cards

  - Physical games:

    - All sports
    - Wrestling and martial arts
    - Jump rope

  - Music, art, theater, and dance:

    - Channel exhibitionistic wishes
    - Enhance confidence in self
    - Channel coordination
    - Sublimate sexual and aggressive wishes
    - Develop abilities that eventually are gratifying in themselves (ego interests)

- If not allowed, children become

  - overly disobedient,
  - destructive,
  - socially isolated,
  - uncooperative,
  - rule-breaking,
  - disorganized in action, or
  - envious of others.

The preceding questions are designed to elicit any (1) inadvertent sexual overstimulation of the child, (2) aggravation of the child's destructive aggression, and (3) blockage of normal outlets for conversion of the child's destructive aggression into constructive activities.

Positive findings are common in children with severe anxiety, inhibition of function (like problems with concentration and motor control), and misbehavior/severe disobedience.

Background Information about This Phase

Research shows that boys and girls discover their genital organs, as part of their body exploration, around 1 year of age (Marcus & Francis, 1975). With the improvement in motor coordination, reality testing, and integration between ages 2 and 3 (Galenson & Roiphe,1980), the child discovers that touching the genitals can produce pleasure. Therefore, the phase of development starting around age 2 and ending at about age 6 or 71/2 is termed the "first genital phase."

Sometimes the term "infantile genital phase" is used because, of course, children at this age are not "sexual" in the sense that post-pubertal human beings are sexual. Nevertheless, children stimulate themselves to a degree and must be taught by caretakers to avoid public exhibition of their pleasurable masturbatory play. Any activity of the parents, whether intentional or inadvertent, that inflames sexual stimulation during this phase is likely to cause problems. The previous questions elicit what those problems might have been during this phase, even if evaluating an older child.

"Aggression" in its many forms is also a major factor during this phase. Children can be astoundingly negative and destructive if left to their own devices. Children's job at this age is to anger their parents—in order to establish a sense of autonomy. Children often use language development (saying, "No!") to frustrate their parents ("the Terrible Twos"). What the parents did to help the child divert destructive aggression and negativism into productive channels is important (technically called sublimation).

Also, how did the parents try to stop the destructiveness? Did they use injunctive techniques (stopping destruction before it happened) or punitive techniques (punishment after the misbehavior or destruction)? (Parens, 1973). The developmental history should include how the child handled verbal criticism and limitation, any corporal punishment or "time-out" efforts by the parent, and how the child responded (Blackman & Dring, 2016).

Further, between ages 2 and 3, the child should have developed a stable attachment and be able to tolerate brief separations (detachment) from the parents without undue anxiety (first resolution of separation-individuation phase). Exploratory play—even with apprehension—is normal for the child at this age. Close friendships at this phase with other children tend to retain "parallel play" characteristics. Don't expect 4-year-olds to run a formation in soccer or develop a BFF (best friend forever), although this sometimes occurs.

Children during this stage have not yet formed an internal sense of fairness and rules. More primitive aspects of the conscience should be appearing— in order to please the parents. Thousands of interactions with parents will eventually result in the child's attitudes toward honesty, stealing, privacy, and violence—first consolidating into a conscience around age 6 (Brenner, 1982b; Sarnoff, 1989). How much do the parents recall about all this? Were parents expecting too much?

In assessing any child, the history of this infantile genital stage (age 2–71/2), given by the parents, is useful. Keep in mind that it is common for parents to have forgotten most of it. The child experiences a "wave of amnesia" just before school (age 6) and, interestingly, so do many parents. Nevertheless, whatever the parents can recall regarding the following points can be quite enlightening regarding the origins of the child's current problems.

Essay

The Oedipus complex (or, more accurately, conflicts in the family among children, their parents, their siblings, and others) is hard to imagine unless you have a child in the first genital phase (3–7½ years old or so). Around age 6½ or 7½, when the first genital phase comes to a close, the contents are routinely forgotten by both the child and the parents (repression). There are actually many variations on the triangular conflicts a child has in this stage—involving not just parents but also grandparents, siblings, schoolmates, and others.

It is easiest to think about the oedipal situation by considering the onset of volitional masturbatory play between ages 2 and 3. This occurs because as children explore their bodies, they realize that touching specific areas elicits pleasure. Then consider how these pleasurable experiences become integrated with the people to whom the child has (hopefully) become attached: both parents, usually the mother first, and then others. (Marcus & Francis, 1975; Krohn, 1978; Blackman, 2010, Chapter 10).

Next, consider that the mental functioning of the child—perception, organization of thought, motor control, and intelligence/curiosity—is also growing in leaps and bounds. Therefore, most kids start asking about reproduction. They usually (although certainly not always) realize that it somehow happens in the parents' bedroom, and a man and a woman are needed—at least in heterosexual marriage situations. In single-mom situations and in gay marriages, of course, other fantasies occur. But children also notice that in the world around them, women get pregnant, and men do not. So regardless of the home situation, the reality of gestation taking place in the abdominal area of the woman becomes clear—though it may be denied or repressed by the child.

Then there is the matter of how the baby is produced. Children don't quite figure it out during the oedipal phase, but if they do, they usually quickly repress it, in the girl because of "feminine genital anxiety" (Lerner, 1976; Dorsey, 1996), and in the boy because of castration anxiety.

When the home includes any type of marriage, ideas about marriage become associated with reproduction. In other situations, reproduction may not be integrated with a concept of marriage. When a child is raised by a man and woman who are married (granted, a dwindling number of cases), the child will usually wish to marry one parent or the other. Simultaneously, the child will wish the unwanted parent gone, so as to have exclusive possession of the wanted one.

Typically, these wishes oscillate quite a bit. Both boys and girls initially imagine being married to the mother figure. What happens after that has infinite variations. Typical nightmares during the oedipal phase are generally due to projections of any hostile-destructive fantasies about either parent. So, when the child wants to run to the parental bedroom—consciously for soothing—there is also an *unconscious* wish to see what the parents are up to. Therefore, it is better to soothe the child in the child's room and let the child go back to sleep there, even if the parent must sit in the room for a while to calm the child's fear of their own aggression.

Freud happened to be a classics scholar, among other things, so when he discovered these triangulations forming the symptoms in adults, he thought of Sophocles's (420 BCE) tragic play, *Oedipus the King*. Hence the Oedipus complex (Freud, 1924). However, that's not quite right. For a total exposition of the myriad possibilities of the first genital phase, see Sandler (1960).

Humberto Nagera (1975) found a proto-oedipal stage in girls, where they want to be the man and marry the mother (very common) or be the woman and be the mother's wife. We have more recent studies that show boys, at times, wish to marry the father and have babies (Lax, 1997). In sum, children during this phase possess what Kubie (2011) called "the drive to become both sexes."

It's only when the girl realizes the difference between the genders (between 1½ and 3 years of age) that the possessor of the penis becomes an issue. She begins, usually unconsciously, to associate father with penis and penis with making babies, somehow (again the actual activity is usually not comprehensible until age 9 or 10, or later).

When boys recognize the difference between the genders, they typically develop a fear that they could be turned into girls by having their genitals removed ("castration anxiety"). Of course, this is a fantasy since males and females have *different* equipment, and one cannot be made into the other, in reality. The effects of such fantasies may be profound—or transient and without much significance.

Incestuous wishes (to marry either parent) trouble children, and adults minimize the overt statements of the children about these fantasies. Nobody wants to look back at this stage of development because the sexual fantasies are terrifying and so are the competitive-hostile ones. So, the child eventually forgets all this stuff ("repression") and identifies with both parents as a defense—especially with the parents' values (Brenner, 1982b).

The first resolution of first genital phase conflicts occurs at the beginning of latency, about age 6½–7½. During latency, most children tend to avoid anything that has sexual overtones. At puberty and during adolescence, the wish for a sexual object is displaced outside the family. A second resolution of the Oedipus complex often occurs in marriage (obtaining a partner for oneself who does not belong to anyone else). More resolution can occur with child-birth and further resolution, no doubt, later with grandparenthood.

Secure attachment preceding the first genital phase is requisite for a loving oedipal situation. At first, the pronouncements of preschool children about reproduction and marriage can sound "cute." But the conflicts surrounding aggression, as well as the depression about failure to obtain the loved object, cause the nightmares and the phobias (5 D's) typical of this phase (see Table 6.1)—when destructiveness and loneliness are projected onto symbolic objects.

In talking with parents, discussion of the "resolutions of the children's fantasies and conflicts about the family" is generally more palatable than the term "Oedipus complex"—which has garnered negative publicity for over a century. The therapist is well advised to mention the repressed nature and uncomfortable features of the first genital phase as material is collected about the actual experiences of a child during those years.

The various fantasies that occur during the first genital phase are less disturbing if the child has developed stable internalizations of parents' images (including a reduction of splitting of parents).

Case Example

The Case of Mikey, Age 5

Symbolic play during the first genital phase reflects not only the internal dynamics of the child but also the real events that have impacted the child's life (Kris, 1956). The following case illustrates the functions of play: demonstration, in behavior, of basic mental functions, attachment matters, defenses, and gratification of wishes (Freud, 1926).

First, meeting with the parents gives an overview of the problems and provides the developmental history. Then the child can be seen alone, and this must involve play-oriented interaction with the child. During the interaction, pay attention to the overall themes—including defenses and conflicts represented in the play—as well as the symptoms and concerns previously described by the parents. Also, pay attention to how the child responds to you in the playroom. Does the child involve you in the play? What roles, if any, are you assigned, and can the child move easily from the fantasy of play to the reality of the session?

The Initial Parent Interview(s)

Note: My understanding of Mikey's activities and verbalizations are in italics

Mikey's parents reported, during their first meeting with me (KD), that Mikey had recently told them that a close male family friend and neighbor had

Table 6.1 Additional Questions and Answers

Questions	Meaning	Problems	Other Considerations
Did the parents read to the child	Attachment, language acquisition, beginning of projections/sublimations	Failures to use verbalization	Persistent misbehavior, introversion
Was the child allowed to run and play?	Discharge of aggression	Inhibition; severe temper outbursts	Persistent disobedience, lack of pleasure
Friendships?	Turning to love outside family	Symbiotic persistence	May lead to lack of friends in school
Ability to be alone/go to preschool	Object constancy developed, so mother's image is stable	Persistent separation anxiety	Some children are OK alone, but are "low-keyed"
Child sleeps in own bed?	Object constancy	Anxieties at night stay due to residual separation anxiety	Parents' wish to soothe the child in the marital bed reintroduces symbiotic issues
Nightmares? How handled?	Elements of Oedipus complex projected and symbolized	Constant sleep issues	Child best soothed in own room
Which of the NORMAL 5 "D" phobias did the child manifest, while awake, if any: • Dogs • Deep water • Dentist • Doctor • Dark • OTHER	Projections of aggression during the oedipal phase, symbols of genital anxieties	Complications from failures in separation, or co-sleeping	Overstimulation Other abuse

Table 6.1 (Continued)

Questions	Meaning	Problems	Other Considerations
Symbolic play: swords, dolls, costumes	Resolution of conflicts in play	Failures to sublimate, persistent aggression, anxiety	Transforming of passivity to activity Assimilation of overpowering affects/experiences Ego mastery/ego strength
Finalization of toilet training	Control of affects Socialization/ability to attend preschool; object constancy; relinquishing of anal pleasure in messing	Regression due to unresolved triangular problems; overstimulation; developmental delay	Play is symbolic of separation from mother; social adaptation, self-confidence in body control occur
Dressing, bathing, locked master bedroom door	Freedom from overestimation or intrusion into self-image, tolerance of being alone, resolution of possessive features of Oedipus complex (locked master bedroom door)	Overstimulation, poor concentration, persistent dependency, regression, clinging	Omnipotence, sense of entitlement, officiousness; possible primal scene exposure
How was child disciplined?	Physical abuse rationalized; time-out causing regression from object constancy; spoiling; verbal control; structure of caretaking; comparison to siblings/gender matters	Increased rage from corporal punishment; identification with the aggressor (attacking other children)	Separation anxiety interferences with early learning of letters, numbers Symbolism interferes with sports, learning
Medical problems, deaths, other traumas	Increased anxiety, self-esteem problems, depression (resolved or not?)	Mistrust, chronic irritability, misbehavior	Apparent hyperactivity, regression in empathy, argumentativeness (negativism); regression to encopresis, enuresis, thumb-sucking

fondled him and made Mikey masturbate him. The necessary legal authorities had been notified. Based on Mikey's memory, his parents believed the sexual abuse had happened about two months prior to Mikey's disclosure and had occurred on at least three to four occasions. The parents were surprised that their neighbor sexually abused Mikey, but they believed their son, so they had taken measures to keep Mikey safely away from the neighbor. A medical examination by Mikey's pediatrician, after Mikey's disclosure, revealed no significant findings.

He had an interview with a forensic mental health worker about one month before the parents came to me, in which he had described the sexual abuse clearly—remarkably consistent with what he had told his parents.

This clarity reflected his secure attachment to his parents, which, I thought, had provided him with sufficient affect regulation to be able to describe the events verbally. His (ego) functions of memory, integration, and language use were also sufficiently developed for him to describe the trauma.

Interestingly, Mikey's early superego precursors involved the concept of telling the truth. Nevertheless, for some days after that interview, he experienced more nightmares, reflecting the age-appropriate limits of his affect tolerance.

At this stage of development, isolation of affect is often not as prominent a defense as it is in latency (see Latency Defense Chart in Chapter 7), but the child seems to have identified with his parents' suppressive defenses and their attention to detail.

Chief Complaints by the Parents Regarding the Child's Problems

The parents reported that prior to the sexual abuse, Mikey had been "well-adjusted." He had an interest in sports, particularly soccer. About two months prior to Mikey disclosing the sexual abuse, however, Mikey's parents noticed the following changes in his functioning:

- He had trouble going to sleep on his own and frequently awoke with nightmares.
- After awakening, Mikey would go to his parents' bedroom and be too afraid to return to his own room.
- He often complained of gastrointestinal symptoms ("stomach hurts").
- He became fearful and had tantrums when one of his parents was not near him, even at home.
- He started hitting and biting his sisters.
- He was having "meltdowns" when asked to comply with parental requests (such as to pick up his toys). Aggressive oppositional behavior had not been a problem previously.
- He engaged in heightened public masturbatory activity accompanied by tantrums if his parents redirected him or asked him to cease the behavior.
- He had two episodes of nocturnal enuresis.
- He was reluctant (cried and had a tantrum) when he prepared to leave home for school.

- He refused to go to school on about six occasions; he became inconsolable and refused to leave his parents' car when they arrived at school. The parents allowed him to return home and do some schoolwork there. He calmed down quickly when he realized he could spend the day at home with his mother.
- He had difficulty focusing on his preschool teacher.
- He had trouble remaining in his seat to do classwork.
- His teacher told his parents that in the past few months, Mikey seemed distracted and irritable.

Other Data Obtained from the Parental Interview

CURRENT FAMILY SITUATION

Mikey lived with his parents, who were both employed in the financial industry. He had one older sister (7) and one younger sister (3). There was no history of significant psychiatric or psychological problems in the family. Prior to the sexual abuse incidents, Mikey's parents indicated he got along with his siblings and was not particularly oppositional or defiant.

PREGNANCY AND DELIVERY HISTORY

Mikey was a planned pregnancy, and his mother had no difficulties with the pregnancy or delivery. She was not prescribed any medications during pregnancy. Mikey was born at term by natural birth and had high APGAR scores. He and his mother went home from the hospital the day after he was born.

MEDICAL HISTORY

Mikey was a healthy child. He had regular pediatric examinations and was prescribed preventive vaccinations. He had no head injuries, seizures, or hospitalizations. He was taking no medication at the time of his evaluation.

Developmental History

First Year of Life

His parents described Mikey as a "happy and easy" baby: when Mikey cried, it was easy to calm him down. His mother took a hiatus from work and stayed home with him. Grandparents also helped. He responded well to breastfeeding, which was done in accordance with his needs, so he gained weight in an expectable way. In comparison to his older sister, the parents said he developed physically ahead of schedule: he was active, enjoyed crawling around the house, and liked playing "chase" games with his older sister and parents.

Socially, he was described as "friendly" and related easily to peers and adults. He walked at 11 months.

Second Year of Life

Speech and language development were age appropriate. He had attachments to both parents, but could also play alone and sleep alone by age 2. He was proud of his ability to look at picture books and fall asleep.

Third Year of Life

Mikey began preschool at 3½ years of age, with no problems separating.

Intellectually, he did well in preschool with learning letters and simple words. He was proud of his ability to write the letters of his name, for example. His teachers described him as intelligent and a quick learner. He is ambidextrous, mostly using his right hand to write. There was some reversal of letters, but his teachers did not believe this was significant.

Socially, he enjoyed school and shared some events of the day with his parents. He had friends at school and was protective of his younger sister.

From a motor developmental standpoint, he was early: at age 4, he was able to ride a two-wheel bicycle.

Toilet training began when he was 3 years old, as the parents followed the child's ability to understand and cooperate (Brazelton Method). He only had two to three diurnal enuretic incidents when he started preschool, but this stopped. He had a good appetite and was in the average range of height and weight.

Masturbatory play was readily managed until after the abuse incidents.

Observation of Mikey (of Necessity, First with His Parents)

After having an interview with Mikey's parents, a separate session was scheduled for Mikey. His parents prepared Mikey, as I had advised, by telling him that he would be seeing a "talk doctor" who would talk and play with him, as opposed to a doctor who gave shots.

Both parents accompanied him to the evaluation session. Mikey sat between his parents on a couch in the waiting room. When I entered the waiting room, he appeared nervous—he quickly moved closer to his mother and held onto her arm. He had not been playing with any toys or games that were available in the waiting room.

After I introduced myself, Mikey was reluctant to talk or answer simple biographical questions in his parent's presence (such as his age and his grade in school). I tried to interest him in a toy in the waiting room, but he rejected this overture and looked at his mother. I asked him if he wanted to see my playroom; he then reluctantly nodded his head. *Noting his apparent separation anxiety* (see Chapter 5), I suggested that perhaps he would like his parents to come with him to the playroom; he again nodded yes. Upon seeing the playroom, Mikey became interested in some of the toys, and on his own began exploring the room with curiosity. I told him he could play with anything in the room.

Periodically, he would show his parents toys, and they expressed interest. After about ten minutes, I asked Mikey if it was OK for his parents to leave the room and wait for him in the waiting room. Mikey agreed, and his parents left.

At that point, I explained to Mikey that we could talk and play games, and that I was interested in whatever Mikey wanted to say, play, or draw.

I "planted a seed" (for Mikey's play associations) by revealing that his parents had called because of what he had said about the neighbor.

I deliberately did not mention the details because that would have been overstimulating and likely would have overwhelmed his suppressive defenses.

Mikey's immediate response was to look worried; he began looking around the room. He asked me if I knew the neighbor. I truthfully said I did not—

to establish myself as a "new object" who would be honest—and not trick him, as the abuser had done. This also set the stage for Mikey to be honest with me.

He then darted from one toy to another.

I waited and watched patiently, occasionally commenting on what Mikey was doing and which toys he used. Mikey interacted very little with me and made little eye contact. He appeared interested in action figures and motor vehicles (apparently familiar toys that afforded him a sense of safety).

I asked him if he liked to draw and color. He said, "a little." As the initial session with Mikey progressed, he was less anxious and more relaxed about exploring the playroom. At the end of the session, I asked Mikey what he thought about coming back to my office to play and talk with me. He said he would like to play with some of the action figures. Mikey rejoined his parents. When they asked him how things went, he said, "It was OK; she has some good toys."

At the beginning of Mikey's next evaluation session, he appeared anxious but was able to accompany me to the playroom without his parents. He asked if his parents would be in the waiting room when he was done playing. When his parents assured him that they would wait for him, he easily trusted this (*indicating object constancy; see previous chapters*).

In the playroom, Mikey played with a family of horses. Interestingly, he stated that something had changed in the horse family. He said a tornado had come and the family was upset.

I thought this indicated that the incident had caused powerful disruption of his own thinking. I already knew from the parents that Mikey worried his family would be mad at him because the perpetrator had been a family friend—so the tornado, no doubt, also symbolically represented the disruption in that relationship.

Because of the tornado, Mikey said the horses would change in physical appearance—their eyes and bodies would become scarier looking.

These statements indicated how Mikey used projection and symbolization to manage (protect himself from) his overwhelming anger and fears.

Since these defensive operations were present (projection and symbolization), I only needed to verbally express, with empathy (through the symbolism of his play), that the horses had a hard time with their powerful anger and fear. Mikey responded that the horses were very afraid and felt they would be blown away.

Mikey's comments, again symbolically, seemed to refer to his fear of being rejected as a punishment ("blown away") due to his awareness that his "honest" report of the abuse would lead to the perpetrator being imprisoned.

Mikey then placed a small horse (which he called "my boy horse") underneath the "mother horse." He said the mother horse would protect his horse from the tornado. His exact words were that the mother horse "pinned down" the small horse under her.

The metaphorical use of that phrase, of course, had many potential meanings: the boy's wish for protection and safety, his regression to a wish for symbiotic fusion with his mother, and a representation of someone being restricted (punishment of him for revealing the activity or possibly punishment of the perpetrator).

Next, Mikey said that a big man horse urinated on Mikey's little horse. Mikey put words into the mouth of the little horse, who said, "It was my fault the big horse peed on me."

Here, he seemed to symbolically blame himself for the abuse and felt guilty about the perpetrator being punished.

Then Mikey explained that the "pee was sticky and gooey."

This no doubt represented Mikey's misinterpretation of the man's ejaculation as a form of urination.

Mikey then said his own horse had had its heart taken out and broken. He said, sadly, that the little horse had done bad things that were unknown to the mother.

After this play, Mikey made the horses crash into each other; he said they were biting, kicking, and then killing each other. *Still leaving his symbolic defenses intact,* I said the little boy horse seemed upset and angry because the big horse peed on the little boy horse, and the mother horse could not save him. Mikey responded that the little boy horse then felt dirty and wanted to go take a shower. Mikey said it was a "mean" thing for the big horse to do.

Mikey, more active now, kept hitting the horses together, saying the little horse was angry that his heart had been taken out. Mikey and I commented similarly on the play for the rest of the session. After a few minutes, Mikey abruptly stopped the play with the horses. He mentioned he was tired of the horses. I expressed understanding, and since it was toward the end of the session, I mentioned that he could leave the horses behind and go do something else. He agreed, although he requested that I keep the horses so he could play with them when he returned.

Here, there was evidence that we had established an early working alliance and that he was not finished expressing his "tornado" of unresolved anger and fear.

When I ended the evaluation and we left the playroom, he was calm, although rather somber, as his parents greeted him.

Recommendations to the Parents ("Interpretive Meeting")

After the completed evaluation, I met with the parents without Mikey present. I expressed my opinion that Mikey's symptomatology did seem to be caused by the trauma of the sexual abuse incidents. From the parents' description and from Mikey's symbolic play, I recommended that he be seen in dynamic play therapy. The parents agreed.

Epilogue

Regarding the parents, I did not find any outstanding psychopathology that needed individual clarification and resolution. I recommended they meet with me each time I saw the child to furnish me with updates. This also gave them the opportunity to express their guilt and anger about the incident having ever occurred, and my nonjudgmental approach to them seemed to help diminish their superego anxiety.

They also relied on me for support and advice in relation to the legal issues that arose as Mikey's perpetrator was prosecuted. For the first month or so of therapy, Mikey was nervous about returning to school. I recommended his mother accompany him until his teacher appeared to walk him to class, but there were a few occasions when Mikey would not leave his mother, and I advised her not to force him to separate.

This approach, based on my impression that his separation anxiety had been a regressive defense to handle his overwhelming anxiety over being hurt, was effective. After several weeks, Mikey jumped out of the car to run into school on his own. I was not required to directly interact with the school or the legal system in this case.

7 Ages 6½–11½ Latency

Key Questions for Parents

- **Where Does the Child Sleep?**

  - Looking for persistent anxiety over nighttime separation (persistent symbiosis).[1]
  - Looking for nightmares caused by overstimulation due to co-sleeping.

- **What Types of Punishments Are Used? Any Hitting? The Child's Response?**

  - Looking for the child's weakness in handling powerful emotions (overwhelmed affect tolerance).
  - Looking for misbehavior and malicious mischief (identification with the aggressor).

- **Does the Child Have Friends?**

  - Looking for empathic, supportive relationships outside the family (vs. autism).
  - Looking for interference (too much anxiety) in interacting with other children.

    - Damaged social skills and judgment
    - Excessive hostile aggression or paranoia

- **Does the Child Have Hobbies and Participate in Sports?**

  - Looking for problems channeling aggression into productive pursuits. (Sublimation of aggression).
  - Looking for poor channeling of [sexual] curiosity into intellectual activities (failure of sublimation).

---

1 Mahler et al. (1975).

DOI: 10.4324/9781003257110-7

- Looking for disturbance of developing morality.

  - Not following rules.
  - No respect for authority: no humility, bullying.

- **How Has the Child Performed Academically and Behaviorally at School?**

  - Looking for interferences with learning caused by emotional conflicts.
  - Looking for disruption in attention (caused by neurological factors, developmental delay, or overwhelming affect).
  - Looking for failures to cooperate with time management.

- **Does the Child Have Intact Reality Testing?**

  - Looking for odd behaviors, hallucinations.
  - Psychological testing, including intelligence, academic, and personality testing, may be useful.

- **Have There Been Interferences with the Child's Development by Television, Cell Phone, or Computer?**

  - What type of controls have parents instituted, if any?
  - Looking for limited social and family interactions, leading to withdrawn, egocentric children.
  - Looking for effects of corrupt moral values absorbed from TV programs or internet (e.g., video games about stealing, violence toward authority figures [e.g., police officers], ethnic, or social groups).
  - Looking for interference with sleep-wake cycle.

Answers to the Key Questions

Where Does the Child Sleep?

- Looking for persistent anxiety over nighttime separation (persistent symbiosis).
- Looking for nightmares caused by overstimulation due to co-sleeping.

Co-sleeping, very common in Asian countries, has gained popularity in the United States and other Western countries. During the latency phase, co-sleeping is quite counterproductive.

First, co-sleeping causes failure in children to develop an independent sense of self—that is, the internal picture children have of themselves as independent people. The internal fusion of the images the children have of themselves and of their parents is normally present, to some degree, until age 2 or 3, but may be prolonged by co-sleeping—technically, this is called *persistent symbiosis*.

It turns out, in practical terms, that co-sleeping is a controversial matter. In China, 79% of Chinese families co-sleep until the child is 6 years old, and 53% co-sleep with the children from 6 until puberty (Huang et al., 2010). In the United States, the percentage has risen to between 53% and 84% in the early years of life (CDC, 2022).

One often overlooked aspect of co-sleeping concerns the details regarding the manner in which the parents proceeded with it. If there is not much skin-to-skin contact, if the parents are modest and are not nude around their child, and if they don't have sexual intercourse in the bed while the child is sleeping with them, the child may develop normally. Those children may retain a stronger "family identity" and experience a slightly greater amount of separation anxiety.

There is also the matter of genetics. Certain children are not affected by co-sleeping, whatever type it may be.

In certain cases, during the first genital phase and latency, a lot of nudity with the parents, including co-sleeping, showering together naked, and the parent dressing in front of the children not only produce symbiotic conflicts but can cause sexual overstimulation, which the children have difficulty tolerating.

The pathological persistence of symbiotic conflicts is one common cause of school reluctance, where the child refuses to go to school because of anxiety. The thought content of the anxiety (that is, exactly what the child is afraid will happen), though sometimes not conscious, may be represented symbolically in the child's complaints of physical symptoms, such as stomachaches and sleepiness, which necessitate the child not leaving home (relieves separation anxiety). Interestingly, such school-age children, while at home, often isolate themselves or argue with their parents (to relieve selfobject fusion anxiety).

Since knowledge of the first genital stage (see Chapter 6) is either unknown or denied by many parents, continuing to co-sleep is frequently unrecognized as causing *sexual overstimulation* of the children. Attentive parents have recognized the child's pleasurable "masturbatory play" between about 2 and 7 (Marcus & Francis, 1975). During latency, repression of sexual fantasy and inhibition of masturbatory activity allows the child to learn and develop "self-stability" (Knight, 2005).

Children cannot generally[2] relieve sexual stimulation until after puberty (when masturbation to orgasm is possible). Although not optimal for mental health, some children volitionally[3] engage in sexual intercourse immediately after puberty (Meers, 1975). Sexual overstimulation during latency can

---

2 There exist cases of latency girls who masturbate to orgasm. They had been sexually overstimulated during the first genital phase.

3 In the past, such children were termed participant victims. This term has recently been dropped.

cause agitation and fidgetiness, which are often mistaken for attention deficit/hyperactivity disorder (ADHD). When children are gently removed from the parents' bed,[4] agitation diminishes. Then, concentration and psychomotor difficulties usually fade away. (For a neuropsychoanalytic view of ADHD, see Levin, 2002).[5]

Finally, the nightmares so characteristic of the first genital phase may become magnified by co-sleeping. The violent fantasies harbored by 2- to 7-year-old children had been managed, during the first genital phase, by use of repression (forgetting) and symbolic play (for example, with dolls and weapons). At night, violent fantasies (toward a loved parent) were also projected, so that the child had fears of monsters in dreams and phobias of various places (such as doctors' and dentists' offices).

During *latency*, if sublimation and repression have been successful, the projections that caused the "typical phobias" of the first genital phase tend to abate. If the child is not sleeping independently, however, family romance fantasies are aggravated,[6] and violent fantasies are not sublimated into competition in school and in sports; instead, nightmares and phobias continue and become exacerbated.

Co-sleeping, if it has been fairly continuous, probably has engendered *persistent symbiosis* as well. To relieve the anxiety brought on by merger fantasies, the child will misbehave using "hostile-destructive aggression" (Parens, 1991). If there is further failure to resolve the triangular family fantasies of the first genital phase, the nightmares, instead of abating, tend to intensify. In other words, parents who soothe the child by allowing co-sleeping (after the child has had a nightmare) actually exacerbate the child's anxiety.

What Types of Punishments Are Used? Any Hitting? The Child's Response?

- Looking for the child's weakness in handling powerful emotions (overwhelmed affect tolerance).
- Looking for misbehavior and malicious mischief (identification with the aggressor).

---

4 We have offered a solution to the co-sleeping dilemma to professionals through the years. To help children who are suffering with persistent symbiotic anxiety *and* inadvertent sexual overstimulation, parents should sit quietly (perhaps reading a book) in the child's room (not in the child's bed) until the child is sleeping. Then, the parent can return to the master bedroom. If the child awakens during the night from fears or nightmares, the child can be told to knock on the master bedroom door. At that point, the process starts over again, with one parent soothing the child and then sitting in the child's room until the child is asleep. It may take a few weeks or even months for the child to sleep separately due to persistent separation anxiety.

5 For further discussion of what is sexually overstimulating and what is not, see the Chapter 9 in this volume.

6 Technically, some aspects of these fantasies are termed "oedipal victory dynamics."

When children are spanked to the point where they cry and lose control of their emotions, this creates a state similar to an erupting volcano. The emotions are like lava that burns through mental structure. Such physical punishment causes inflammation of rage, fear, and pain. The creation of these intense emotions tends to weaken the developing mental structure[7] for handling powerful emotions—similar to the breakdown of the bedrock of earth when a magma chamber (in a volcano) becomes overheated (https://www.twinkl.com.br/teaching-wiki/volcano).

In addition, spanking tends to injure children's self-esteem and may cause them to feel a sense of mistrust toward all authorities (such as teachers).

Physically abusive parents tend to minimize the amount and severity of their use of corporal punishment, so the evaluator must have an eye toward that possibility.

It must be remembered that children during latency are imitating their parents and other authorities, both consciously and unconsciously. So, when parents advise a child, "Do as I say, not as I do," this is usually ineffective. Two untoward effects of spanking then become clear: one is that children may become destructive and hit other children, animals, siblings (and sometimes their parents).[8] Other misbehavior and malicious mischief (bullying) may develop.

Another problem with spanking is that the children may *not* make the parents' values part of themselves, as they should be doing during latency. Criticism will stay external, so these children will not obey any authorities unless they are really threatened (often with a negative consequence).[9]

Nota Bene. These questions should be specifically asked, but obviously, this is a touchy area. Nevertheless, many parents may understand that hitting other adults is considered a crime (battery). If parents have been victims of rationalized physical abuse themselves, this may need to be aired, along with the parent's minimization of the effects on them.

Does the Child Have Friends?

- Looking for empathic, supportive relationships outside the family (vs. autism).
- Looking for interference (too much anxiety) in interacting with other children.

---

7 A capacity technically called "affect regulation" (Bretherton, 1992).

8 The terminology for this mechanism is called "identification with the aggressor" (Blackman, 2003).

9 Technically referred to as persistent externalization of the superego (Johnson & Szurek, 1952).

- Damaged social skills and judgment.
- Excessive hostile aggression or paranoia.

- For mental health, the child must begin to make friends during the latency phase. Parallel play is diminished, and cooperative play, demonstrating the development of empathy for others, should increase. When this does not happen, there may be several reasons:

  - The child is developmentally delayed in establishing stable images of others and has too much fantasy in consciousness (some form of autism).
  - The usual ways of playing with other children (by the rules) have not been learned by the child or taught to them (lag in superego development and in social skills).

Shame over assertiveness can cause an *inhibition* of play. In these situations, any assertiveness is often associated with "doing something wrong." The child may become more paranoid if the self-image is already damaged from earlier phases of development since the failure to separate images facilitates the projection of hostility (which is now seen in others).

Does the Child Have Hobbies and Participate in Sports?

- Looking for problems channeling aggression into productive pursuits (failures in sublimation of aggression).
- Looking for poor channeling of curiosity into intellectual activities (sublimation of sexual curiosity).
- Looking for disturbance of developing morality.

  - Not following rules.
  - No respect for authority: no humility, bullying.

One of the most salient features of latency is the process of modifying hostile-destructive aggression into friendly competition and ambition. Input and support from parents and teachers are necessary.[10] It helps with sports if the child already has an inborn capacity, such as eye-hand or eye-foot

---

10 When my (JSB) son was 7, I was trying to teach him to play tennis. He hit the ball so hard, it flew over the fence. As I was advising him not to hit the ball so hard, the tennis pro walked by and heard me. The pro corrected me. He said, "No! The aim is not to hit it softer. The aim is to control the power!" Today, my grown son has a killer topspin forehand, which he delights in using against me when we play tennis.

coordination. Then the aggression becomes associated with the already developing function we call "psychomotor control," and the aggression is easily channeled.

Sports are not the only channel for aggression. Dancing is also excellent. Competition in intellectual areas is also useful if the child has intellectual abilities; examples would be spelling bees, math competitions, and science projects.

We see problems if there has been no outlet for hostile-destructive aggression offered to the child. Then frustration provokes anger, which may conflict with guilt, causing the defense of turning on the self—and suicidal ideation or attempts (self-cutting and dangerous behavior). DeMijolla-Mellor (2009) points out how failures of sublimation can lead to the development of perverse activities (especially sadism and masochism).

Violent video games probably occupy a gray area. They certainly represent, symbolically, violent fantasies that are projected onto (played out in) the game. Games may not fulfill the next developmental step, however (i.e., become sublimations), unless the games are played with friends in good-natured competition and do not become an obsession. Several astronauts have admitted to getting their start by playing space video games as a child. In other words, if the symbolic play eventually becomes linked with physical skill, learning about computers and aviation, a sublimated activity develops.

On the other hand, if parents don't monitor and limit the latency child's use of video games, the child may become preoccupied with the games to the exclusion of social, academic, and physical development (Akhtar et al., 2011).

Collecting is essentially a sublimation of anal interests (amassing things) but can be beneficial. Stamps, coins, Pokémon, Yu-Gi-Oh, baseball cards, and dolls remain favorites. Trading for social interaction and learning about real persons can stimulate intellectual pursuits and friendships.

The masturbatory play of the preschool years is usually mostly repressed (shut out of consciousness) in healthy latency kids. Sexual curiosity (about the difference between males and females, and about reproduction) is likewise repressed and hopefully sublimated. This means that children become interested in "looking into things," such as the biology of animals, detective stories, science, and math.

In addition, the "family romance" ("family conflict" [Blum, 2010]) fantasies of the first genital phase (stories of abduction, kidnapping, royalty, and the parents' histories) will hopefully be displaced into reading. The material that children of this age usually like involves anthropomorphized animals and royalty/magic. Other content involves the children knowing more than the adults (e.g., *Hardy Boys, Nancy Drew, Red Wall, Harry Potter*). Comic heroes and heroines represent fantasies of powerful children.

Ideas of right, wrong, fair, unfair, misbehavior, and punishment are characteristically developing. Nuances of values are not usually present. Children are not particularly aware of their internal development, but concretely know who follows rules and who cheats.[11]

At the beginning of latency, external enforcement of rules is necessary. Gradually, in normal children, these rules are internalized, so by age 9 or 10, normal kids have ideas of their own regarding fairness and improper behavior. They are also capable of criticizing others. As Sarnoff (1976, 1989) points out, many children do not reach this level and continue to cheat, lie, and steal unless there is an imminent punishment threatening them.

Looking for Disturbance of Developing Morality

No respect for authority: Bullying, no humility, not following rules.

Although we expect teenagers to challenge authority and standard societal beliefs, this attitude is not characteristic of the latency stage. Again, more or less normal latency children have internalized their respect for authority and idealize their parents and teachers. Defiance, at this stage, is generally indicative of pathology, or at least delay in conscience development. In some cases, children have become like a corrupt parent through "identification with the aggressor."

Bullies and self-appointed officious children manifest narcissistic pathology and sometimes have identified with parents who have spanked, intimidated, or sexually abused them. The use of projective blaming adds to the picture and may be accompanied by extreme excuse-making ("rationalization").

How Is School Performance?

- Looking for interferences with learning caused by emotional conflicts.

  - Perfectionism leading to fear of failure.
  - Rebelliousness against anything required by authority.
  - Narcissistic entitlement (spoiled children).
  - Grandiosity (defense against poor self-esteem).
  - Acting out a wish to not grow up (Peter Pan Syndrome).

---

11 In lecturing to a group of elementary school teachers, I (JSB) was asked for my opinion of "values clarification groups." When I explained that I was not familiar with this, the teachers explained that in their curriculum, at the time, they were required to put their class in a circle and ask the children to each discuss their own "values." When I heard this, I tentatively responded that I did not think that would be a good idea with latency children, who are just developing values through identification, who had limited abstraction ability, and who generally could not engage in introspection. Two of the teachers then thanked me for my opinion. It turned out they had had trouble with this assignment. Many children, when asked to discuss themselves, started crying or ran out of the room. The teachers said they would use my opinion to argue with the administrators who had asked them to do this. I don't know what became of this issue, but I thought the experience of the teachers demonstrated the state of ego functioning during latency quite well.

- Looking for disruption in attention (caused by neurological factors, developmental delay, overwhelming affect) or learning.

    - Rule out specific developmental delays in concentration, impulse control and motor control (ADHD).
    - Limited intelligence or academic functioning in specific categories, for example, dyslexia, dyscalculia, and dysgraphia.
    - Visuomotor integration problems.
    - Auditory or visual limitations.
    - Physical or sexual abuse → decrease in affect tolerance.
    - Emotional abuse or neglect → apathy and lethargy.
    - *Neurotic inhibition* due to symbolic meanings of learning:

        - Children who refuse to read due to the unconscious gender symbolism of reading certain subjects.
        - Children who have been exposed to their parents having sexual intercourse (or who have been sexually abused) often associate new knowledge and understanding with being exposed to something overwhelming or forbidden.
        - Success causes guilt, which then leads to inhibition (Freud, 1916).

    - Looking for failures to cooperate with time management.

        - Fights about bedtimes and getting up on time (separation conflicts).
        - Food pickiness (rebellion and fight for autonomy when parents are too strict).
        - Obsessional development leads to overwork and loss of time.
        - Procrastination as a way of delaying the "play-to-work" developmental line (A. Freud, 1956).
        - Parents prematurely demanding that latency children understand abstract concepts like "stretches of time".

Does the Child Have Problems with Reality Testing?

- Looking for odd behaviors, hallucinations.
- Practical jokers (Arlow, 1971).
- Talking to themselves.
- Isolation for hours.
- Suicidal threats or attempts, including dangerous behavior that is potentially self-destructive.
- Misunderstanding simple social concepts (Knight, 1954).
- Hearing voices.
- Seeing "ghosts".
- Odd sleep cycles.

- Thumb-sucking and nail-biting.
- Focusing on toys and other matters of interest to much younger children.
- Difficulty distinguishing reality from fantasy.
- [Drugs, cigarettes, and alcohol abuse].[12]

Has There Been Interference by Television, Cell Phone, Computer?

- What types of controls have parents instituted, if any?
  - Overcontrol – not allowing some computer and cell phone use.
  - Undercontrol – allowing too much computer and cell phone use.
- Looking for poor social interactions and family interactions, leading to withdrawn, egocentric children.
  - Parents who insist on no electronic devices – interfere with socialization.
  - Parents who allow extensive use of electronic devices instead of socialization.
- Looking for effects of corrupt moral values absorbed from television programs or the internet.
  - Heavily influenced by normal-appearing external sources of authority.
  - Corrupt websites.
- Danger of child pornographers.
- Video games about stealing or killing vulnerable animals and people.
- TV shows that glamorize and minimize real situations that are highly difficult, challenging, and illegal.
- Looking for interference with the sleep-wake cycle.
  - Allowing children to stay up all night on electronics.
  - Failing to awaken children on time.
  - ADHD stimulant medication.
  - Punishment by withholding food at dinner (going to sleep hungry).
  - Co-sleeping.
  - Not talking to and soothing children who awaken with nightmares or night fears.

Essay

Latency is not always so latent (Sarnoff, 1976, 1989). Freud initially described this phase (1905) as the period of time when the intense fantasies and nightmares of the first genital phase (ages 2½–7½) seemed to calm down. The latency child should be channeling destructive aggression into sports,

---

12 Unusual during latency, but they do occur.

competition, music, art, and dancing. The child should also be channeling "infantile" sexual curiosity into the developing intellectual function so that the motivation to learn is enhanced.

In addition, children's conflicts over aggression during the preschool years (wanting to be rid of one parent or a sibling vs. loving the same parent or sibling) seem to get resolved by the development of a new mental structure: the conscience (superego) (Brenner, 2006). The 6-year-old child identifies with the values of the parents, meaning the child incorporates the parents' values (both through being taught and through imitation). This development has a powerful effect on the child's values. Superego development governs whether the child will be obedient and well-behaved or disruptive and disorderly.

The Superego

Because of the importance of sublimations (channeling of childhood wishes) and identifications in the development of the superego (Bornstein, 1951), it is important, when assessing children who are between the ages of about 6 and 11, to know to whom they have been exposed. Have they spent a lot of time with their parents, grandparents, nannies? What has been the attitude of those people toward the child, particularly when it comes to values about work, treating other people in a certain way, handling money, regulating one's life, being on time, and obeying authorities? Did the child incorporate those values, or because the caretakers were too lenient or too strict, did the child act even more impulsively (indicating either rebellion or disidentification)?

Many theoreticians believe that value systems should be taught to children; this is partly right. Some of the superego develops as a result of what children are taught during this stage, although children may easily reject what they are taught. Religious teachings, various moral teachings by parents, and instruction by other children about how to do things usually cause (intrasystemic) conflict in children about their own value system.

In addition, the culture in which the child grows up greatly affects the values and ideals comprising the superego. Ideas about work, gender roles, marriage, child-rearing, and management of competition are all affected by government policies, movies, and a large variety of internet websites and podcasts.

The third factor in creating the superego is the child's own perspective of the world. Children have their own minds, so no matter how much they may identify (or disidentify) with parents, and no matter what they are taught, children may develop a set of ideas that is somewhat at odds with all of that.

Ego Functions

Aside from developing a superego, the child needs to develop various autonomous mental functions which hopefully will be encouraged by the parents. These functions include the use of intellect, particularly in reading and learning, and moving from play to work—a very difficult transition (A. Freud, 1956).

There are millions of pages of literature on how to help children learn. The problem of getting them to concentrate on work rather than play is a persistent one. The majority of children do not take easily to work. They would rather play or daydream. The superego is just starting to develop. Latency children are therefore easily misdiagnosed as having ADHD (see Appendix 1).

Two impediments to diagnosing school problems in latency children have been (1) the failure to recognize that children have trouble moving from play to work and (2) not taking into consideration the status of their superego development.

Attachment and Socialization

During the first genital phase, from ages 2½ to 7½ (more or less), children experience conflicts with the people who love them. We have to look at each household individually to determine how the triangular conflicts of the first genital phase have played out. A missing parent, parents who divorce, and other situations affect the child's resolution of their competitive and loving feelings during the first genital phase. These individualistic resolutions, in turn, affect the types of values the children develop later through identification.

Further, we hope that children during latency have developed self and object constancy (by the end of their third year) so that they have capacities for empathy, trust, and emotional closeness with others. When this has happened, even in the face of other difficulties, they will be more likely to develop shame and guilt when they transgress against someone they care about. Absent those types of attachments from early childhood, the superego is much more difficult to instill. Therefore, those children tend to be less obedient, to be less governable, and to have more difficulty learning.

By the time they are in latency, mentally healthy children should have developed secure-organized attachments, not disorganized or insecure ones.

The evaluator can check this by getting a history of whether the child has any close friends, whether the child helps out in the home, whether the child has trouble separating from the parents to attend school, and whether the child has begun to adapt to the parents' schedule. Many aberrations in the normal scheme may occur and should be noted.

Drive Activity

Aggression and sexuality should have been tamed somewhat by age 6. Although children during the preschool years "play doctor," run around naked, and engage in masturbatory play, this should have come to a halt somewhere between the ages of 6 and 7. Repression plays a large role unless the parents are overstimulating the children—which interferes with repression. As we described elsewhere (Blackman & Dring, 2016), inadvertent overstimulation may occur when parents are trying to soothe their children. However, the notion of the family bed, whether in the United States or other countries, generally causes sexual overstimulation in the child.

Children are not aware exactly of what sexual stimulation feels like, and they do not yet possess the physical capacity for relief. Therefore, the usual result of overstimulation is that the child is agitated during the day and has more difficulty sitting still. If the parents respond by disciplining the children more severely (often with corporal punishment), the child may be intimidated into obedience. But the child's suppressed, seething anger will remain unconscious only until adolescence when abject passivity evaporates and delinquent aggression arises in its place (Meers, 1974).

The evaluator is advised to inquire as to where the child sleeps and how often. As noted, frequent sleeping with the parents is often a major cause of disturbance in latency. Receptive parents may be willing to gradually move their children out of their bed and stay in their children's room with them for a few minutes (while the children are in their own bed) until the children are sleeping. This enforces the idea that a child should be sleeping alone. As parents institute this gradual separation, residual conflicts over symbiosis are resolved. Simultaneously, as sexual and aggressive overstimulation are eliminated, the child should be able to relax and the agitation and passive-aggressive withdrawal from working should diminish.

Defensive Operations in Latency

Aside from latency disturbances being based on developmental delays, some disturbances in latency children occur due to various defensive operations being used to handle conflict. Before latency, most children can relieve painful emotions by forgetting, denying a reality, or projecting their feelings onto something. But during latency, because of maturation and superego formation, a large number of defensive operations can be instituted.

A defense is a mental operation that removes some part of mentation from consciousness (Blackman, 2003, 2021). Emotions can be defined as being made up of a sensation (pleasurable or unpleasurable) plus a thought (conscious or unconscious). So, anxiety consists of an unpleasurable sensation plus a thought that something terrible will happen in the future. Depressive affect can be defined as an unpleasurable sensation plus a thought that something terrible has already occurred (Brenner, 2006). Anger consists of an unpleasurable sensation plus a thought of doing harm (Blackman, 2010).

Defense mechanisms operate something like circuit breakers—when affects threaten to overload the mind, defenses shut the sensation out of consciousness ("isolation of affect"), or shut off the thought content ("repression"). (Also see Arlow & Brenner, 1964.) Defenses can also be likened to breathing: they are occurring automatically all the time, outside of awareness, but they can be drawn into awareness and used on purpose ("I don't want to go there!").

Any mental operation can be used defensively. One hundred and one plus have been defined (Blackman, 2003, 2021). A man plays golf to avoid his wife, who makes him angry—**golf** as a defensive operation. A woman blames her mother for all her troubles—**projective blaming**, which relieves her shame over causing her own problems (Friday, 1997). A latency child forgets an assignment to dress as a bumble bee until bedtime the night before it is to be worn at school—**repression** (forgotten but stored memory, until triggered to consciousness).

Until the school-age years, as mentioned, children have only a handful of defenses to manage emotions: denial, repression, and impulsivity, for example. During latency, however, maturation and resolution of conflict lead to a larger variety of defensive operations. Some of the most common are listed in Table 7.1 (Defenses in Latency).

Compromise Formations

Figure 7.1 shows the five components of a *compromise formation* (wishes, reality, guilt-shame, affects, and defenses), and how they interact with one another. This can be used by the evaluator to integrate the information gathered from the key questions, observations, psychological testing data and other sources of information.

Any symptom (like a phobia) or negative character trait (such as ignoring work or defying rules) is a compromise formation. For example, a latency age child, Bill, who refuses to do homework, is expressing a hostile-destructive wish (against parents) and an oral dependent (libidinal) wish (to be lazy and have everyone take care of him). These wishes conflict with reality, which is that he needs to do his homework for school. At the same time, unconsciously he feels ashamed of wanting his mother to coddle him, and he feels guilty over his hostility—these conflicts, involving his superego, produce anxiety and depressive affect, respectively. Bill relieves his superego anxiety by provoking punishment (defense) and relieves his shame over dependency by inciting his parents to pay attention to him (but the wish is repressed). His resistance to schoolwork is partly a compromise formation—which includes all five elements simultaneously.

After a few years of not doing homework, Bill will not have enough information to learn new material easily – he will have developed what has been described as a "de facto" developmental delay, caused by his solutions (to conflicts) that impaired his learning (Blackman, 1991). This type of delay must be distinguished from an idiopathic lag in the development of his intellectual functioning, and this must be further differentiated from other developmental delays such as a failure to move from play to work, and other "learning disabilities" related to a lack of focus and attention (often labeled as ADHD).

Table 7.1 Defenses in Latency

What is managed	Latency defense (Technical Names)	Effect	Reason for it
Sadness	Denial Of Affect	"Mr. Spock"[1]	Shame over loss of control
Anger	Isolation Of Affect	Not experience sensations	Relief of guilt
Masturbatory play	Repression	Unintentional forgetting	Relief of affect
External sexual stimulation	Suppression	Intentional forgetting	Relief of affect
Genital anxieties	Ipsisexual Friends	Friends of same sex	Avoid cooties[2]
	IDENTIFICATIONS WITH		
Depressive affect	Fantasies	Become like superhero	Compensation for inability due to phase
Sexual or hostile misbehavior	Parents' Unconscious Wishes	Act out parents' wishes	Relieve parents' conflicts
Grief	Survivors	Become like survivor	Adapt to losses
Insecurity	Ideal Objects	Enhance motivation	Relieve identity worries
Destructive aggression	Aggressors	Bullying/sadism	Relief of anger and fear
Guilt and shame over helplessness of parent	Victims	Victimization/masochism	Relief of guilt
Loss-based depression (Anaclitic type)	Lost Objects	Imitation of lost person	Avoidance of grief
Ambivalence and obedience	Introjects	Early conscience	Please the parent
Fear of reality person	**SEDUCTION OF THE AGGRESSOR**	Teacher's pet coquette	Reality benefits, relieve real anxiety
Guilt	Provocation	Criticism by other	External relieve of guilt
Guilt and Shame	Rationalization	Making excuses	Avoid tension, guilt, or punishment
Guilt	Rumination	Overthink, poor concentration	Relieve guilt, poor self-esteem
Real fears of environment	Counterphobic behavior	Dangerous jaunts	Relieve anxiety about danger

Table 7.1 (Continued)

What is managed	Latency defense (Technical Names)	Effect	Reason for it
Competitive aggression	**Intellectualization**	Focus on elite concepts and language	Relieve guilt and other affects
Loneliness	**Socialization**	Focus on external friendships	Avoid upsetting things
Social anxiety	**Emotional distancing**	Loneliness	Avoid fusion anxiety and social ostracism
Gender-based anxieties	**Instinctualization of ego function**	Irrationally associate a particular type of work with gender	Avoid insecurity about sexuality or hostility
Guilt	**Inhibition of ego function**	"De facto" defect in major function	Shutoff of function to relieve guilt
Self-image insecurities	**Idealization**	Overvaluation of others	Relieve shame, disappointment
Self-esteem	**Devaluation**	Condescend to others	Preserve own self-esteem
Unpleasant reality situation	**Daydreaming**	Distract from concentration	Relieve boredom

1 Mr. Spock, a well-known TV icon at the time of this writing, was a character on *Star Trek* (1966–1969), who was half human and half Vulcan (a fictional planet). Because of his hybrid nature, although he experienced human emotions, when asked about them, he always responded that he did not know the reference point of the humans.

2 For those non-American readers, "cooties" refers to a common fantasy of latency children that the other gender is infested with an unspecified but disgusting insect. The "insect" is usually symbolic of unconscious sexuality of the opposite gender, which frightens the latency child.

BLACKMAN'S FIVE-POINTED STAR COMPROMISE FORMATION

REALITY

Loved one's personality
Complications with schoolwork
Actual losses or traumas
Other impediments

WISHES

Oral – *to be taken care of*
Sexual – *with a forbidden person*
Hostile-destructive – *toward a
loved one*
Object related – *for attachment,
closeness, love*
Ego related – *success, interests*

SUPEREGO

Guilt – *over destructive wishes*
Shame – *over oral & sex wishes*
Fairness
Integrity
Punctuality & reliability

DEFENSES

Repression
Isolation of affect
Denial
Rationalization
Intellectualization
Symbolization
Displacement
Projection
Concretization
Inhibition of function
Regression
Projective identification
Identification with the aggressor
Externalization
Humor

AFFECTS

Anxiety
Depression
Anger

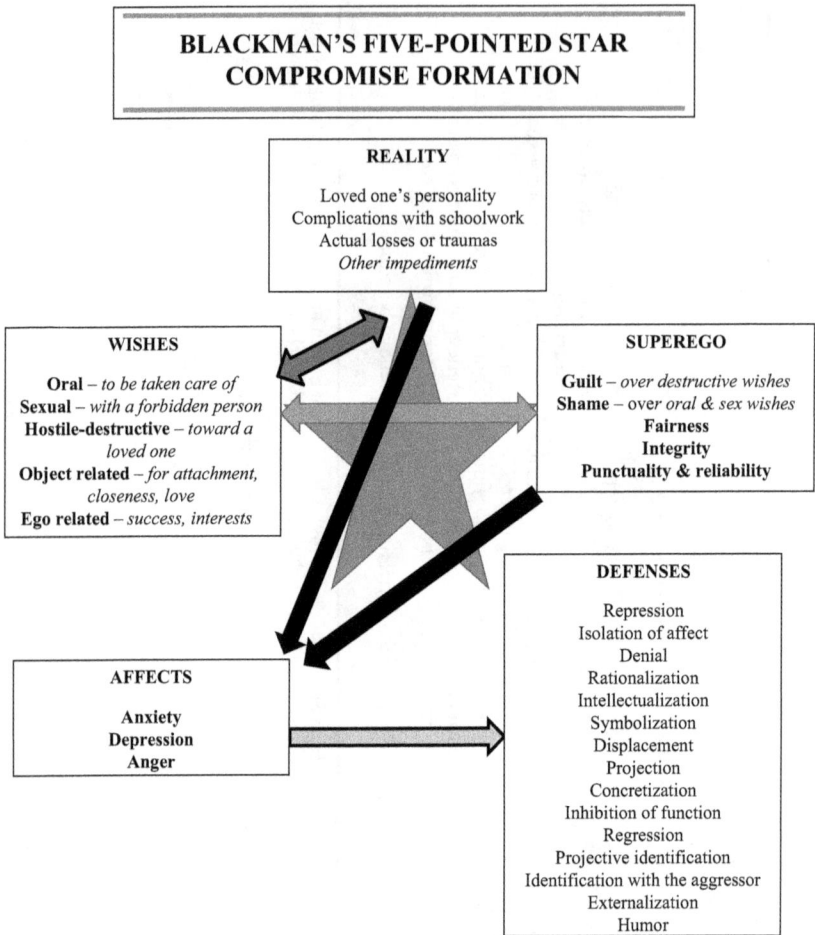

Figure 7.1 Blackman's Five-Pointed Star: Compromise Formation

Psychological Testing

It is not surprising that parents of latency age children frequently request psychological testing. Many children are entering full-day academic settings and are faced with new challenges and demands. The increased time at school requires the child to function more autonomously. Cognitively, during latency, most children enter the period of concrete operations (Piaget & Inhelder, 1969) and have increased abilities to organize and solve problems mentally, rather than through actions.

Two major developmental changes are occurring during latency. *Intrapsychically*, the child enters a stage where the prior first genital phase (family intrigue) conflicts should dissipate (Freud, 1924). In addition, the superego becomes prominent in development. *Cognitively*, the child is developing increased intellectual, abstraction, and organizational abilities. Each of these developmental activities influences the other. If there is a lag or deficit in one of these capacities, the child may manifest behavioral, interpersonal, or learning problems. Mahon (1991) discussed the intermingling of cognitive changes and the resolution of oedipal conflicts in latency, as follows:

> [I]t is easy to see how one might influence the other maladaptively. It is easier to repress desire and identify with society's dictates when the ego's psychological skills and cognitive skills join forces in a developmental alliance that paves the way for the progress of mental health and the process of adaptation.
>
> (pp. 632–633)

While children generally adjust to these changes relatively well, many parents face educator recommendations to evaluate (and ameliorate) below-average academic functioning as well as behavioral problems related to oppositionality, impulsivity, hyperactivity, and inattention. Some children manifest anxiety about the separation from their parents while attending school. Psychological testing is often a useful adjunct to the psychodynamic clinical interviews we outlined in this book. The testing often meets educational/legal requirements for documentation.

The majority of graduate psychology programs de-emphasize personality assessment (Stedman et al., 2001), and few psychoanalytic training programs offer education regarding personality testing. This is ironic since the majority of mid-20th century efforts toward personality testing were made by psychoanalysts (Rappaport et al., 1945; Bornstein, 2010). Bornstein (2010) advocates for a return to using psychodynamic principles for conceptualizing and integrating personality testing data (see also Sugarman & Kannur, 2000).

Currently, the trend in psychological assessment and testing is atheoretical and not tied to psychodynamic personality or developmental theory. Most psychological assessment of children involves evidence-based biological and cognitive behavioral models (Meersand, 2011). In our opinion, the atheoretical approach has been fueled by laws and U.S. federal regulations that place emphasis on empirically based assessment of learning disabilities.

There are few assessment articles, textbooks, or even educational courses that use psychodynamic theories of development, defenses, transference and countertransference concepts, the meaning and quality of the child's fantasies, the status of basic mental (autonomous ego) functions, the influence of sexuality, or aggressive struggles around separation and identity. We believe that personality assessment and evaluation of children must consider these factors in order to arrive at a proper diagnosis, give proper feedback to the parents, and make proper recommendations for interventions. Much of this information should be forthcoming in the answers to the key questions we suggest. Psychological testing offers more information, if needed.

There is a wide range of psychological assessment instruments commonly used with latency age children. The following descriptions address the common reasons for referral, as well as the psychological assessment measures associated with these complaints.

Specific Learning Disorders – Since the enactment of the Education for All Handicapped Children Act of 1975 (P.L. 94-142), the number of children in the United States diagnosed with a learning disability has increased by more than 300% (Sotelo-Dinoga et al., 2018). Four issues complicate the assessment of learning disabilities:

1   The necessity to consider a complex layer of U.S. federal and state law mandates designed to protect the legal rights of children.
2   The lack of emphasis on psychodynamic principles, especially the concepts of defense, symbolism, and compromise formation (Freud, 1926; Brenner, 2006; Blackman, 2010). Reliance on standard psychological testing alone may inhibit the integration of vast amounts of data from clinical interviews, collateral sources, and observations.
3   Multiple classification and diagnostic systems for learning disabilities create confusion or inconsistency in definitions, to wit: *Diagnostic and Statistical Manual of the American Psychiatric Association, 5th Edition, Text-Replacement (DSM-5-TR)*, *International Classification of Diagnoses 10 (Clinical Modifications) ICD-10-CM*, *Individuals with Disabilities Education Improvement Act* (IDEA, 2004), and the *Psychodynamic Diagnostic Manual-Second Edition (PDM-2)*.
4   The definitions and interpretations of what classifies as a learning disability are unclear. The measures used to make empirical determinations of learning disability are also variable. For many years, the key element in defining learning disability was an analysis of the discrepancy between a child's intellectual ability versus performance as scored on standardized achievement tests. The analysis of this discrepancy focused on identifying *unexpected underachievement*. While many school districts still rely on this method, it has come under criticism (Ysseldyke, 2005), including that it overidentifies minority students (Bradley et al., 2002).

An alternative to discrepancy analysis, the Response to Intervention (RTI), is a multi-tiered assessment system. RTI, initially done in school, tries to identify students with academic problems, primarily in reading. A teacher or counselor monitors a child's performance by looking at test results and getting input from teachers and reading specialists. If a child continues to function below the expected level in reading or other subjects, more intense "interventions" are recommended. A child's response to the first set of interventions will determine if a higher "tier" of intervention is needed.

A third way to identify learning disabilities involves the evaluation of patterns—of strengths and weaknesses—based on academic achievement and cognitive abilities (Flanagan et al., 2010).

Whatever method is chosen to assess a learning disability, most assessments for latency age children involve a broad-based combination of intellectual, achievement, behavioral, and emotionally focused measures. Many of the listed measures (see the following section) were developed in response to referrals for mood disorders, problematic intellectual or organizational functioning, family problems, and attentional difficulties. (For more information on ADHD assessment, see Appendix 1). The following list is not exhaustive.

Intellectual Assessments

- *Wechsler Preschool and Primary Scale of Intelligence–Fourth Edition (WPPSI-IV)*. Appropriate for ages 2 years, 6 months through 7 years, 7 months. This is an individually administered tool for assessing cognitive functioning (Wechsler, 2012). (For a review of the WPPSI-IV, see Syeda & Climie, 2014).
- *Wechsler Intelligence Scale for Children-V (WISC-V)*. This is an individually administered intelligence assessment, appropriate for ages 6:0–16:11 (Wechsler, 2014). (For a review of the WISC-V, see Sabrina & Burns, 2016).
- *Kaufman Assessment Battery for Children–Second Edition Normative Update (K-ABC-II-NU)*. This is an individually administered measure of cognitive skills, appropriate for ages 3–18 (Kaufman & Kaufman, 2018). It is culturally sensitive and may be used if a child has language difficulties.
- *Stanford-Binet Intelligence Scales–Fifth Edition (SB-5)*. This is an individually administered test of intellectual ability for ages 2–85 (Roid, 2003). (For a review of the SB-5, see DiStefano & Dombrowski, 2006).

Broad-Based Achievement Tests – These measures generally provide indicators of learning problems in reading, mathematics, and writing. If a more specific determination of subsets of learning disabilities is needed, the following tests can suggest specific areas of weakness that need further investigation.

- *Woodcock-Johnson-IV Test of Achievement (WJ IV ACH)*. This is an individually administered test appropriate for ages 2–90 (Schrank et al., 2014). It can be used to assess, diagnose, and monitor progress in reading, writing, and mathematics.
- *Wechsler Individual Achievement Test–Fourth Edition (WIAT-IV)* (NCS Pearson, 2020). This is an individually administered academic achievement test appropriate for ages 4–50:11. (For a review of this instrument, see Beaujean & Parkin, 2022.)
- *Kaufman Test of Education Achievement–Third edition (KTEA-III)* (Kaufman & Kaufman, 2014). This is an individually administered measure of achievement appropriate for ages 4–25. (For a review of this measure, see Frame et al., 2016.)

Specific tests for abilities in reading, mathematics, and writing/spelling:

- *Reading* – The evaluation of reading disorders, including dyslexia, is complicated by the multiple psychological processes involved in developing reading abilities: phonemic awareness, phonological processing, decoding, perception, recognition of printed words, prosody (emotional tone), retrieval, fluency, vocabulary, working memory, and executive function (Feifer, 2018).

The *Feifer Assessment of Reading (FAR)* – (Feifer & Gerhardstein-Nader, 2015) is a comprehensive reading measure used to assess underlying cognitive and linguistic processes important for reading development.

- *Mathematics* – Mathematics learning disabilities are not consistently defined. Generally, the assessment involves looking for poor number skills, slow or inaccurate arithmetic fluency, inefficient strategy used during problem-solving, and atypical math errors. (For an overview of mathematical difficulties, see Mazzocco, 2007.)
- *Writing* – Written expression is made up of many skills, including fine motor skills, oral language, reasoning, spelling, and the ability to put thoughts into writing. In young children, early warning signs of writing difficulties are noted by awkward pencil grip, illegible handwriting, avoidance of writing tasks, or tiring quickly when writing (Mather & Wendling, 2018).

Behavior-Related Assessments

- *Conners Parent-Teacher Rating Scale-Revised (CPR)*. This assesses ADHD and related problems in children ages 3–17 years (Conners, 1997).
- *Child Behavior Checklist (CBCL)*. This is a component of the *Achenbach System of Empirically Based Assessment (ASEBA)*. The ASEBA is used to detect behavioral and emotional problems in children and adolescents. The CBCL is completed by parents. There is also a teacher and a self-report form for older children.

The CBCL divides the child's problems into internalizing vs. externalizing factors. There are eight syndrome scales: (1) anxious/depressed, (2) depressed, (3) somatic complaints, (4) social problems, (5) thought problems, (6) attention problems, (7) rule-breaking behavior, and (8) aggressive behavior (Achenbach, 2011).

Emotional Functioning

- *Children's Apperception Test (CAT)* (Bellak & Bellak, 1949). This is a projective test for children ages 3–10. Children are asked to look at a series of pictures and cartoons, and then asked to tell a story based on those images. Reality testing, judgment, control of drive fantasies, defenses, and level of autonomy can be assessed by the CAT. (For a description of the application of the CAT to a psychoanalytic discussion of an 8-year-old child, see Tuber, 2004.)

- *Personality Inventory for Children–Second Edition (PIC-2)* (Lachar & Gruber, 2001). This evaluates psychopathology and emotional/behavioral problems in children ages 5–18 years old. It is completed by the parents.
- *Personality Inventory for Youth (PIY)* (Lachar & Gruber, 1995.) This assesses emotional and behavioral adjustment, family interaction and attention-related academic functioning in individuals ages 9–19 years old. (For a discussion of the validity scales on the PIY, see Wrobel et al., 2000).
- *Roberts Apperception Test for Children–2 (RATC-2)* (Roberts, 2005). This test uses free narratives to assess adaptive social perception and the presence of maladaptive or atypical social perception. The children are shown pictures (which depict children in everyday experiences) and then asked to tell a complete story about each. The pictures have been updated to include three parallel sets depicting Caucasian, African-American, and Hispanic children.
- *The Children's Developmental Play Instrument (CDPI)* (Chazan & Kuchirko, 2017). The CDPI is a multidimensional scale designed to assess play activity among children. It is based on the psychoanalytic concepts of coping and defensive strategies. The CDPI was constructed to measure functional variables in the following areas: play engagement (initiation and/or facilitation of sustained play), symbolic function (thematic play, ending play with satiation, imagination, representations, substitution of one object for another), adaptive play (uninterrupted forward-moving effort toward mastery), inhibited/conflicted play style (lack of expression of emotions, inhibitions), impulsive/aggressive play style (lack of continuity in play and modulation of affect), and disorganized play style (high levels of anxiety indicating feeling overwhelmed, withdrawn, and avoidant interactions).

Case History

Ryan, age 9, was discussed with me (KD) by Dr. Smith, a psychologist, regarding whether psychological assessment for ADHD and/or learning difficulties would be helpful in making a differential diagnosis. Dr. Smith also sought guidance about psychotherapeutic interventions with Ryan and his parents. The consultation involved discussions with Dr. Smith regarding her meeting Ryan's parents and Ryan. Ryan's parents had engaged Dr. Smith for help with the following problems regarding Ryan:

1) Preoccupation with water dripping from the bathroom faucet, which caused him to recheck it several times before bedtime.
2) Refusal to do homework unless his mother "helped" him by being physically available and doing some of the homework for him.

3) Defiantly yelling at his mother and father, refusing to do chores.
4) Fear of germs and need to clean his desktop and shower after using them.
5) Phobia of sitting in the car while his mother drove through automatic carwashes.
6) Joking and refusing to take school seriously, somewhat inattentive to classwork.
7) Recently, Ryan expressed a wish to die.

Developmental History

(Italics indicate the consultative opinions shared with Dr. Smith).

Pregnancy

Surprise pregnancy, but both parents wanted the child. No illnesses during the pregnancy.

0–1 Year: Oral, Attachment, "Normal Symbiosis" and Early Hatching (Separation Phase)

Slept in bed with parents. Often, his father slept in a different room because he had to get up early to go to work. No feeding problems. Mother volunteered part time at a blood-donation center. Father, a professional, worked long, irregular hours.

The pattern of co-sleeping set the stage for persistent conflicts about symbiotic attachment and separation.

1–3 Years: Symbiotic and Later Separation Phases Leading to Self and Object Constancy

Ryan continued sleeping with his mother, although at times, his mother slept with his older brother, and his father slept with Ryan. Mother was busy assisting his older brother (5 years old) with academic work. When Ryan sought help, however, his father told Ryan to ask his mother to assist him.

Toilet training was begun at 18 months; Ryan was afraid of the toilet being dirty. Also, he was afraid that flushing it would drown him after he fell into the toilet.

Precursors of (or precocious) superego development (conscience, i.e., shame and guilt) were seen as the child had difficulty establishing self and object constancy (see prior chapters); therefore, extra destructive aggression was projected (imagined to be outside of him) onto the toilet and "germs." Some of his fear was also an introjection (taking into his thinking) of his mother's overconcern with cleanliness and her fears of his death. In addition, because of early sibling rivalry (wish to kill his brother), which was projected, he imagined himself dying (being killed).

Toilet training was not completed until age 4, with continued periodic night-time bed-wetting until age 9.

Since the rapprochement subphase of separation-individuation runs from about 16–25 months, his continued co-sleeping exacerbated Ryan's conflicts about symbiotic fusion and separation affects. In addition, the periodic bed-wetting and co-sleeping with his mother suggest that he was sexually overstimulated, and the later latency repression (ages 6–9) did not occur successfully.

At age 3, he was afraid to go to preschool and cried severely. Once at preschool, however, Ryan would calm down. When he saw his mother at noon, he cried again, and sometimes refused to go with her.

Here we have further evidence of internal failure of self and object constancy. The problems that occurred when his mother came to pick him up suggest that he suffered with insecure or ambivalent attachment.

At preschool, he was inattentive and uncooperative during reading time. Later, his teachers noticed that he knew the letters—he was refusing to comply.

Oppositional defiant behavior, associated with aggressive strivings for self-constancy, now was becoming symbolically linked with other authorities, and Ryan, therefore, rebelled by resisting learning.

His father, who soon entered his own individual analytic therapy, was depressed, passive with his wife, and had been preoccupied with work stress for several years.

The father's passivity also made it difficult for Ryan to internally separate his self-image from the image of his mother, since he did not have a consistent father to turn to for support in forming that separation.

Age 3–6 Years: First Genital Phase and Object Constancy

Ryan continued sleeping with his mother, but sometimes went into the other room and slept with his father. His father would make fun of him and call him "wifey."

During this first genital phase, his father's "jokes" were experienced by Ryan as castrating, and he seemed to stick to his mother for protection in a symbiotic way. At times, he yearned for his father's love, but his father's sarcasm interfered with Ryan's identification with his father.

Ryan was a good athlete, but would not stay with any game. He would walk away. No children came over to stay at the house.

The parents' failure to encourage some socialization and stick-to-it-iveness, and his mother's persistent co-sleeping reinforced Ryan's separation conflicts and prevented sublimation of aggression. The lack of sublimation of aggression interfered with playing games with other boys. Instead, he became a practical joker (Arlow, 1971), and this continued into latency (see the following).

At 4, his mother nagged him not to touch his penis in public, but he continued to grab at his genitals periodically, provoking his mother to scold him. His father would sometimes yell at him, supposedly as a joke, "Cut it out or it'll fall off!"

Again, these interactions with his parents, during this phase, increased Ryan's cas-tration anxiety and interfered with his self-esteem regulation and identity formation. In addition, some elements of "oedipal victory" caused an exacerbation of severe self-criticism due to identification with his father's aggression toward him (and with his own projected aggression toward his father).

Age 6–9: Latency (Self and Object Stabilization, [Knight, 2005])

Ryan's mother was insistent that Ryan's clothing be well pressed and match-ing. She also insisted that his books be stacked neatly in his backpack and that Ryan wash his backpack with a cloth at least every few days. He complied.

Here the attitude of the mother led Ryan to identify with her obsessional neatness and germophobic propensities as a defense against his hostile aggression toward her for her invasiveness and control.

Ryan became terrified that dripping water would kill his mother and that germs would kill him.

These fantasies seemed to symbolize his (unconscious) wish to kill his mother as well as his fear of his own projections (that she would die) and his developing guilt.

He began cleaning the faucets and checking them for drips.

Here, the cleaning was a reaction formation against the guilt over matricidal wishes.

At other times, he squeezed toothpaste into his parents' and his brother's shoes.

The practical jokes symbolized his hostility toward his mother and brother, as well as anal regression of making a mess (Freud, 1926). The toothpaste squeezing and bed-wetting seemed to indicate his response to his mother's previous sexual overstim-ulation of him as well.

Ryan continued to insist that his mother assist him with all of his home-work and answer homework questions for him.

This showed the persistent symbiotic tie (relief of separation anxiety) and grandi-ose defense development consistent with oedipal victory. We can see here the evolu-tion of his problems in a developmental sequence.

Ryan's mother took him to his family doctor at age 7, at the beginning of school, because she was worried that his penis was too small. The doctor reas-sured her that he was within normal limits.

This doctor visit contributed to Ryan's castration anxiety and interfered with his self-confidence and identification with his father.

Ryan's mother took baths with Ryan in the nude until he was 9. Ryan's mother also indicated that during the baths, Ryan would try to grab her breasts, which made her uncomfortable. She also assisted in his toileting if he had a bowel movement that she thought was "too messy." His mother was concerned because Ryan expressed a wish to die shortly before the parents requested the evaluation.

His mother's overstimulation, invasion, and infantilization and his father's cas-trating jokes all produced a perfect storm. Ryan became obsessional, oppositional at school, played practical jokes, had difficulty separating from his parents, and expressed a wish to die.

I suggested to Dr. Smith that she discuss with Ryan's parents the importance of having Ryan sleep in his own bed and do his toileting independently. I also advised that the parents not bathe nude with Ryan or expose him to parental nudity. The parents were accepting of this when these recommendations were brought to their attention by Dr. Smith. The parents correctly predicted that Ryan would have trouble adjusting to being more independent and sleeping on his own.

Apparently, Ryan had developed homicidal aggression toward his mother for invading him but had turned this onto himself, causing suicidal rumination. He also developed a fear of germs due to the projection of those hostile wishes.

Ryan excelled in soccer due to natural eye-foot coordination, but he often quit a game if he fell in the mud. He would go inside and wash his clothes. Because of his athleticism, the other boys chose him to play games during recess, and the girls liked him for his mischievousness and loquaciousness.

Ryan's parents were concerned that he was underperforming at school, and the teachers worried that he might have ADHD and learning disabilities. Ryan's school recommended he be evaluated for medication management of his inattentiveness and impulsivity. Ryan was resistant to working and complained about the amount of homework.

Because of the family history and Ryan's apparent actual abilities in school, dynamic psychotherapy was initially considered the treatment of choice. ADHD seemed like an unlikely diagnosis, considering his multiple symptoms and personality traits. Performing an ADHD assessment might have resulted in a concretization by him and his parents (belief that his problems were not symbolic or developmental).

In addition, moving toward testing for ADHD could lead to Ryan's parents' minimizing the seriousness of his symptoms and not seeing their own contributions to those symptoms. Instead, dynamic play therapy seemed indicated.

Superego functioning was unintegrated: he lied about the amount of homework he had, often cheated at games, and once stole money from his parents.

The parents criticized Ryan frequently but rarely punished him. There was no corporal punishment.

Punishment, at this point, was considered to be antitherapeutic. Instead, help with separation, diminution of castration threats, and modeling for superego development seemed indicated.

One area of conflict between Ryan and his parents surrounded playing video games. Ryan would argue about his right to play. He lied that he was doing homework when he was actually playing a war-themed video game. His parents had allowed him to have a computer in his bedroom.

During discussion with Dr. Smith, I recommended that the parents monitor Ryan's video game involvement and remove the computer from Ryan's bedroom.

Ryan's obsessive use of his cell phone was also interfering with the time he spent doing homework and engaging in hobbies and interests. Ryan's parents were nervous about limiting him because they knew he would get argumentative. Their passivity would need to be handled during treatment.

I recommended to Dr. Smith that the parents receive concomitant support and advice since they correctly anticipated conflicts with their son over his grandiosity. Without their cooperation, Dr. Smith correctly anticipated that Ryan's problematic symptoms and behavior would persist. The parents agreed that supportive child-oriented counseling for them would be helpful.

Persistent superego pathology would continue unless his parents intervened to limit his obsession with electronics. Conflicts could be anticipated during therapy due to his persistent symbiotic gratifications with his mother, alternating with his hostility toward her to effect separation (identity formation). These conflicts had become symbolized by not doing homework, by abruptly leaving sports activities, by obsessions with germs, and by "addiction" to video games (Akhtar et al., 2011).

Meeting with the Child (Continuing the Evaluation)

Ryan showed no reluctance to separate from his parents and enter the playroom. He played with some toys, showed interest in age-appropriate games, and was quite talkative. He was not shy or nervous. At times, he would move from one area of the room to another.

He was willing to draw. His first drawings were "populars," of trees, a house, sun, sky, and grass. Later drawings were filled with scribbling, guns, and mess. Sharks were under the water threatening to eat a woman. Odd-looking monsters making a mess of everything were common. When Dr. Smith commented on the mess, Ryan laughed and said, "Oh yeah. A big mess," and scribbled over the drawing.

When discussing his fear of germs, he responded to Dr. Smith's opinion that it was "impossible" to die from germs in the sink or toilet. Ryan challenged, "But not 100%!" This was answered "Yes, 100%!" He asked, "How do you know?" She responded, "Because I went to school for a long time and studied biology." That made Ryan ask, "Then why am I afraid of germs?" He eventually agreed that there must be some meaning to it—indicating that he had capacity for mentalization and symbolic thinking.

When he jumped to a different part of the room, Dr. Smith to commented to Ryan, "You don't like to follow rules." Ryan smiled and turned a toy animal upside down. He said, "Now I'll put the cow away," while referring to a toy elephant.

He played one quick game of checkers with her and won. Then he asked if her feelings were hurt (*indicating guilt over aggression*).

Initial Formulation and Discussion with the Parents

For meeting with the parents, alone, I advised Dr. Smith, and she reported back that she had accomplished the following:

She began by pointing out the child's strengths and healthy functioning to the parents. Ryan had excellent intellect and the ability to play sports with other kids, and he was verbal. In addition, there did not seem to be any damage to major functions, such as his knowledge of reality and his ability to understand and think about himself (mentalization). He was able to trust and form a relationship with the therapist during the evaluation.

Dr. Smith recommended dynamic play therapy for Ryan. His parents were supportive and attentive, and willing to acknowledge their own contributions to the problems. (This is often not the case.) But because of Ryan's symbiotic tendencies, it was predictable he would want to stop therapy periodically.

Ryan's presenting problems were then tentatively explained. Since the parents had been so thoughtful in answering key questions in the developmental history, they were anticipating many of the formulations presented to them. Ryan showed obsessions regarding dirt and water, consisting of symbolic projections of anger that were brought about by guilt (defense mechanisms). He was rebellious about homework, although he could concentrate when he wanted to. This distinction militated heavily against a diagnosis of ADHD. All his symptoms suggested he needed therapy directed at understanding the origins of his hostility, laziness, guilt, and shame. He had already shown some ability to handle this approach with play materials.

Practical jokes were also complex, involved in what is technically called a "character perversion" (Arlow, 1971). They were made up of hostility generated by the destabilizing interactions he had with both parents, which were managed by the defenses of denial and projective identification.

His insistence on co-sleeping (and co-studying) seemed to be developmental delays (including persistent symbiosis and dependency gratification), which would need child-centered parental counseling. His laziness seemed due to parental spoiling (they agreed with this), which also needed correction by the parents.

His fear of carwashes (a compromise formation) was tied to bathing with his mother; the sexual overstimulation caused by her nudity with him conflicted with shame and guilt, causing him to repress the sexual thoughts, symbolize them (bathtub = carwash), and externalize his guilt onto the carwash (fear of punishment to relieve his guilt). She agreed to stop bathing with him.

Dr. Smith suggested that the father spend more time playing games with Ryan. Other athletic activities seemed indicated, especially since Ryan enjoyed sports. Overall, Ryan needed more identification with his father's healthier superego functioning

The parents agreed to bring Ryan to individual dynamic therapy sessions once a week. The mother and father eventually requested separate therapists for individual analytic psychotherapy. In addition, the parents agreed to meet with Dr. Smith frequently to formulate solutions to Ryan's problems with co-sleeping and disobedience.

8 Ages 10½–Puberty
Preadolescence

🔑 Key Questions for Parents

- **Have You Noticed an Increase in Emotional Volatility?**
    - What behaviors have you noticed? Any antagonism?
    - How have you handled it?

- **Has There Been an Upsurge in Interest in the Other Sex (~95% of the Time in Boys, 85% of the Time in Girls)?**
    - Approach behavior in girls toward boys?
    - Curiosity in boys about girls, glancing interest in prurient visual materials?

- **Have You Witnessed Withdrawal in the Child?**
    - Has the preteen rejected being seen with you?
    - Is there an avalanche of interest in connection with friends or rejection of friendships and hiding?
    - Have social awkwardness, language difficulty, and impulsivity suggested an autistic pattern?

- **Has There Been Symptom Development?**
    - Anorexia – conscious, willful food avoidance
    - Bulimia – overeating followed by self-induced emesis
    - Obesity – overeating for pleasure

- **Has the Child Been Punished? How?**
    - Looking for escalation of autonomy matters.

DOI: 10.4324/9781003257110-8

- Looking for runaway behavior.

- **Any Drug Abuse or Sexual Acting Out by the Preteen?**

  - Has menarche or spermarche been reached?
  - Is the preteen allowed to lock the bedroom door at night?

- **Has the Preteen Become a Bully or Been Bullied?**

  - Looking for management of upsurge of aggression and effects on the self-image.
  - Looking for passivity and inhibition of self-preservation function.

- **Has the Preteen Dropped any Favorite Activities?**

  - Looking for rebellion interfering with sublimatory channels.
  - Any family disturbances affecting the child?

Answers to the Questions and What They Mean

Have You Noticed an Increase in Emotional Volatility?

- What behaviors have you noticed? Any antagonism? Girls, in particular, become argumentative with their mothers and somewhat dismissive of their fathers at this stage. Parents must handle girls' sensitivity with understanding and some firmness. If not, the girls' ego strengths of impulse control and affect tolerance may be damaged.
- How have you handled it?

  - If parents have punished the child for "bad mouth" or forbidden the child to speak in certain ways, the child's beginning autonomy will suffer delay. On the other hand, if parents are overly lenient, and allow the child to get his/her way all the time, the capacity for affect tolerance will not develop, self-esteem may become falsely elevated, and there may be damage to the developing sense of fairness and responsibility (superego).
  - If parents have punished children for their "anal regression" to stubbornness (see the "Essay" in this chapter), verbal unresponsiveness, and tendency toward dirtiness, the children may "go underground" and stop communicating with the parents at all. Any child's tendency toward passive aggression at this age, if aggravated, frequently leads to resistance to schoolwork. On the other hand, if the parents do not insist on a reasonable degree of cleanliness and responsibility, the child may become grandiose, a bully, or a delinquent.

Has There Been an Upsurge in Interest in the Other Sex (~95% for Boys and ~85% for Girls[1])?

- Approach behavior in girls toward boys? About 85% of girls actively approach boys they like—in school, through social media, or on the phone. About 15% of girls, as of 2021, seem to be interested in other girls. Problems during pre-adolescence include severe gregariousness or severe emotional withdrawal.
- Curiosity in boys about girls, glancing interest in prurient visual materials? Even before consciously manipulated ejaculations are attempted, boys' "part instinct" of looking (for sexual excitement) leads many of them to watch at least pornographic movies.[2]

Have You Witnessed Withdrawal in the Child?

- Has the preteen rejected being seen with you? Many preteen kids have already started the process of creating their own identities. Internally, this involves separation of their own internal image of themselves from the images of their parents ("introjects"). To do this, preteens often wish to visit friends in public places (like shopping malls) before being picked up by parents.
- Pre-adolescents who are having difficulty may
    - cling to their parents and not make friends; these kids are vulnerable to "bullying" in school and may request a withdrawal from school; or
    - reject parents entirely and become disobedient.
        - Show an avalanche of interest in friends in lieu of studying or activities
- Various versions of the autism spectrum syndromes become more pronounced during pre-adolescence, and if present, usually manifest themselves in odd social gestures, inappropriate language usage, a tendency toward compulsive rituals, and a resulting lack of friends.
- Lack of emotional closeness with parents.

Has There Been Symptom Development?

- So-called oral symptoms, so frequently noticed in girls, are remarkably under-reported in boys. The key is whether the oral activities are consciously motivated regarding weight:

---

1 Murez (2021).
2 In the movie, *There's Something about Mary* (Decter et al., 1998), the male protagonist masturbates, before a date with Mary, while looking in the newspaper at black and white drawings advertising women's underwear.

- Anorexia – conscious, willful food avoidance and refusal, usually to feel separate and independent from parents—at the same time forcing parents to take care of them and control them.
- Bulimia – overeating is usually a defense used to relieve tension from myriad sources, both internal and external. The following self-induced emesis is done to prevent obesity, but sometimes also has symbolism.
- Obesity – pre-adolescents almost universally show some regression—handling depressive feelings, anger, or anxiety by overeating. If there is trouble in the home, eating may give the only pleasure available.

- The effects of impending puberty – body hair, body changes, voice changes, may cause anxiety if growing up is associated with some type of unpleasure—this has sometimes been referred to as the "Peter Pan Syndrome."
- Disturbances of rational thought (intrusion of "primary process" – that is, symbolic, condensed ideas into consciousness) may show up here—leading to paranoid thoughts about classmates and occasionally frank auditory and visual hallucinations. Although overt schizophrenic illnesses are more common in adolescence and early adulthood, some prodromal symptoms—such as disorganized thought, paralogical thinking, social oddities, and excessive withdrawal into fantasy—may be picked up during evaluation.

Has the Child Been Punished? How?

- Looking for escalation of autonomy matters—punishment, after latency is over, is relatively dangerous to the development of the preteen, although surprisingly common. Many parents don't realize that the struggle for autonomy has already begun and still insist on the children modeling themselves after adult family members—as would be helpful during latency. Overpunishment routinely leads to severe violent reactions and is found later in most delinquent teenagers.
- A different group internalizes punishments, hates themselves, and thereby becomes overwhelmingly depressed. They often present with concentration and memory problems mimicking attention deficit hyperactivity disorder (which, in contrast, comprises specific developmental delays *not caused by emotional overload*).
- The same problems are found in preteens who are underdisciplined (such as not being required to help around the house and do homework); neglect by overworked or dismissive parents may have the same effects.
- Runaway behavior, which can occur at almost any developmental phase, becomes more dangerous in preadolescence. It is usually a response to corporal punishment (physical abuse), sexual abuse, or emotional abuse.

Any Drug Abuse or Sexual Acting Out by the Preteen?

- Has menarche or spermarche been reached? As discussed in the "Essay" (later in this chapter), the boy's first ejaculation and the girl's first menstrual period are the usual signals that the pubertal body and hormonal changes have arrived. When either of these events involving the genital organs occurs before age 10½ in girls or 11½ in boys, pre-adolescence may not take place. Emotional shock reactions are not uncommon in these children, who often need extra discussions, and sometimes dynamic psychotherapy, to ease their anxiety.
- Is the preteen allowed to lock the bedroom door at night? The statistical findings that boys supposedly purposely masturbate more frequently than girls (Clower, 1976) have recently been revised. It seems that girls tend to be more secretive about it. In either case, allowing preteens to lock their bedroom doors when they go to sleep ensures their privacy about their masturbatory activities. This prevents primal scene trauma should a parent walk in on the preteen while the child is in the middle of masturbating.
- The other meaning of relative privacy to the preteen is support for their autonomy. The closed door is symbolic of the solidity of the incest barrier—a relief to the parents and the preteen regarding self and object boundaries (internally).

Has the Preteen Become a Bully or Been Bullied?

- The upsurge of aggression that is just beginning to be felt—sort of the "foothills" of puberty—may produce bullying behavior in some preteens. Often their victims come for therapy. But at times, these children have gotten into trouble at school or during play, and this disturbance is reported to the parents. This behavior is serious. At times, bullying is encouraged by identification with bullying parents. Identification with the aggressor is a major factor there. Other causes of bullying include counterphobic mechanisms, sadistic pleasure, and avoidance of feminine identifications (Blackman, 2013, pp. 75–79).
- Looking for passivity and inhibition of self-preservation function. The self preservation function requires coordination with the aggressive drive. During preadolescence, because of the rise of the aggressive drive, all preteens need to integrate some aggression with protecting themselves, verbally, and sometimes physically. Extremely passive preteens usually are guarding against shame, are identifying with victims in their families (MacGregor, 1991), or have been inhibited during latency in expressing themselves and developing sublimated activities.

Essay

The pre-adolescent phase, as described by Peter Blos (1970), has been updated by the work of Rhona Knight (2005). Her research suggests that latency ends for girls, on average, around age 10½, whereas for boys, on average, latency ends around 11½.[3] If pre-adolescence is defined as the period between the end of latency and the onset of puberty, pre-adolescence will start at 10½ or 11½ based on the birth gender of the child. Because of the variability in the onset of puberty, pre-adolescence may last many years or be prevented from occurring entirely. The average age of menarche in the United States has been calculated to be about 12 years of age.[4] The average age for "conscious ejaculation" in boys has been calculated at about 13½ years of age,[5] although it is likely that nocturnal emissions (ejaculation while asleep) occur somewhat before that.

Secondary sexual characteristics, such as voice changes, body shape changes, and hair growth may precede puberty proper and cause disruption to the child. Common maladaptive defenses include asceticism and intellectualization (Blackman, 2003, 2021). How the parents have discussed these changes (or not) has a major effect on the comfort with which the changes are handled.

From this vantage point, a girl who begins menstruating at age 9 will have bypassed pre-adolescence altogether; she has jumped from late latency to adolescence. This often causes many psychological problems. Appositely, a boy who has not had a nocturnal emission (or volitionally masturbated to orgasm) until age 16, will have experienced a pre-adolescence of 4½ years, also likely to have caused emotional difficulty.

Of course, other matters must be ascertained. Blos (1960, 1962) points out the frequency of libidinal regression—e.g., a previously hygienic and neat latency child has become more slovenly and resistant to bathing. There is a concomitant regression in impulse control, and an object relations regression to more narcissistic thinking (rather than object-related considerateness).

Parents may behave in pathogenic ways, but not be aware of the disruptive impact it has upon their children. Examples include but are not limited to the child still sleeping with one or both parents and grandparents. Parents may also shield the child from losses in order to protect preteens from grief over a traumatic loss, deaths, and other overwhelming experiences that have affected the child. Such suppression of the facts often leaves the child with unresolved

3 As noted previously in the chapter on latency, Knight's work also suggests that latency begins in boys at approximately 6½ years of age, whereas it begins in girls at about 7½ years of age. The boy, therefore, generally has a latency period of five years, compared to a latency period in girls of three years. Knight feels this difference, which gives boys two years more time to develop self-image stability (and ego strengths), helps explain the commonly noted greater emotional volatility in girls during pre-adolescence (average 10½–12).

4 Martinez (2020).

5 Laron (2010).

grief. Sexual abuse can cause major disruptions in the child's ego functions, ego strengths, and object relations.

And, of course, as in latency and later adolescence, sublimated activities are critical to healthy development. The fewer sublimations and the less mastery the child has developed, the more likely the child will become depressed and irritated.

An essay on this phase of development, as well as about latency and adolescence proper, would not be complete without mention the issue of electronic devices, cell phones, and the internet. A lot of good can be said about the internet connecting people, offering *gratis* educational experiences, and offering immediate news. Overuse of the internet in preteens and teenagers, however, is almost epidemic (Akhtar et al., 2011). Overuse of video games, computers, and cell phones is by now known to cause damage to socialization, self-esteem, and study habits. Parents must limit the use of these media, in the face of strong objections from the child, the child's friends, and the culture at large.

Case Example

Background and Presenting Problem

Jane requested treatment of her 11-year-old daughter, Gayle, two months after Gayle witnessed a physical altercation between her mother and father (Tom). After the altercation, Jane and Gayle went to live with a relative while Jane instituted divorce proceedings. During the physical altercation between Jane and Tom, Jane's face was bruised, and Tom tripped on the rug in the kitchen and broke his arm. Since that time, Gayle had resisted going to school. She could not do her homework, was restless, avoided socializing with friends, and was complaining of depression.

Gayle had a younger brother, seven years her junior. Her parents had been married for 13 years. The father's paternal grandfather was reportedly schizophrenic. Gayle had had regular contact with her maternal and paternal grandparents, who lived nearby. Her maternal grandparents were supportive of her and her mother at the time of the separation.

First, I (KD) interviewed Jane alone. She provided background information and the developmental history. Tom, at the suggestion of his lawyer, agreed to an interview. He turned out to be guarded, apparently due to the legal proceedings against him for the alleged assault as well as the divorce action. Finally, Gayle was interviewed to complete the initial evaluation.

Interview with Jane, the Mother

Jane was 36 years old and worked part time as a nurse. Gayle had witnessed the parents fighting while she hid behind a door. Jane managed to call 911. When the police arrived, they questioned Gayle, and she witnessed her father being arrested.

Jane did not require medical help, but she did have a large bruise on her face where Tom had hit her. Jane recalled that Gayle appeared frightened, angry, and agitated after the incident. As part of the divorce action, Jane went to court and obtained a restraining order. The court hearing resulted in the requirement that Tom complete "anger management" treatment before being allowed unsupervised time with Gayle.

Jane explained that she and Tom had argued frequently over the past two years, mostly about his alcohol abuse. When drunk, he would angrily throw things, but this had been the first time he had been physically assaultive. Tom's use of alcohol had increased during the past year.

Since she moved out, Jane acknowledged feeling depressed, and she had been ventilating to her daughter about marital problems and the divorce (*a prototypical reversal of roles*).

Jane, as she was describing this, seemed unaware of how her inappropriate sharing with Gayle might have been distressing to Gayle.

Gayle had a mild stutter, which had begun when she was 3 years old and been successfully treated when she was 5. It had now returned.

Gayle was attending a school for gifted children (sixth grade). In addition to Jane's initial worries, Jane noted that Gayle, for the last two months, had dropped off the volleyball team. Gayle was forgetting her homework assignments and procrastinated on school projects. Before the violent incident, Gayle had been relatively happy, an A/B student, and had socialized with many female friends. Now, Gayle would simply come home after school, stay in her room, and not call her friends or get together with them on weekends. She had cloistered herself in her room playing video games—mostly World of Warcraft.

Interview with Tom, the Father

Tom was a 38-year-old physician's assistant with an orthopedic surgery group. He expressed a wish to see his daughter and was resentful toward Jane, alleging that she had poisoned Gayle against him. He averred that he did not need anger management treatment; now that he was separated from Jane, he claimed he was much less angry. He did not furnish data regarding the specifics of their arguments.

He stated that since the problems in his marriage had nothing to do with Gayle, there was no reason he should not see his daughter. He expressed little remorse regarding the domestic violence incident and asserted that he was not an alcoholic. He blamed Jane for using this "minor" incident to get custody of Gayle. Tom also argued that Gayle had a close relationship with his family; therefore, it was important for Gayle to see them.

Tom described having a "good relationship" with Gayle and emphasized the time he spent coaching her volleyball teams. He expressed worry that all the time and effort he had put into developing her volleyball skills would be wasted because Jane had dropped off the team. Tom bragged about his own athletic skills, including having played baseball in college.

Before Gayle went to kindergarten, Tom admitted that Jane had been the main caretaker for Gayle since he spent long hours at the office or the hospital. He claimed to have a close relationship with Gayle, including helping her with her homework. Tom called Gayle "my tomboyish, little princess."

Tom denied all substance abuse or overuse. He said Jane exaggerated his use of alcohol; he "never missed a day of work" due to drinking. He had never taken psychotropic medication and never had psychotherapy.

Developmental History

Pregnancy and Immediate Postpartum Period

Jane suffered no untoward effects during pregnancy. Gayle was born at term and was healthy. The mother did not experience post-partum depression. Jane denied using any substances or being prescribed medication during her pregnancy with Gayle. Jane said that both she and Tom were looking forward to the birth of Gayle, although Tom seemed disappointed that they had not had a boy. Jane had planned to be a full-time mom and return to work when Gayle entered kindergarten.

0–1 Years of Age

Gayle was breastfed until she was 6 months old and then transitioned to a bottle with no reported difficulties. Gayle was described by her mother as "an easy baby" who fell asleep and began sleeping through the night by 10 months of age. Gayle showed a social smile at about 2 months of age and was a "happy baby" who responded to her mother's smile and presence. Gayle walked at 11 months.

1–3 Years

Gayle did not co-sleep with her parents. She could speak a few sentences by 2 years of age, but at age 3, she developed a mild stutter when she was upset. Jane noted that some of the stuttering occurred during toilet training, which occurred between 2 and 3 years of age. Gayle had no significant separation anxiety as a toddler, easily slept in her own room, and engaged in the usual darting and returning behavior.

3–6 Years of Age

Gayle had no illnesses and was not prescribed any medications.

The pediatrician told them to wait until she was about 5 years old to consider speech therapy; she thought that Gayle would likely grow out of it. In fact, by age 5, the stuttering had abated.

Gayle did not have excessive nightmares. She readily separated from her parents to begin a full day in kindergarten and excelled academically until the recent incident (*secure attachment, object constancy*). Gayle had suffered no significant emotional traumas or losses in her life until her parents' separation.

There was little indication that Gayle had developed much closeness with her father during this phase of development.

6–10 Years of Age

Socially, Gayle made friends easily, and her teachers reported she was "well-liked" by both other students and teachers. She had been voted captain of her last two volleyball teams. Her father did coach her, although there were problems (see "Interview with Gayle"). Academically, she excelled and was noted to be advanced in reading.

Before her parents' separation, Gayle was popular with a close circle of friends. Her friends liked her sense of humor, athleticism, and intelligence. In athletics, especially volleyball, she was fiercely competitive, but always fair and played by the rules (superego functioning). At one time, her goal was to get a scholarship to play collegiate volleyball (identification with father). After the domestic violence incident, she stopped attending volleyball practice and did not keep up with her friends on social media.

Apparently due to depression, ego regression (in skills), disidentification from her father, and acting out anger at her father.

Age 11

Gayle had always been within normal height and weight for her age. Since the incident, however, she had gained ten pounds but was not severely overweight.

Interview with Gayle

Gayle wanted to talk to me. Because of her verbal capacities, play materials were not needed.

Gayle immediately stated she did not want to see her father, did not trust him, and did not feel safe with him. She blamed her father's violence on his use of alcohol. She reported he was "a different person when he drinks." Gayle indicated her father had never "hit me, but he yelled a lot."

Gayle would not respond to any requests by her father for contact or visits. She expressed sadness about her parents' separation but was relieved that her parents would be apart and not fighting any longer. She felt guilty about her anger toward her father but also felt depressed about the loss of her intact family.

Gayle was conscious of guilt over not having protected her mother on the night of the reported domestic violence. She had hidden behind a door because she was too afraid to get between them.

Gayle now felt responsible for protecting her mother emotionally, but this responsibility caused her loneliness and anger. When Gayle discussed these matters, she noticeably stuttered, suggesting a connection between her emotional conflicts about the incident and the language difficulty.

When I interpreted that it was difficult for her to discuss her parents, Gayle responded that she had been keeping secret just how angry she felt; it was painful. She acknowledged she kept her feelings secret both to protect her mother and to avoid feeling guilty about her anger at both of her parents. Gayle confirmed that she did not want to upset her mother or risk making her father angry. She also feared her mother might not love her as much if she expressed anger toward her mother.

Regarding her father, she was afraid that if she told her father she was angry at him, he would yell at her and not understand.

Concerning her social functioning, Gayle nervously admitted she had a crush on a boy in her class. She had called him on the phone several times—although he had little to say. She had been excited when she learned they would be in some of the same classes. She told me how she used to laugh when her friends teased her about how "cute he is." She did not think it was funny anymore, and it irritated her when her friends discussed him (*disruption of social development and identity, disavowal of sexual feelings*). Gayle felt so sad when she saw the boy talking with another girl at lunch that she ran to the girls' bathroom, cried, and kicked the bathroom stall door (similar to her father's manner of expressing anger).

This discussion led to her expressing further anger at her friends for teasing her about stuttering and about her crush on the boy. She continued complaining about school. Her teachers gave her too much homework. She would not speak up in class because she was embarrassed about her stuttering. Gayle remarked, "On the inside, I feel really frustrated and angry, but on the outside, I show my mother, my friends, and my teacher a smile."

Regarding volleyball, Gayle rationalized that it took too much time and that she hated the team shorts for revealing too much of her legs. She was embarrassed that her legs were "too muscular."

Gayle said she had always been close to her mother. She had shared with her mother many of her thoughts and feelings. Recently, she had limited this because she did not want to upset her mother (*issues of autonomy but significant loss*). Gayle was worried about her mother "crying a lot" and about the divorce (*reversal of roles*). Gayle had recently become closer to her maternal grandmother, who apparently tried to maintain emotional neutrality when discussing Gayle's parents' situation.

Gayle would not discuss her parents with her friends because "they would not get it" (*impact of trauma; identity issues*). She felt she did not fit in with her classmates because she had "seen and heard too much" (*trauma description and impact*).

Gayle talked about a friendship with an older girl (14) who lived in the neighborhood. This neighbor girl was showing Gayle how to use makeup (*identity and anxiety about adolescence*). Gayle expressed interest in being "pretty like the girls on television." Although her mother did not approve of this friendship (*oppositional; independence*), Gayle said this friend was the only one who seemed to understand. Her parents were separated also.

Gayle said her relationship with her father was mostly focused on athletics. He would attend her volleyball games but was not involved in other parts of her life. She disliked him putting pressure on her to get good grades (identity diffusion anxiety; ambivalence about her father's ego ideal; self-esteem) as well as his urging her to practice volleyball. He wanted her to get an athletic scholarship to college—so he would not have to pay for it.

Gayle said her father and mother fought a lot, but the recent incident was the first time her father hit her mother. She wished her father would stop drinking alcohol. She blamed his alcohol use for her parents' difficulties (rationalization; defense against loss, and defense against anger at her mother). Gayle noted that this was also her mother's position.

Gayle saw her father as smart and athletic, but was afraid of his temper, especially at volleyball games. He criticized her in front of teammates when her team lost a match. Gayle was embarrassed about this; she said her dad made her teammates nervous.

Unlike many pre-adolescents, Gayle wanted to openly talk about things that were worrying her. She expressed a wish to talk to a therapist about how nervous she felt when she is at home with her mother, especially when her mother asked her questions about school and friends. Gayle complained that her mother treated her like a kid.

She also wanted to talk to someone about "boys who are so weird; they can be nice and then so mean." Finally, Gayle said she was worried that she was not pretty enough. Boys used to like her because she was good at sports, but now she thought they ignored her. Regarding her family situation, she said she just wanted to forget it, and not see her father (*suppression and minimization defenses*).

Mental Status Assessment

Gayle was cooperative and open during the initial interview. She was an attractive 11-year-old, who was dressed in fashionable athletic clothing. Her vocabulary and language were above average.

There were no problems with her memory, concentration, and attention. She was not physically jumpy and there were no indications of impulsivity. She was oriented in all spheres. Her cognitive and intellectual abilities were well above average. Gayle had an average general fund of information, and she showed precocious abstract reasoning abilities. She liked to read and write poetry.

Gayle denied hallucinations or delusions. Her thought processes were coherent and logical. Her reality testing was intact.

Her sleep was erratic, with frequent awakenings at night. She acknowledged staying up late at times playing video games. She hid this from her mother.

Gayle was so depressed that she did not want to see her friends. She had lost her desire to perform academically and participate in sublimatory activities (volleyball). This regression seemed to be defending her against anger at both parents and over grief about the loss of her intact family.

Her anxiety stemmed partly from increased feelings of vulnerability after witnessing the violent conflict between her parents. She seemed to regress in her sense of autonomy.

Gayle had no significant deficits in her ability to be honest, fair, and trustworthy. She demonstrated internalized guilt and shame, causing some of her depressive affect. She did not blame herself for her father's alcohol use or her parents' separation.

Formulation

Gayle's parents' conflicts, resulting in their separation due to her father's violence, seemed to be interfering with her developmental trajectory. Specifically, the transition from latency to pre-adolescence, which comprises a second individuation, had been interrupted by inflamed external conflicts (with peers and family). Her problems suggested difficulty in the early restructuring of her own and parental introjects (internal images).

In pre-adolescence, she had been moving away from the family as the main focus of attention and had been broadening her peer group. So, at a time when she was just becoming a bit more autonomous, Gayle was forced to struggle with anger at a father from whom she was keeping distance and at a mother who was depending upon her emotionally. This situation created internal conflicts involving guilt, which led Gayle defensively to withdraw socially, give up on schoolwork, and regress in her sublimatory activities.

Other defensive operations included inhibition of her autonomous ego functions of planning and organizing, as well as symbolic rejection of her father by avoiding volleyball.

Gayle's recent weight gain seemed defensive in several ways. First, the oral regression relieved anxiety about upcoming uncontrollable changes in her prepubescent body. She compared herself to older female acquaintances who were experiencing breast development, axillary, and pubic hair growth (secondary sexual characteristics).

Her drive derivatives included an interest in makeup (aggressively contrary to her mother's wishes) and a sexual interest in boys. Her weight gain, from overeating, also seemed to ameliorate tension caused by the severe emotional disruptions she had recently experienced from witnessing domestic violence.

Her depressive affect seemed related to the loss of her intact family. She also felt guilty over her rage at her father and hopeless about his ability to give up the use of alcohol. Gayle experienced frustration regarding consoling her depressed mother, but any anger came into conflict with guilt—leading her to fear a loss of the closeness she previously felt with her mother.

Self-esteem problems were associated with "not fitting in" with her friends. She had become more sensitive to their playful teasing about her crush on the boy in her class—apparently connected to increased shame over the situation with her parents. Her regression in her attachments to her friends complicated Gayle's autonomous development of self-image as separate from her family.

Gayle consciously hid her angry feelings in order to protect herself from the disapproval of people she cared about. The masking of her true feelings served as a barrier to validation of her self-worth, to identity formation, and to what she might have excelled at doing.

Diagnostic and Treatment Recommendations

Gayle showed obvious depressive and anxiety symptoms, which seemed to be triggered by the trauma of witnessing the domestic violence incident. Her parents' longtime conflictual relationship had bothered her and caused her ambivalence about their impending divorce.

When she was placed in the role of caring for her mother, Gayle felt a loss of the past closeness and support from her mother, as well as irritation. She then rebelled by seeking out an older friend (mother figure), which irritated her mother. Gayle's loss of closeness with her mother seemed to contribute to her depression. Her depression seemed secondary to her pushing away her friends (to avoid shame).

In sum, Gayle felt pressure to grow up too fast; but she was not emotionally ready for all the responsibilities of later adolescent and adult roles.

Her inflamed emotions seemed to cause an interruption in her previously normal trajectory of development. She also manifested conflicts about autonomy, reorganization of relationships with family members, body image, and peer relationships. She was agreeable to individual psychodynamically oriented therapy, which would involve her mother periodically.

Epilogue

Gayle decided to pursue therapy with me (KD). She was seen once a week for eight months. During that time, Gayle openly discussed her questions and anxiety about puberty and her worries that she would not be "girly enough." She also felt more comfortable discussing this with her mother as therapy progressed.

We could see, together, that the anger she felt toward her father conflicted with her wish to have his approval, causing her agitation. This disruption was interfering with the development of her burgeoning sexuality, body image, and identity.

As we discussed her anger about her father's treatment of her mother and understood his effect on her identifications (she didn't want to be his "tomboyish princess" any longer), she could see how his narrow focus on her athleticism had contributed to her exaggerated self-consciousness about her body, her sexual interests, and the changes she anticipated with puberty.

She then could reintegrate her identity and return to gratifying closeness with her female friends. She also returned to feeling more comfortable about her interest in boys.

Gradually, her father regained her trust in their supervised visits by abstaining from alcohol while they were together. She grew more comfortable with him and felt more able to express her feelings to him directly. With remarkable maturity, she also saw that until he stopped using alcohol, his personality would not change much. She knew that she did not want to be around him when he drank. Her father agreed to accept her condition.

At termination, Gayle was no longer depressed. She decided to return to playing volleyball, although not on the team—she did it her own way, not her father's. Gayle also became interested in school again; she obtained all A's on her last report card for her sixth-grade year. She was looking forward to the following year in school.

During treatment, Gayle realized that her self-imposed isolation had caused her to miss seeing her friends on weekends. She had contacted them and was meeting them at the movies and at the mall. Gayle also obtained relief after joint sessions with her mother, where she could express the anxiety and frustration she felt when her mother cried and talked to her about the divorce. Jane was dismayed and surprised to learn of the deleterious effect this was having on her daughter. Jane thereafter obtained her own individual therapist and ended the reversal of roles where Gayle had acted as her mother/husband/therapist.

That summer, Gayle attended a two-week summer camp focused on writing and creativity. She made many friends at camp and was looking forward to middle school. While at camp, she had her first menstrual period; she felt prepared and relatively comfortable about the changes in her body.

Gayle visited her father, who had maintained his promise not to drink around her. The acrimony between Gayle's parents gradually diminished. Gayle felt her therapy had progressed well. She and I discussed how she was doing. She felt she was ready to end therapy, and I agreed. Her mother, in the meantime, had made progress in her own therapeutic work and no longer "parentified" her daughter.

9   Ages 13–20+ Adolescence

Key Questions for Parents of Adolescents[1]

Ego Functions of Language, Integration, and Reality Testing

- **Is There Evidence of Maturation and Autonomy?**

  - Can the teenager verbalize disagreements without violence?
  - Is the adolescent's demoralization regarding the parents proceeding without severe depression?
  - In what areas has the teenager developed mastery?

- **Can the Teenager Organize Schedules and Study Independently?**

  - If the teenager cannot organize working and playing, this portends badly for the post-high school years, whether they be in college or work.
  - Can the teenager avoid excessive peer pressure and ostracism? If not, depression and misbehavior may occur.

- **Has the Teenager Developed Adequate Social Skills?**

  - Needed for group functioning.
  - Needed for interacting with authorities.

- **Has the Teenager Had Very Unrealistic Thoughts or Hallucinations— Serious Mental Illness**

  - Schizophrenia frequently arises during this stage, earlier in boys.
  - Looking for referential thinking (the idea that things going on around you have reference to you, e.g., "people at the next table who are talking, must be talking about me"), persecutory feelings (e.g., "those people at the next table are actually plotting against me").

---

1 The same questions are pertinent to early, middle, and late adolescence. The answers and the meaning of the answers will vary depending upon the age of the adolescent. Generally, more control and autonomy are expected as the adolescent gets older.

DOI: 10.4324/9781003257110-9

- Looking for history of suicidal thinking, attempts, and/or self-cutting behaviors.
- Chaotic, abusive family history may predispose to a "psychotic core."

Ego Strengths

- **Can the Teenager Verbalize Disagreements Without Violence?**
  - This is needed to contain the many frustrations of adolescence.
  - If parents limit their teenagers' verbalization (and/or do not model by engaging in discussion with their teenagers), this can lead to teenagers engaging in destructive actions.

- **Has the Teenager Become Immersed in Computer Games, Social Media, or Substance Abuse?**
  - Teenagers need time for some laziness (Blackman, 2016b) but may not move from play to work.
  - Addiction to games or substances weakens impulse control.
  - Has the teenager engaged in substance abuse? If so, what substances, how long, and how much?

- **Can the Teenager Control Emotions and Impulses Fairly Well?**
  - Has the teenager become "addicted" to pornography and masturbation?
  - Does the teenager have temper tantrums?

Object Relations

- **Does the Teenager Maintain Close Friendships?**
  - Does the teenager have any friends who can be trusted?
  - Has the teenager become withdrawn from friends (schizoid)?
  - Has filial piety been kept in balance with individual desires and identity?

- **Regarding Friendships, Can the Teenager Maintain Individuality or Be Easily Influenced?**

- If the teenager is not developing some identity stability, the teenager will be vulnerable to gangs, cults, and cataclysmic fads.
  - Dedifferentiation from parents or friends (giving up identity and values, to avoid peer pressure and ostracism) can lead to depression and misbehavior.

- Looking for disturbances of separation where the teenager withdraws to their home and possibly fails academically.
- Looking for running away behavior due to a wish to avoid home.
- All teenagers will rebel against a value of their parents—but assess whether this rebellion is self-destructive or illegal.
- Is some rebellion allowed by the parents? If not, the teenager can become severely inhibited or potentially violent.

Superego and Ego Ideals

- **Is There Evidence of Ideals for a Career in the Future?**

    - If there is no future focus regarding careers, this may indicate damage to self-esteem from many sources. This will likely lead to a decrease in ambition.
    - If confused, the teenager should be testing reality to discover strengths.

        - For example, if the teenager wants to be a professional baseball player, but could not make the varsity baseball team in high school, this indicates divergence between the ego ideal and real abilities. Depression may result from this divergence.

    - Depression over failures may also be due to inhibition of function conflicting with reasonable ideals.

- **What Kind of Morality Is the Teenager Developing?**

    - Regarding sexual activity? Regarding violence?

        - Is sex treated cavalierly? If so, there are dangers of sexually transmitted disease and a lack of integration of sex and love.
        - Is there severe sexual inhibition? Painfully shy teenagers may have difficulty establishing committed relationships later.

    - Regarding community activity:

        - Can the teenager help with projects?
        - Is the teenager concerned with the people in the environment?

            - If not, narcissistic elements may pervade the character.
            - Spoiled teenagers will lack ambition and may have life failures.

- **Is There Evidence of Ideals Regarding Family? What Is the Evidence?**

    - If the teenager becomes demoralized about the value of a family, close and committed relationships can become inconsequential.

- Lack of respect for the other sex may continue and interfere with later work and personal relationships.

- **Is the Decrease in Idealization of the Parents Proceeding Without undo Grief?**

  - Reality of the parents' personalities needs to be clarified and accepted.
  - Complete rejection of the parents is a sign of possible rejection of all authorities in the future.
  - If the parents are too damaged, the teenager may become suicidal to relieve their painful realizations (and guilt) about their parents.

Conflicts, Defenses, and Compromise Formations

(See "Essay" for a more complete description of compromise formations, which can be formulated from the material during evaluation).

- **Has the Teenager Become a Daredevil?**

  - Counterphobic defenses can lead to injury and death.
  - Thrill-seeking can lead to injury to others or illegal behavior.

- **Sexual/Puberty Issues**

  - Has the teenager developed a sexual relationship with anyone? If so, how did the parents respond to this?
  - Is the teenager using contraception?
  - Has the teenager had a human papillomavirus (HPV) vaccine?
  - Has the teenager expressed a gender identity?
  - Is the teenager able to lock the bedroom door at night?

    - Looking for interference with autonomy, especially regarding masturbation.

  - When did the teenager reach puberty?

    - Looking for precocious or delayed puberty.
    - Looking for parents' and teenagers' responses to puberty.

- **What Hobbies (Sublimations) Has the Teenager Developed?**

  - Without some success in these "sublimated" areas, there is a danger of developing destructive or sexual impulsivity, recklessness, or perverse activity such as voyeurism, compulsive masturbation, fetishes, and suicidal proclivities:

- Sports – looking for sublimations of aggression.
- Dancing – looking for sublimations of aggression and exhibitionistic wishes.
- Music, art – looking for sublimations of sexual curiosity.
- Math, physics – looking for inhibitions of special intellectual abilities.
- Other clubs/social groups – looking for inhibitions or delay of social skills.

Late adolescence is complex. In fact, a multitude of books have been written about this phase. It is difficult to condense the many variables that must be considered into one chapter. Because people live longer today, and because between 66% and 72% of Americans go to college,[2] late adolescence may be prolonged, starting at around age 16 but not culminating until well into the mid-20s. Today, most people do not get married just after completing high school. According to the latest U.S. Census, the "estimated median age to marry for the first time was 30.4 for men and 28.6 for women."[3]

Late adolescents must complete several tasks. After ascertaining the chief complaint and the family structure, the answers to the previous questions give much information about the development of their personality, abilities, and emotional problems.

The following are the meanings of the answers to those key questions.

Meanings of Answers to Questions

Ego Functions

Is There Evidence of Maturity and Autonomy?

- Can the teenager verbalize disagreements without violence?

  - It is a truism that teenagers need to move from motor expression of emotions to verbal expression. Those who have not developed language capacity and those who are having difficulty organizing their thoughts tend to become more impulsive. The impulsivity may take the form of acting without thinking. This is particularly a worry in the area of drive activity, where overeating is a big problem, particularly in the United States (where about 20% of adolescents [Reinberg, 2022] are considered obese). Other drives that may be acted on without thought include sexual matters and, of course, violence.

2 https://admissionsly.com/percentage-who-go-to-college/.
3 https://www.census.gov/newsroom/press-releases/2021/families-and-living-arrangements.html.

Is the Adolescent's Demoralization Regarding the Parents Proceeding without Severe Depression?

- As teenagers develop better reality testing and abstraction ability, they notice their parents' personalities somewhat more fully. This may not be a highly developed impression until they are in middle adulthood, but opinions about their parents' values and opinions about their parents' behavior become more formed. As teenagers begin to have a complete picture of their parents, they, of course, notice their parents' flaws and idiosyncrasies. If they have idealized their parents during latency, they will expectedly become demoralized and feel somewhat depressed. Sometimes the demoralization is severe and causes a melancholic picture of loss, brooding, and cynicism.

In What Areas Has the Teenager Developed Mastery?

- Here, we are looking for sublimated activities where the teenager has developed a considerable amount of ability, often rivaling those of adults. Certain achievements as in mathematics, physics, language capacity, dance, art, and the like, are all evidence of this. Some teenagers in Canada, for example, immediately join the National Hockey League after graduating from high school.

  i   School subjects_____
  ii Athletics_____
  iii Other activities_____

  - Without some success in these "sublimated" areas, there is a danger of developing destructive or sexual impulsivity and recklessness, or perverse activities, such as peeping, compulsive masturbation, and fetishes (Hartmann, 1955; Loewald, 1988; DeMijolla-Mellor, 2012).

Can the Teenager Organize Schedules and Studies Independently?

- We hope that teenagers, by the time they are 16, 17, and 18 years old, can organize their schedules by themselves, and not need many reminders from their parents. Many teenagers in the United States are driving cars by this point, so they must make decisions regarding their own safety.
- "Secondary process" (Freud, 1900; Blackman, 2010) is the technical term for time-oriented thought. Early teenagers very often still do not have a good sense of time. Mature teenagers at 17 or 18 should be aware of the passage of time and engage in *time management*. Of course, this capacity continues to develop, and even in older teenagers and adults, it can be a residual developmental problem.

- Peer pressures can enhance organization (as in China, where getting good grades is considered admirable by peers). On the other hand, peer pressures can interfere with work in favor of playing and horsing around (Graham, 2004).
- Looking for development of good or poor social skills.

  - Superficial social skill is not necessarily related directly to warmth, empathy, and closeness.[4] Rather, social skill refers to the teenagers' ability to interact with people on a more superficial level, to make connections, to engage in certain activities with other people, and to develop a hierarchy of friends that are more or less close. Comfort during adolescence often depends on this early type of "networking." Team and club participation offer social settings that help the teenager not feel alone as the sense of separateness is forming.

Has the Teenager Had Very Unrealistic Thoughts or Hallucinations— Serious Mental Illness?

- Schizophrenia frequently arises during this stage, earlier in boys. Damage to abstraction, integrative functioning, reality testing, and self-preservation are frequent elements of this disease.
- Chaotic, abusive family history may predispose adolescents to a "psychotic core." These cases look similar to schizophrenic illnesses but have a different etiology. Chronic abuse and distortions throughout development can also destroy the main functions of abstraction, integration, reality testing, and self-preservation. These cases are noted in the *DSM* as "Other" types of psychoses.

Ego Strengths

Can the Teenager Verbalize Disagreements without Violence?

- This is needed to contain the many frustrations of adolescence.
- If parents limit their teenagers' verbalization (and/or do not model by engaging in discussion with their teenagers), this can lead to teenagers engaging in destructive actions.

Can the Teenager Control Emotions and Impulses Well?

- During early adolescence, teenagers are quite volatile. Some teenagers tend to be verbally explosive. Others tend to withdraw and stop talking, or perhaps throw something. Affect tolerance (what the capacity for tolerating powerful emotions is technically called) should be developing

---

4 Many of Sandra Brown's books deal with this type of teenager (e.g., *Hello, Darkness*, 2003; and *Overkill* 2022).

gradually during adolescence. By age 18, if teenagers are still exploding, cutting their wrists, or running away because of shyness or anger, this damaged affect tolerance is associated with borderline personality organization (Kernberg, 1975, et seq.).

Has the Teenager Become Immersed in Computer Games, Social Media, or Substance Abuse?

- Teenagers need time for some laziness (Blackman, 2016b) but may not move from play to work.
- Severe laziness can be due to depression, narcissism, rebellion, lack of social skills, or failed sublimatory activities. It is important to ask what, if any, restrictions they have attempted to impose on the adolescent.
- Addiction to games or substances *weakens impulse control.*

Has the Teenager Engaged in Substance Abuse?

- Teenagers can use different substances to effect some type of "high." This is an experience of dizziness often accompanied by relaxation. The pleasure, no doubt, is a replication of the feelings of infants just after nursing, when they get drowsy and fall asleep (Blackman, 2010). But teenagers rarely consciously think of using substances this way.
- In evaluating teenagers who are using substances, there are questions about degree, frequency, and etiology of their motivation toward it. The causes include but are not limited to, relief of social anxiety (especially fears of ostracism) by identifying with others, relief of inner tension, fantasies of being a he-man, counterphobic defenses, grandiosity, mastery of uncontrolled hallucinations (in paranoid schizophrenic patients), relief of depression, relief of boredom, undoing (breaking one's own rigid restrictions), rebellion against parents, laws, and social restraints. That's the short list.
- There is a vast literature on the treatment of adolescent substance abuse. Suffice it to say that the higher on the progression list the teenager's use is, the more dangerous, and the more likely that hospitalization and/or institutional treatment may be necessary. Intensive outpatient therapy for the teenager and the adults in the home is usually necessary. Whether psychoanalytic interpretations of the causes can be helpful depends greatly on the intactness of the teenager's abstraction ability, integrative function, reality testing, self-preservation functions, as well as impulse control, capacity for trust, and superego development. All those factors contribute to the teenager's motivation.

Object Relations

Does the Teenager Have Very Close Friends?

- "Schizoid object relations" means that the teenager is focused on the self and does not invest energy or love (friendliness) toward others. These teenagers may stay by themselves, read, watch television, play video games but never develop intimate friendships with anyone. Sometimes these teenagers are very good students, but they are often terribly preoccupied with themselves, and much more comfortable when they are alone.

These teenagers tend to have massive anxiety about identity diffusion, but this cause of the withdrawn qualities needs to be differentiated from teenagers who are shy about sexual interests. Both etiologies can result in teenagers who avoid social interactions.

Those who are self-preoccupied need treatment for narcissism and withdrawal, whereas those who are ashamed need treatment aimed at understanding their defenses and conflicts regarding sexual matters, shame, and social anxiety complicated by externalization defenses (Blackman, 2003).

Can the Teenager Maintain Individuality or Be Easily Influenced?

- If the teenager is not developing some identity stability, the teenager will be vulnerable to gangs, cults, and cataclysmic fads.
- Teenagers show "object hunger"—wishes for new people to care about and to identify with. Boys and Girls Clubs were created by Ernest Coulter in 1904 to provide alternatives for teenagers who were going astray.
- Faulty identity development will also predispose teenagers to develop narcissistic traits and have difficulty making independent decisions about their careers and romantic interests.
- Dedifferentiation from parents or friends (giving up identity and values to avoid peer pressure and ostracism) leads to depressions and misbehavior. This can be seen in teenagers who never rebel at all.[5]

Superego and Ego Ideals

Is There Evidence of Ideals for a Career in the Future?

- Regarding ambition, healthy teenagers usually have developed some concepts (fantasy as trial action) regarding their careers. Have they organized their thoughts about these ambitions, tested reality by working briefly in the field, talked with people who are in those fields, and given more thought to their plans? At times, parent support and guidance can be helpful.

Ambition, in general, is healthy, and teenagers who lack all ambition may flounder after high school. Diagnosing disturbances of ambition must include recognition that sometimes these ambitions are grandiose and out of touch with the teenagers' actual abilities. At other times, teenagers underestimate their abilities and set their ambitions too low. From a therapeutic standpoint, teenagers who have not been able to organize their thoughts about their ambitions accurately will need help in that direction.

---

5 Nonrebellious teens are more common in China than in the United States.

- When study habits are inhibited, teenagers may be intelligent, but other people will notice that these teenagers are their own worst enemies. This type of inimicality is found in very depressed teenagers, and as a defense against guilt in teenagers who are neurotic. Guilt may derive from several sources, such as identifications with strict parents, massive hatred toward parents, being pampered by parents for no good reason, and other intrafamily disturbances.

  In any case, whether guilt is conscious or unconscious, teenagers who feel this will, very often, without wishing to, feel inhibited about studying and concentrating. They may even become self-destructive through suicide attempts.

- A more mundane cause of study difficulties is laziness (Blackman, 2016b). Laziness represents oral regression in teenagers, where they want everybody to take care of them, and they do not want to work. Sometimes, regression in the superego appears in failures to be responsible; this often will result in the teenager suffering quite a bit. Hopefully, only one or two bad grades may convince them of the error of their ways, and their laziness will be tempered. Parents' reaction to the laziness of their teenagers has a powerful effect, either positive or negative.

What Kind of Morality Is the Teenager Developing?

- Regarding sexual activity
  - Is sex treated cavalierly? If so, there is danger of sexually transmitted disease, lack of integration of sex and love.
    - Both teenage boys and girls in the United States commonly complain of boredom with sexual intercourse. "Casual sex" may lead to this situation. Male and female promiscuity have become so common in adolescence that HPV vaccines are now recommended by many pediatricians for all postpubertal kids.
  - Is there severe sexual inhibition? Painfully shy teenagers may have difficulty establishing committed relationships later.
    - Some "practice" with physical contact with other teenagers tends to promote comfort in future relationships.
    - At either extreme, it is important to inquire whether the teenager has suffered from sexual abuse or has been sexually overstimulated.
- Regarding community activity
  - Can the teenager help with projects?
    - Building, repairing, cleaning the house, and babysitting are common activities that help the teenager integrate superego functioning (responsibility) and object relations (caring for others).

- Is the teenager concerned with the people in the environment?

  - If not, narcissistic elements may pervade the character.
  - Spoiled teenagers will lack ambition and may have life failures.

- Regarding helping in the house, will the teenager pitch in?

  - Housework is needed for living neatly and hygienically;
  - Assess whether the teenager has a lack of knowledge in this area or if the parents have not modeled and encouraged this behavior.
  - If the teenager refuses to participate, this may lead to damage to self-care in the future.
  - Assess whether the teenager is behaviorally rejecting the parents (disidentifying from them and rebelling against them).

- Community interests also suggest that teenagers value forming relationships outside of the family that help them with their autonomous development.

  - Assess how supportive parents are of these activities.
  - Community activities also increase opportunities for sublimation.

- Regarding school and other forms of work?

- Has the teenager been able to move from play to work?

  - If the teenager has difficulty balancing play and work activities, playing games may dominate.
  - If the teenager cannot move from play to work, this may result in failure to establish motivation to become self-sufficient ("failure to launch").
  - Assess patterns to determine if the teenager's inability to move from play to work is due to depression, poor self-esteem, or, more seriously, a withdrawal from reality.

Conflicts: Drives, Defenses, and Compromise Formations

Has the Teenager Become a Daredevil?

- Counterphobic defenses can lead to injury and death.

  - Charles Krauthammer, MD, for example, described how diving into a pool without looking, as a late adolescent, led to his broken neck and its resultant quadriplegia.

- Thrill-seeking can lead to injury to others or illegal behavior.

  - Ask about driving habits and whether the teenager has had motor vehicle accidents. Also, inquire about other injuries and visits to the emergency room.

Can the Teenager Organize Studies and Show Ambition?

- Teenagers can have many skewed preoccupations regarding studying. Some are workaholics who avoid other people. Some are antiestablishmentarian to the point where their parents feel they must yell at them to get them to even pick up a book.
- Ask about changes in academic motivation and performance.

Many teenage boys in the United States associate studying with being feminine (Parker, 2008). These teenage boys will avoid studying and preoccupy themselves with sports or violence, which they associate with masculinity.

Some teenagers associate studying certain subjects with forbidden areas. Those who are having trouble in chemistry often have sexual inhibitions, for example.

As opposed to the diminution of the importance of SATs in the United States, in China, studying for the college entrance exam becomes all-consuming. Parents may actually move across a city, lease a separate apartment for their teenager, and live with the teenager part time so that the teenager can attend the best high school and study constantly.

Has the Teenager Developed a Sexual Relationship with Anyone?

Some teenagers are quite immature in organizing their thoughts about others. In some countries, even kissing is not experienced until an adolescent is in college. In other countries, including the United States, in most areas, teenagers do engage in physical contact with each other. By age 18, approximately 50% of American teenagers have had sexual intercourse (CDC, 2017).

According to the CDC, "An estimated 55% of male and female teenagers have had sexual intercourse by age 18,"[6] and only 80% used contraception during the first sexual experience.

Teenage relationships can be very difficult and sometimes result in a pregnancy. Sexually transmitted diseases are common, which is the reason that HPV vaccinations are recommended at the beginning of adolescence for all teenagers in the United States.

On the other hand, some teenagers, by late adolescence, have developed a loving relationship with consideration, thoughtfulness, loyalty, and mutual pleasure, with another person. Those teenagers show remarkable maturation in those capacities.

Essay

Introduction

In *Three Essays on Sexuality* (1905), Freud discussed puberty ("Ephebic transformation") as a time when genital sexual impulses intensify, along with the

---

6 https://www.cdc.gov/nchs/pressroom/nchs_press_releases/2017/201706_NSFG.htm.

establishment of new objects of sexual desire. During puberty, oral, anal, and infantile genital pleasures become incorporated into mature genital wishes. In healthy development, object-related love also gets integrated with sexual pleasure.

Developmentally, Freud outlined two fundamental tasks of adolescence: disconnecting from ties with parents and establishing nonincestuous sexual relationships (Barish, 2020). In doing so, teenagers must come to terms with changes in their bodies, in their identities, in their relationships with parents, and in their morals and values. In later theoretical modifications, as described next, Freud's initial discoveries still provide a foundation.

Previously, Hall (1904) had stirred research and controversy regarding adolescence as a prolonged, separate stage of development (Gilmore & Meersand, 2014). He proposed that adolescence was a time of "*Sturm und Drang*"[7] characterized by reality conflicts with parents, self-awareness, depression, and expressions of sexuality (also see Blum, 2010; Blackman, 2018b). Offer and Schonert-Reichl (1992), contrarily, suggested the storms of adolescence were not requisite; the adolescent passage could have relatively few crises. Perhaps both are correct, in different situations. Adolescence as a developmental stage no doubt involves more psychological upheaval than other stages of development, however (Arnett, 1999; Gilmore & Meersand, 2014).

During puberty, intensification of sexual desire leads to a revival of oedipal-style conflicts—in the family and with peers. The affects generated by the conflicts among sexual wishes, reality, and the superego lead adolescents to use defenses such as repression, displacement, acting out, provocation of punishment, ego and libidinal regression (Freud, 1926), reaction-formation, and, hopefully, sublimation. These factors contribute to character formation (A. Freud, 1958).

The changes in sexual drive activity are manifested in fantasy and masturbatory activity (Novick & Novick, 2022). The associations between adolescent masturbation and developmental progression are profound: "Genital masturbation is again phase-specific in adolescence and further aids in establishing object-relatedness and gradual subordination of pregenitality to genitality" (Marcus & Francis, 1975, p. 42).

During adolescence, there are forward and backward movements. Sometimes, changes in behavior represent maladaptive defenses (Jones, 1922). At other times, regression occurs "in the service of the ego" (Bellak, 1989).

Regressions (backward movement developmentally) can be seen in impulse control (of oral, genital, and hostile-destructive wishes). Progressions are condensed with symbolized thoughts and behaviors to "learn" (Solms, 2021b) from experience. Thereby teenagers should eventually show better affect tolerance, speech and language usage, motor control, and social skill (A. Freud, 1956; Blos, 1970).

7 The well-known German phrase meaning Storm & Stress.

Puberty and Adolescent Stages

Adolescence is usually defined as beginning at puberty—which involves several biological changes. A growth spurt occurs, secondary sexual characteristics appear, and fertility is achieved. Girls experience their first menses and boys their first ejaculation. The timing of these events is variable. Girls' menstruation can begin anywhere from age 8 to 16 or 17. Boys' may experience a first ejaculation (from masturbation or nocturnal emission) anytime from 9 to 15 years of age (Kipke, 1999).

The teenager must psychologically adapt to these bodily changes. Asynchrony—such as very early menstruation in girls or early growth and ejaculation in boys—may eliminate their preadolescent phase entirely. (Menarche before age 11, e.g., places the girl at risk for depression and substance abuse. See Gilmore & Meersand, 2014.)

Neurological research indicates that during adolescence, the brain develops faster neural processing—meaning an uptick in cognition and abstract reasoning (Kipke, 1999).

Psychoanalysts generally divide adolescence into stages, but the age designations vary. This is not surprising due to the significant differences in cognition, biology, relationships, and emotions in different adolescents. In particular, the criteria for the closing of adolescence are in some dispute. In some teenagers, adolescence seems to extend through college and graduate school, whereas in others, it ceases at the end of high school (about age 18). Blos (1967), recognizing this variability, offers an approximate division of adolescence into three stages:

Early adolescence (11–13 years old)

- Puberty.
- Growing sexual interest.
- Increased cognitive capacity, especially abstract thought.

Middle adolescence (14–18 years old)

- Less pubertal drama.
- Life goals appear.
- Distance from parents starts.
- Adjustments to body become more routine.

Late adolescence (19–21 years old)

- Firmer identity.
- Better ability to delay gratification.
- Increased empathy.

Identity and Object Relations Theories

Tausk (1924) mentioned identity development as a lifelong process beginning in childhood (Akhtar, 2009). Erik Erikson (1950a) put forth an "epigenetic" theory of development in which "identity vs. role confusion" was viewed as a key conflict during adolescence. According to Erikson, "The sense of identity provides the ability to experience one's self as something that has continuity and sameness, and to act accordingly." Erikson's definition of identity includes influences from both intrapsychic and environmental pressures (so-called psychosocial factors).

If adolescents do not develop self-definition integrated with prior identifications, they are at risk of experiencing *identity diffusion*. Under stress, teenagers with poor identity development tend to become what others demand and do not develop unique ideas or opinions (Erikson, 1968). Persistent identity diffusion anxiety puts the teenager at risk for severe character pathology (especially narcissistic and borderline disorders), social isolation, juvenile delinquency (Aichhorn, 1935), a sense of emptiness, body-image disturbances, and delay in the ability to work (Akhtar, 1984, 1992; Kernberg, 2006).

Edith Jacobson (1964) viewed identity formation as an intrapsychic process necessary to become autonomous and separate from others in reality. She disagreed with Erikson's view that the self was associated with sociocultural influences. Jacobson saw self-development as beginning in the first few years of life; by 2–2½, toddlers discover their own identity and can recognize differences between themselves and others. Though Jacobson and Erikson disagreed, autonomy and separateness are still considered important developmental tasks of adolescence. Lachmann (2004) also pointed out that adolescents need to de-idealize and become less controlled by their parents as part of resolving symbiotic attachments.

Daniel Stern's (1985) ideas about infant self-development were later incorporated by others to apply to adolescent individuation. Through his four senses of self—emergent self, sense of a core self, sense of a subjective self, and sense of a verbal self—the infant slowly puts together an image separate from, as well as connected to caretakers. Stern's self-theory was applied to adolescence as the "underpinning of identity," where the agglomeration of past identifications integrates with current and future proprioceptions. During the teenage years, flexibility in tolerating both wishes for merger and autonomy are needed for mental health (Beebe and Lachman, 2002; Lachmann, 2004). Moreover, struggles over merger vs. autonomy are present throughout life (Marcus, 1973).

Blos's theory of adolescence's *second individuation* has relevance for identity formation. The second individuation involves the adolescent task of mourning the loss of connection and symbiotic attachment to parental representations. Mourning is needed to establish independence and autonomy.

According to Blos (1983),

[T]he most painful task which faces the adolescent is the de-idealization of the self and object. With this statement I wish to convey the developmental fact that many of the narcissistic supplies which the young child receives from the "holding environment" (Winnicott, 1969) are drying up with the advent of puberty.

(p. 579)

Pursuant to Blos's theory, adolescent identity development includes conflicts between independence and dependence, idealization and rejection, merger, and autonomy. The resolution of these conflicts is a crucial aspect of what Blos (1976, 1983) termed *adolescent closure*.

A thorough adolescent assessment requires examining identity development. Akhtar (2009) describes this healthy state as follows:

- feeling of self-sameness or displaying roughly similar character traits to varied others,
- temporal continuity in the self-experience,
- genuineness and uniqueness,
- sense of inner solidity and the associated capacity for peaceful solitude,
- subjective clarity regarding one's gender,
- an inner solidarity with an ethnic group's ideals, and
- a well-internalized conscience.

Toward the end of adolescence, object relatedness should include the following features: warmth, empathy, trust, holding environment, identity, closeness, and stability in relationships (represented by the mnemonic device Warm-ETHICS) (Blackman, 2010, 2018c).

Problems in object relations are suggested by the following:

Warmth –	You can't feel warmly toward others
Empathy –	You can't "put yourself in the other guy's shoes"
Trust –	You can't trust even those who are close
Holding Environment –	You fear all will change
Identity –	You don't know who you are, stably
Closeness –	You must get distance somehow
Stability –	You change toward people, splitting their images into loving and hating
Ethics –	Your sense of propriety has not developed because you haven't been attached to anyone, so you don't care

(Taken from Blackman, 2010, p. 110).

Superego Development

The superego is a psychic structure that develops throughout life, beginning with the child internalizing parental values, prohibitions, and injunctions.

The superego is made up of multiple features that are connected to the conscience. Deficits in the superego generally stem from interpersonal problems between children and their parents during latency and adolescence (Blackman, 2010).

Superego development includes children accepting responsibility for and criticizing their own thoughts, feelings, and behaviors. Gradually, the older adolescent and young adult will look to their own superego for judgment about morality and ethics, and rely less on the external parental authority. This process in superego development requires more complex abstract thought and ego strengths, which become more refined in adolescence (Blum, 1985).

As adolescents broaden their experiences and disengage from their parents, their superego is influenced by others who take the place of parents as ideal models, such as teachers, coaches, and peers (Freud, 1926). Adolescents' increased autonomy, along with the characteristic regressions and progressions of adolescence, bring about significant changes in their superego (Blos, 1967; Jacobson, 1964; Blum, 1985). The complications of regression and progression in superego development were described by Blum (1985) as follows:

> The superego is thus assessable to changes in both the child and the parents, to cultural change, and to regression and progression within its own structure. Regression, which is normative as part of adolescence, will often reveal the earlier dimensions of its structure, and particularly early fantasies may demonstrate childish notions of morality or specific castration threats. The regression is usually partial and selective and [can affect drive development and basic (ego) functions such as intellect and judgment]. The resulting picture may be very complicated, and because of the selective regressive alterations, their presenting clinical pictures will not be a direct replication of the past or present.
>
> (p. 89)

The fluctuations in the superego throughout adolescence increase the difficulty in assessing the teenager's psychological functioning. When evaluating an adolescent who is rebelling and engaging in disruptive behaviors, it may be problematic to differentiate enduring psychopathic behaviors (severe damage to the superego—where there is no guilt) from more transient rebellious behaviors brought on by a wish to provoke punishment to relieve harsh guilt.

During early adolescence, the superego becomes more integrated into the personality but may conflict with other aspects of the personality based on childhood ideals. With the advent of powerful sexual desires and confusing bodily changes at puberty, adolescents begin to realize that the mores taught to them by their parents and their prior identifications with their parents are out of sync. This situation represents a significant change from latency, when most children adhere to and accept parental prohibitions.

In middle adolescence, the teenager often looks to others such as peers, idealized sports, music, or celebrity figures to replace family ideals and values.

These trial identifications and role modifications allow teenagers to broaden their autonomy and abstract morality (Akhtar, 2009). Idealizations also produce feelings of inferiority, as adolescents realize they cannot match the abilities, looks, or fame characteristics of such celebrities. When the ego ideal is greater than adolescents' actual abilities, they can suffer depressive mood fluctuations resulting from these narcissistic injuries (Gilmore & Meersand, 2014).

In late adolescence, the superego tends to become more differentiated from family and peer values. Teenagers usually become more tolerant of ambiguous moral situations. There may be others who still influence the adolescent in college or work settings, but late adolescents make more individual moral choices based upon their own identity and values.

Late adolescents develop a view of the world, or *Weltanschauung* (Freud, 1936; Jacobson, 1961), in which they form opinions, ideas, and ideals of their own, including moral and ethical standards. This development requires reality testing, experience, conscious thought, and reworking of identifications with their parents (Jacobson, 1961). (For a complete overview of superego functions, deficits, and how these relate to diagnosis, see Blackman, 2010).

Our view is that studies of the interconnections of brain development (Willoughby et al., 2014), emotion, and behavior are in their infancy. Recent studies indicate that understanding an individual adolescent's emotional functioning requires an appreciation of brain development. On the other hand, the vastly more well-understood elements of the mind (the manifestations of the brain), should be considered: object relations, ego development, identity features, family and other interpersonal experiences, drives, superego, affects, defensive operations, and the effects of the environment and culture.

By late adolescence, most superego features should be functioning adequately, although professional ethics, morals, and concepts of self-preservation continue to develop throughout adulthood. In Tables 9.1a and 9.1b, superego and ego-ideal functions, the meanings of these, and what deficits in the functions look like clinically, are depicted (Blackman, 2010, p. 132).

Substance Abuse

Many substances that affect the brain cause a drowsy feeling, including alcohol, marijuana, sedative medications, opiates (both medicinal and recreational), and certain naturally occurring substances, such as melatonin. Long-term or chronic use of these substances is toxic to the brain and interferes with mental development. Short term, they can be fatal if taken in large doses or used by certain vulnerable people (cf. Len Bias, in Schmidt & Kenworthy, 1986). Fentanyl, a synthetic opioid used legally for years for medical anesthesia, has, as of this writing, been sold illegally. It has become a favorite among opiate addicts and led to many deaths, especially when mixed with other toxic compounds.[8]

---

8 The TV series, *Breaking Bad*, dramatized this widespread, dangerous social problem.

Table 9.1a Superego Deficits

Superego Function	Meaning	Deficit
Fairness	Sense of equity, sharing	Greediness, cheating
Integrity	Stands by what one says	Does not mean what is said
Reliability	Will do what is promised	Will slide out of promises
Ethics and respectfulness	Has a code of correct behavior	Has no sense of correctness
Lawfulness	Obeys the law	Breaks the law
Ideals	Aspires to goals	Does not aspire to much
Guilt	Feels self-critical, accepts fault	No fault felt for transgressions
Honesty	Generally, tells the truth	Generally, lies
Trustworthiness	Can be trusted with secrets	Cannot be trusted with secrets
Shame	Cares what others think	Does not care what others think

Mnemonic: *F I R E L I G H T S.*

Table 9.1b Ego-Ideal Deficits

Ego-Ideal Facet	Meaning	Deficit
Behavior, manners	Thoughtful to others	Offends others, thoughtless
Intellect	Values intellectual achievement	Abhors intellectual achievement
Work	Expects to work	Attempts to cheat the system
Athletic capacity	Values body agility	Decries body agility
Kindness to others	Values understanding, help	Selfish, sadistic
Community involvement	Participates for good of group	No care for overall good

Cocaine and amphetamine class substances alter mentation by causing agitation. LSD, psilocybin, peyote, PCP, Ecstasy, and other similar compounds seem to cause some relaxation, some disorganization, and a variety of distortions of thought— including hallucinations and pseudohallucinations (distortions of actual things).

Alcohol addiction in the United States was so severe at the beginning of the 20th century that many groups organized to pass a constitutional amendment (the 18th in 1917) making all alcohol illegal. The unintended consequence of this amendment was that it fostered organized crime. Finally, in 1933, the United States adopted the 21st Amendment, which repealed the 18th.

Today, the age at which teenagers can legally drink alcohol varies in different countries. In the United States, the drinking age is 21—due to an unusual deal between the Federal government and the state governments in the 1980s; before that, the drinking age in many states was 18 (Britannica, 2022). In many western European countries, the minimum legal drinking age is much lower.

Substance usage has different levels, sometimes called "Progression" (Waranch, 2022). The stages of usage commonly are listed as follows:

- No use
- Experimental use
- Social use
- Habitual use
- Abuse
- Dependency

Teenagers who use substances in the first three categories are at somewhat less risk than those who get into the last three. Regardless of why the teenager uses any substance (for rebellion, soothing, provocation of punishment, relief of social anxiety, e.g.), the more intense their abuse of substances is, the less treatable they will be with solely outpatient dynamic therapy. Often, detoxification in a facility, rehabilitation, and support will be necessary. On the other hand, those who have experimented or used socially are generally more reachable with an outpatient, insight-directed approach to the origins of their behavior.

Defenses and Conflicts

Interpersonal, reality-based, and internal emotional conflicts occur in all teenagers. The components of the conflicts include, but are not limited to, the following:

- Wishes[9]
    - Dependent wishes (to rely on someone else for soothing and financial support)
    - Sexual wishes (for pleasure, and/love, and/or orgasm)
    - Aggressive wishes (to outcompete/succeed, to obtain things, to engage in physical activities, to protect oneself, and to destroy or take revenge)
    - Symbiotic vs. autonomy wishes (to become someone else, to tie someone else to you, to feel separate, to know who you are)

These conflict with

- Reality
    - The need to work

9 Solms (2021b), in his paper on redefining drives, points out that biological LUST-based wishes must be coordinated with learned behavior in order to bring about sexual gratification with another human being. He argues that the enteroceptive sexual urges require attachment to another human being to satisfy concomitant attachment wishes. The biologically based urges have different brain determinants from the learned behavior requisite to attain an object for gratification of other wishes simultaneously (attachment and love, for example).

- The availability of what one wishes for
- Dangerous physical and political situations

The wishes also conflict with

- Superego
  - Guilt
    - Remorse – over hurting someone else
    - Regret – over having hurt oneself (made an error) (Akhtar, 2018)
  - Shame – overexposing
    - A weakness in a function
    - A conscious drive element
  - Sense of fairness
  - Integrity – meaning what one says, saying what one means (Carroll, 1865)
  - Responsibility

These conflicts generate

Affects

- Anxiety – unpleasurable sensation plus a thought that something bad will happen in the future
- Depression – unpleasurable sensation plus a thought that something bad has happened already
- Anger – unpleasurable sensation plus a thought of doing harm to something or somebody

The affects generated often cause the mind to shut something out of consciousness—i.e., to use defenses.

- **Definition of Defense (Blackman, 2003, 2021)**

Defenses are mental operations, often automatic, that take one aspect of an affect (or another aspect of thinking) and make it unavailable to consciousness. Depending on the constellations of defensive operations, different syndromes can be described.

Typical defensive operations during adolescence include the following:

- Impulsivity – e.g., a 19-year-old college student decides to have sex with a boy at a fraternity party to relieve her inner tension regarding her conflicts about sex and morality.
- Counterphobic action – e.g., someone who fears deep water goes on a scuba-diving trip.

- Procrastination – e.g., a senior boy in high school puts off his final English paper, unconsciously relieving himself of anxiety about leaving home.
- Verbal argument – e.g., a teenage boy argues with his parents about the existence of God.
- Denial of danger – "It's no big deal," says the teenage boy who is planning on driving through a high-crime area of the city at night.
- Rationalization of transgressions possibly with projective blaming – e.g., a student copies someone else's homework because the teacher was sadistic and gave too much homework over a holiday weekend.
- Intellectualization – an adolescent decides he needs antidepressant medication due to depression after the end of a relationship.
- Symbolization – refusal to do (home)work represents a teenager's fight against being "controlled."
- Hostility (to establish autonomy) – a teenager who used to enjoy playing tennis with a parent now complains that the parent is not good enough and stops playing with the parent.
- Extreme shyness – boys and girls avoid interacting with others in social situations to relieve shame over exposing wishes for love and sex.
- Group formation and identification with idealized figures – a teenager only wears clothes with the symbol of a favorite professional baseball team.
- Disidentification from parents' values – a teenager refuses to apply to college, and both parents are teachers.
- Displacement of extreme rage (originally toward parents) onto the environment/government – a teenager vandalizes school property and writes profanity on the walls.
- Humor – guards against real fears and disappointments.
- Deidealization of parents – mother is a conservative Republican, so teenager joins the campaign of a liberal Independent candidate.
- Emotional distancing (to guard against identity diffusion anxiety) – a boy likes a girl in his class but insists on texting her for two months before he talks to her on the phone. This relieves his anxiety about getting too close.

Compromise Formations in Adolescence

The revision of structural theory (Freud, 1923) suggested by Brenner (2006) attempts to explain symptoms, behavior, and character formation using the concept of compromise formation. Compromise formation means that five different forces of the mind occur simultaneously. The forces are wishes, reality, superego, affects, and defenses (Figure 9.1).

Conscious or unconscious conflicts can occur between elements of the mind ("intersystemic conflict"—I hate you, but I feel guilty about it, e.g.) or within one system (intrasystemic conflict—I love you, but I want to kill you, e.g.).

Example

A male sophomore in high school wishes to beat up his English teacher (hostile-destructive aggressive wish) because reading *Romeo and Juliet* (Shakespeare, 1597) is so boring. But the student knows the reality that he will get arrested if he hits the teacher. The conflict between his hostile-destructive wish and reality produces anxiety ("*realangst*"). To manage his anxiety, he institutes the defenses of suppression (says nothing) and regression (he falls asleep in class). The sleeping protects him from getting arrested and from acting in a hostile-destructive way; simultaneously, he expresses hostility by falling asleep (rudeness to teacher).

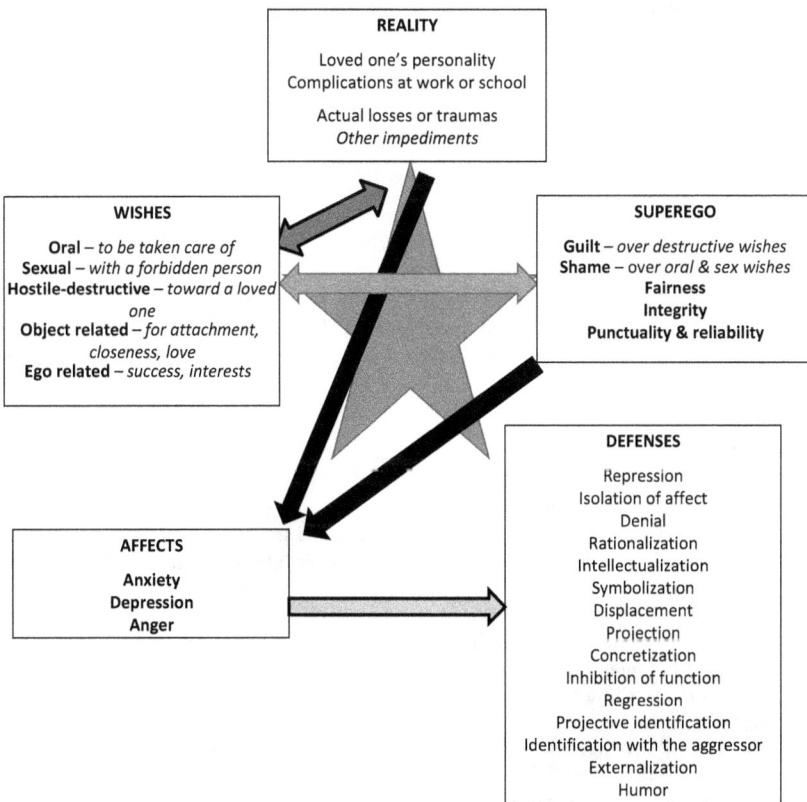

Figure 9.1 Blackman's Five-Pointed Star: Compromise Formation in Adolescence.

Blackman (2003) pointed out that libidinal and aggressive wishes are not the only types that come into conflict. Wishes to separate identity and wishes to fuse identity (with others) can also come into conflict with shame (superego feature).

Example

An 18-year-old girl, who had co-slept with her mother until 13 (menarche), is accepted to a university in Spain, after recommendations from her Spanish teachers and encouragement from her parents.[10]

In July, after she had planned to go to Spain, she suddenly announced to her parents that she no longer wanted to go to Spain. She wanted to stay home and not go to university at all. After consulting an analytically oriented psychologist, it was discovered that going to Spain was originally her mother's idea. Her mother had always wanted to study in Spain, herself. For years, she had told the girl how wonderful she thought Spain was.

In the evaluation session with the girl, she told the therapist,

> "Let my mother go there, if she loves it so much. I want to stay here and be an interior decorator. She's the romantic who wants to know 15 languages and have men play the guitar for her! That's not me!"

Taking this all into consideration, the therapist could formulate ideas about sexual wishes, shame, and the defenses of distancing, symbolization, and avoidance, but that would be insufficient. The girl was also talking about (1)

---

10 There is currently a serious problem with so many teenagers dropping out of high school in both the United States and China. They routinely have developed mildly paranoid ideas about their classmates, feel mistrustful of everything, and are unable to study. In those cases, with the details provided, it seems that lengthy co-sleeping had exaggerated their wish for symbiotic fusion (merger of self and mother images in the mind). At the same time, they experience intense separation anxiety when not with their mothers (similar to infants) and are afraid of the outside world. In these cases, the co-sleeping can be deleterious in that the co-sleeping has interfered with the development of self and object constancy—because of persistent identity diffusion.

A professional woman reported that her friend's daughter, 18 years old, would periodically climb into bed with her mother when the girl was home on vacation—for "pillow talk." The professional woman asked if that were normal. The answer is the following. First, in this situation, the woman and her mother were not naked. Secondly, they did not cuddle and fondle each other. So, there was no evidence of sexual overstimulation.

her wish to be separate from her mother to form her own self-image and (2) her wish to not separate from her mother—she wanted to stay home! She also guarded against her shame over her wish to stay with her mother by using intellectualization, defiance, and repression—which kept her wish to merge her self-image with that of her mother unconscious; at the same time, she partly acted on that wish.

In other words, the concept of compromise formation can also be applied to teenagers suffering from identity diffusion anxiety due to conflicts over separation.

Blackman (2003, 2013, 2018c) has also pointed out that compromise formations take place at each stage of development. Each new stage brings new compromise formations into the picture, while older ones don't disappear—the older conflicts usually are incorporated into the next phase's conflicts.

Example

A 16-year-old girl's father had died in an automobile accident when she was 13. At 16, she fell in love with a boy in her biology class, after joking about the sexual anatomy of a frog. Within months, they had sexual intercourse. The boy then broke up with her, which broke her heart.

She then became obsessed with schoolwork and had no special contact with boys until her senior year of college, at age 21. He was a medical student, age 24. Within three months of dating, they began having sex.

At 30, she presented to a therapist with marital problems. She mentioned that she had initially gotten pregnant after she and the medical student boyfriend had been dating for about ten months. She purposely had gotten pregnant because she did not want to lose him, and she knew from what he had told her that he would marry her if she got pregnant.

Here, we see that the loss of her father was never grieved. Instead, at age 16, she got intensely involved with a boy who was not that stable. The loss of that boy added to her depressive affect over the loss of her father. But still, she did not grieve (depressive affect caused by painful loss). Instead, she used the defenses of avoiding boys and studying intensely. She also did this to avoid shame.

Finally, at 21, after becoming sexually entangled with a young man, she purposely got pregnant to defend against her fear of another reality loss. He married her, but later, they were getting into petty arguments over control. The interpersonal conflicts over who controlled whom was also a regression to adolescent identity diffusion matters—"Can I be my own person?" Apparently, her husband also suffered some sense of being controlled when he felt "forced" to marry her.

Neuropsychoanalysis, Neurobiology, and Brain Development

Solms (2021b) redefines drive theory by pointing out that both exteroceptive and interoceptive factors play a part. Possibly most importantly, he points to brain research showing that (1) consciousness is not entirely located in the cerebral cortex and (2) affects are not entirely located in the limbic system and hippocampus (also see Solms, 2021a).

The brain's changes after puberty (Casey et al., 2000) are "the most dramatic and important to occur during the human lifespan" (Steinberg, 2010).

Neuropsychological reorganization begins at puberty and may continue until approximately age 23 (Stortelder & Ploegmakers-Burg, 2022). Along with reorganization, the lengthy period of neuroplasticity creates vulnerability to psychopathology (e.g., substance abuse and stress-related disorders) but also presents opportunities for therapeutic intervention (Wallace, 2016). Changes in the brain, especially in early adolescence, seem to be reciprocal with the adolescents' behavior and interests (Kuhn, 2006). That is, behavior influences the brain, and vice versa (Feinstein & Bynner, 2004; Luna et al., 2004).

In total, adolescents must develop a separate identity at the same time they are incorporating interventions, supportive guidance, and instruction from parents, social activities, and input from authorities—all of which affect brain-behavior development (Schriber & Guyer, 2016).

Changes in the prefrontal cortex seem to be involved in decision-making and cognitive control. Prefrontal neural connections, during adolescence, should be strengthened through an increase in myelination (increased insulation) as well as through synaptic pruning (reductions). These features, along with increased connectivity with other areas of the brain, seem connected to the efficiency of information processing (Kuhn, 2006; Willoughby et al., 2014).

The prefrontal cortex is the area most responsible for the regulation of emotions, but it is the last to mature (Casey & Jones, 2010). By middle to late adolescence, there are fewer but more selective and effective neuronal connections than in childhood (Kuhn, 2006). The brain's neurochemical changes (Steinberg, 2010) seem to affect executive functioning (decisions about risk and pleasure). Emotional crises during adolescence are associated with the remodeling of the brain's dopamine system (Beckford & Wallace, 2016).

Despite the complexities in the interface between adolescent brain structure and behavior, there has been a tendency to oversimplify the mechanisms of this interface, especially in the matters of adolescent dangerous behavior and poor self-control—which show up clinically as self-injury, addiction, reckless driving, and suicide attempts (Dahl, 2004). Suicide is the second leading cause of death (the first being accidents) in adolescents (Sharma & Fowler, 2018).

Brain-related explanations for dangerous behaviors have had a powerful effect on the U.S. criminal justice system. Defense of teenagers in criminal cases often includes diminished criminal responsibility and limited ability to make choices (Casey & Caudle, 2013), to wit: "all gasoline, no brakes, and no steering wheel" (Bell & McBride, 2010).

Actually, significant individual variation is seen in adolescents' self-control, so generalization can be inaccurate. Moreover, traumatized children, who suffer damage to their self-control, are likely to show increased vulnerability as teenagers (Somerville et al., 2011; Casey & Caudle, 2013).

Conflicting theories of neurobiology are ever-present. The "imbalance theory" of brain development proposes that subcortical connections—responsible for motivation and emotion—develop earlier than connections in the prefrontal cortex (Somerville & Casey, 2010). Following an adolescent brain imaging study, Casey and Caudle (2013) concluded that poor decision-making and risky behavior are not due solely to a less mature prefrontal cortex but to a "tension within neural circuitry involving the ventral striatum, implicated in reward processing, and the prefrontal cortex, implicated in control processing" (p. 85). In contrast, social development research—regarding mortality and morbidity rates across the lifespan—suggests that risk-taking does not reach its peak during middle adolescence, even though that period shows the most asynchrony in brain structure development (Willoughby et al., 2014).

Our view is that studies of the interconnections of brain development, emotion, and behavior are in their infancy. Recent studies indicate that understanding an individual adolescent's emotional functioning requires an appreciation of brain development—but must also consider the vastly more well-understood elements of the mind (the manifestation of the brain): object relations, ego development, identity features, family, and other interpersonal experiences, drives, superego, affects, defensive operations, and the effects of the environment and culture.

Case History

Presenting Problem and Background Information

Dmitri, a 17-year-old boy, was referred by his mother's therapist. He had just failed his first months of college because he was getting drunk, smoking pot, playing video games, and not going to class. The college had put him on a six-month suspension, and he would be allowed to return to college, pending a note certifying that he had received mental health treatment and was able to proceed with school.

I (JSB) first had two meetings with Vera, Dmitri's mother, who was a practicing attorney. His father, Peter, a plastic surgeon, was in Peru at the time with an international group that did charity surgeries on children who suffered with cleft palates and lips. Peter and Vera also had a 9-year-old son who had never been very close with Dmitri.

Vera was quite distraught. She was angry at Dmitri for wasting their money on Tier 1 university tuition, although she was ashamed to admit this. She was conscious of disappointment and fear about his future. She was very motivated to get him help, and after our initial meetings, she and I had a good rapport.

Dmitri had been a good student in high school and had never been a behavior problem. She complained about his relationship with his father, who, it seemed, was hardly ever home. Peter worked and traveled too much, according to Vera. She, herself, had been unhappy with Peter for some time. Vera struck me as warm, though a bit invasive and guilt-ridden. She frequently blamed herself for Dmitri's problems without specificity.

Vera explained that she and Peter had immigrated to the United States several years after the collapse of the Soviet Union in 1991. She had worked for the government of the USSR, in Moscow, for some years after obtaining a law degree from what was then Leningrad State University. She had met her husband in Moscow while he was at Moscow Medical Academy. In May 1998, they decided to move to the United States to take positions in Texas. Dmitri was 6 years old and began school in September of that year. He barely spoke English at the time. They all moved to Virginia when Dmitri started junior high school at age 13.

Developmental History (Taken from the Mother)

Pregnancy and the Postpartum Period (in Russia)

Dmitri was a wanted baby. He was full term and healthy. His mother breastfed him without difficulty. Peter was just beginning work and was too busy, to Vera's dismay, but she was not severely depressed; her sister helped her.

0–1 Year of Age

Vera nursed Dmitri for a year, after which he was easily weaned to a cup. He stopped nighttime bottles when he was about 15 months old. Vera had stopped working for that year to care for him full time. Dmitri slept in a crib in his own bedroom from the beginning, but Vera responded to his crying almost immediately, and he never suffered from colic.

Vera became depleted emotionally, however. To relieve her stress, when Dmitri was 3 months old, she hired Lara, an older widowed woman, to live with the couple and help as a nanny. Dmitri formed a powerful attachment to Lara, which continued until the family left Russia. Vera returned to work full time when Dmitri was 1. He walked at 11 months and was a curious and happy baby.

Lara became the primary psychological mother; Dmitri smiled mostly at her at 4 months of age. He was less demonstrative with his mother. There had been a shift of attachment at 3 months of age, making his attachment to his mother less secure. However, he seemed to develop a secure-organized attachment to Lara.

1–3 Years of Age

Vera returned to her government position when Dmitri was 1. Lara continued to be close with Dmitri. Dmitri's language skills were precocious. He could read letters (in Russian) when he was about 3 and enjoyed his mother reading to him at night. Peter continued to have an erratic schedule, often being called in to help with trauma cases, as well as doing elective reconstructive surgery.

Dmitri often cried when his mother went to work but was soothed by Lara. Vera brought work home with her, which she did at home after Dmitri was sleeping. However, Dmitri never developed a steady sleep pattern. Often, Lara would have to sit with him until he went to sleep, or she had to read to him late into the night.

Dmitri continued to have some persistent symbiotic wishes toward Lara as well as continuous separation anxiety at night.

Toilet training began when Dmitri was 2. It was primarily done by Lara and was gentle, although Dmitri did not learn to urinate standing up until kindergarten. He was mostly trained by age 3, so he could attend preschool for five hours per day.

He cried when he left Lara but accommodated preschool once he was there.

In other words, he had some difficulties with object constancy with Lara, although these were not severe.

He continued to have nocturnal enuresis until grade school. His mother was not happy about this but would change his sheets in the middle of the night when he awakened wet.

In retrospect, it seemed that part of the problem was incomplete toilet training. This represented some trouble with separation anxiety and anger over loss (of mother and Lara). More about this in the following section.

3–6 Years of Age

Dmitri went to kindergarten, at age 5, with no trouble, and seemed to like school. When he returned home, he frequently played with Legos by himself. Occasionally, a male friend would spend the night, and the boys would play Pac-Man.

Dmitri's social skills were developing within the normal range, and he was able to play alone. These behaviors indicated some healthy developmental progress.

Vera did not recall Dmitri engaging in masturbatory play. She did not recall if he engaged in rough and tumble play with other boys.

She had apparently repressed much of this.

Dmitri did not co-sleep with the parents and apparently did not try to. Vera did not recall if he had nightmares or phobias.

Vera did not consider Dmitri's nocturnal enuresis, which continued until age 6, a problem. She, herself, had been enuretic until she was 10, so she figured his enuresis was hereditary (she may have been at least partly correct). She did not punish him for this; she simply changed his sheets. He seemed humiliated and frustrated with himself.

Vera and Peter did not tell Dmitri they were going to emigrate from Russia to the United States when he was 6, although it had taken two years to obtain the necessary work visas from the United States. They wanted to protect him, and they had some of their own anxiety about the process. When the family left, they simply told Dmitri they were going on a long trip. Vera recalled that Lara cried a bit, which confused Dmitri as they hugged goodbye. Lara did not accompany them. When I asked her, Vera guiltily explained that she and Peter never discussed with Dmitri that he would never see Lara again.

It later turned out that Dmitri experienced the move to the United States at age 6 as a traumatic separation from Lara and other relatives, which inflamed his affects regarding the partial separation from his mother at 3 months, the separation he experienced at age 1 when she returned to her practice, and the later move at age 13 to a new state in the United States.

6–10 Years of Age

Dmitri's main problem in first grade was language. Vera recalled that there was some difficulty with making friends, but quickly added that by second grade, Dmitri spoke English without the accent she and her husband retained. He did well academically.

Dmitri now made many friends. He did well in soccer and was a regular starter on his local team. The coaches liked him. He followed rules well.

Dmitri abandoned Legos and became fascinated with computer games. His mother felt guilty that she had allowed him a computer in his bedroom because she knew he frequently sneaked playing games late at night and was sleepy and hard to awaken in the morning. He also frequently played video games with friends, although they also wrestled and played basketball.

Vera, with some pleasure, told me how Dmitri had learned cooking from her; he was a good cook. He still liked making Russian dishes.

Sublimated activities had developed, as well as close friendships with other boys. Superego development seemed to include fairness and obeying rules. This sounded age appropriate. Cooking Russian dishes also symbolically defended against his grief over leaving "home" and Lara.

11–13 Years of Age

Vera only recalled that Dmitri had started growing. She did not know much about his relationships with girls. She thought he had reached puberty around age 13 but was not sure.

13–17 Years of Age

Dmitri did well in school, excelling in math and languages. He was recommended for the gifted program and attended at age 14 for one year. Vera minimized Dmitri's decision to drop out of the gifted program at age 15. She said he appeared bored with it, but noticed that Dmitri did not have to organize his homework or studying as assiduously.

Although the mother minimized Dmitri's decision, this was an early indication of his rebelliousness regarding studying and was the beginning of a disidentification from his parents.

Dmitri now played football and did well. He had friends on the football team. At age 17, his mother recalled he had a girlfriend, whom the mother liked. The girl sometimes ate dinner with them.

Dmitri decided he wanted to become a language scholar, which to some extent disappointed Vera, who had wanted him to go to law school. She seemed to idealize law and medicine. She only mentioned this feeling to Dmitri once; he scolded her, "Mom, I'm not you or Dad!"

Autonomy conflicts now appeared between Vera and Dmitri.

17–17½ Years of Age

Vera was proud that Dmitri did well in high school and would go to a Tier 1 university in New York. Graduation involved some relatives visiting from Moscow. Lara did not make it.

Peter and Vera took Dmitri to college by plane. They accompanied him to his dorm room and were disappointed that it seemed to be in shambles. Vera was irritated that they were spending so much money for the school and that the dorm seemed rundown. She also did not like the boys and girls sharing bathrooms and living on the same floor. Dmitri seemed blasé about all this, at least in front of her.

Vera tried calling him several times a week, but he only spoke to them on some Sundays. She and Peter told him they would visit at the end of October, and this is when he admitted that he had failed all his classes, was drinking, smoking pot, and was "addicted" to video games. His parents helped him contact the appropriate officials. The result was that the college allowed him "Incompletes" on his transcript with an opportunity to change these to grades if he retook the courses later.

Evaluation Interviews with the Teenager

I evaluated Dmitri over three sessions, one with his mother present, at my request. The reason I added the conjoint meeting is that I felt some of the problems had to do with Dmitri's conflicts over his choice of career being different from what his mother wished.

I began by introducing what I had learned from his mother: the apparent problems he had with drinking, pot smoking, video game addiction, and not going to class.

Dmitri immediately said he knew he was "fucking up" but sort of got into a rut.

This crude statement indicated to me that he had a relatively harsh superego, suggesting that one cause of his misbehavior was self-destructiveness in an unconscious attempt to relieve guilt.

First, he said he did not do homework, so he was embarrassed to go to class. Then, he got behind, and never caught up. So, he started drinking too much with friends and playing video games. I expressed an opinion that he sounded like he was critical of himself for not being organized, then got depressed, and that perhaps he had been drinking and smoking pot to relieve his bad feelings. He said he knew that was part of it, but that he didn't want to use that as an excuse. I said he might relieve shame and guilt by making excuses. He laughed and agreed, "Yeah, I'm good at that!"

His response to these defense interpretations indicated that, although he had been using substances heavily, he had self-observing capacity, and thus might be treatable as an outpatient with dynamic therapy.

He said his relationship with his mother was OK, but he felt she was too "pushy" in a subtle way. She never said she wanted him to be a lawyer, but he knew she had gone to a prestigious law school in the Soviet Union ("which couldn't have been fun"), and she expected him to excel at the prestigious university he was attending in New York.

He then said he had actually been kind of down about something else, but it was "weird." He had lost interest in sex. He had gone to parties at the beginning of the school year and met many girls who just wanted to get high and have sex with him. At first, he kind of enjoyed it, but after a while, he felt it was all meaningless.

I commented that it sounded like he had gotten demoralized about relationships with girls. He added that he had had a girlfriend in high school whom he loved, so the sex with her was different.

It sounded to me as though unresolved grief over the breakup with his high school girlfriend had been part of the problem. There was also an indication that he had reached whole object relatedness, as he loved his high school girlfriend. He appeared to be turned off by the later, impersonal sexual relationships with girls.

Past Family History

Dmitri recalled fairly clearly his attachment to Lara, and that his parents had not told him the truth about their immigration. He showed no emotional reaction at the time or when he described this to me.

Isolation of affect seemed to guard against mourning in this case. Later, his therapist in New York told me one dynamic of Dmitri's failure in school concerned an unconscious wish "to go home." This had been interpreted to him successfully, as well as the embarrassment he felt about it, which caused him to isolate the affect and act out in ways that ensured that he would have to "go home" from college without having to ask.

He also related that he felt lonely during his first year in the United States. It took him that long to really be able to speak English so that other children would play with him. He was unaware of any anger at his parents regarding the move or how it was done.

He openly told me he "hated" his father for ignoring the family. He loved his mother.

Relating to his decision to drop out of gifted classes in high school, he admitted he was "lazy." In fact, he thought he got too stuck on himself because he rarely studied but got good grades anyway.

Later, during therapy, the grandiosity engendered by his ease of studying in high school turned out to have been damaged when he got to college and the work required him to study—he experienced the need to study as a narcissistic injury.

Mental Status Assessment

Dmitri was a fit, athletic boy with longish hair and the five o'clock shadow fashionable among young men. His hair was a bit unkempt.

His ego functions of orientation to person, place, and time; concentration and memory; sensorium and psychomotor control were all intact. His intelligence, abstraction ability, integrative capacity, and reality testing were also intact. Self-preservation and self-care were somewhat dysfunctional, but he had never considered suicide or attempted it. There seemed to be inhibition of his work function. His capacity to observe himself was good ("mentalization").

Ego strengths of affect tolerance and containing primary process thinking were intact, but his impulse control (regarding substances and video games) seemed, at best, immature for his age. He was capable of sublimating.

Object relations functioning seemed to have reached whole object relatedness with peers and his high school girlfriend. However, he had regressed when he left home and left his girlfriend, and formed more narcissistic ties with girls. There seemed to be some anxiety about identity diffusion regarding his mother's pressures on him regarding his career. His self-image was not completed, although not terribly age inappropriate. He was interested in languages but not sure of his final decision. I felt there might be some splitting—loving his mother but hating his father.

His sensitivity to regression in object relatedness seemed to be due to early interferences with object constancy in infancy—when his mother resigned as his primary caretaker and Lara took over. He seemed to develop self and object constancy with Lara, but she was taken away when he was 6, and he was isolated for a year because of language—both factors leading to some self and object deterioration, as well as disturbance in secure attachments.

His superego was overactive. He was critical of others, himself, and his mother and father. The drug abuse, which might have been considered a lacuna (Johnson & Szurek, 1952), I suspected served various defensive purposes. He did, however, have difficulty avoiding playing StarCraft (a real-time war-in-space game) on his computer, thereby shirking his study responsibilities.

His conflicts seemed to include using substances to relieve unconscious grief over his lost high school girlfriend, mother, Lara, and home country. He also relieved grief about losing his homeland by becoming expert in cooking Russian food. Playing video games, I thought, was a compromise formation that allowed him to displace violent anger (originally directed at his parents for lying to him and taking Lara away); at the same time, he punished himself (by losing sleep and skipping classes—leading to failure) and established autonomy from his parents and their wishes for him to obtain higher education. Simultaneously, he regressed to early adolescent pleasurable wishes to be lazy, play games, and ignore responsibility.

Some of his depression also seemed to be due to early adult demoralization about the state of the culture at American universities (Wolfe, 2004). Some of the depression also seemed to be due to turning anger on himself.

Interpretive Meeting with Vera and Dmitri

After the evaluation was completed, I had a conjoint session with Dmitri and his mother. I discussed my opinion that Dmitri should be treatable with analytic therapy designed to help him understand himself. He agreed to stop drinking and smoking pot while he was living at home with his parents. He was more ambivalent about stopping video games; this would have to be dealt with during therapy.

I explained that other approaches could include treating his depression with antidepressant medicines, Cognitive Behavioral Therapy, tutoring, and coaching but that, in my opinion, analytically oriented treatment would be better since Dmitri could observe himself, and he seemed to be conflicted. Medication had side effects such as interference with sexual functioning. When Dmitri heard that, he immediately rejected it. CBT involved a therapist trying to change Dmitri's ideals and giving him homework. Dmitri, I thought correctly, opined that that would not be good because he was rebellious about homework.

I offered to treat him dynamically for the rest of the fall and spring semesters, while he was living at home. I recommended he come three times a week and that I meet with his mother once a week with or without him. They agreed to that structure. The following September, he returned to New York, and I referred him to a colleague for further treatment.

Epilogue

Dmitri called me when he graduated from college with a degree in Russian language. He had already interviewed with the State Department for a job. His mother was disappointed with his choice but relieved that he had finished college. He had stopped self-destructive drinking and pot, and was dating one girl steadily, he said. He still played video games with his male friends periodically, but this was not interfering with his sleep or his life.

Appendix A
Autism Spectrum and Attention Deficit/ Hyperactivity Disorders

Regarding ADHD, ASD, and Psychological Testing

We cannot write a book about the evaluation of children without mentioning autism spectrum disorders (ASD), which are relatively rare, and attention deficit/hyperactivity disorder (ADHD[1]), the symptoms of which are commonly reported. These areas are quite expansive; the literature about them is copious; and the differential diagnosis is contentious.

ASD

Autism spectrum disorders (ASD) have a prevalence rate of between 1 and 2% of all children (CDC, 2021). The statistical methods used to calculate those percentages, by the Centers for Disease Control and Prevention's (CDC) own admission, are quite flawed (and have generally been collated for children who are 8 years old) (Lord & Mutter, 2012). Some testing has been devised for younger children (Constantino, 2022).

The prevalence rate of ASD in boys is 1 in 34 (about 3%), whereas the prevalence in girls is 1 in 144 (about 0.7%) (CDC, 2014).

An enormous differential diagnosis exists, including

- childhood schizophrenia,
- developmental delays ("neurodevelopmental disorders") and sensory disorders (hypersensitive or hyposensitive regarding auditory, visual, or dermal stimuli),
- speech and language developmental disorders, and
- *defensive inhibition*[2] of various functions, such as integration, speech and language, and social skill.
- Severe anxiety/depression (or other affect overload).

---

1 Throughout the rest of this chapter, we will refer to the common usage, as of this printing, of ADHD as the usual diagnosis. For the past 80–90 years, this diagnosis has morphed from Minimal Brain Damage to Minimal Brain Dysfunction (MBD) to ADD to ADHD.
2 Blackman (2003). Defense #48.

There are multiple etiologies of cases that look like autism but are not. Many symptoms in non-ASD cases can be caused by overwhelming emotions connected to malign parental input, but many cases are not directly attributable to parental attitudes and behaviors toward the child.

By definition,[3], autism spectrum disorders can involve delays in the development of speech, organization of thought, and psychomotor control. Frequent pathological findings include perseveration, stereotyped behavior, rigidity in habits and expression of emotion, and damaged sense of self and others leading to inappropriate social interactions (based on age). Inappropriate or lack of smiling is common, accompanied by lack of eye contact from early in life.

Based on the noted statistics, 97%–99% of the time children should not be diagnosed with ASD. Taking into account that referrals to therapists will be greater than the prevalence in the population, the number of cases seen would predictably be approximately 1%–3%. The number of cases reported over the last ten years seems to have increased by about 10%. The reasons for this are debatable (The Team at Elemy, 2022).

Lack of social reciprocity and delay in language development are often cited as pathognomonic for ASD. We propose that other factors aside from simple delay also be considered when looking at what may cause those two important problems. In each chapter of this book, we outline and then discuss the long list of factors, throughout development, which could result in problems with socialization- for example, object relations and developmental conflicts at different psychosexual phases.

The problems with use of language may also be the result of disturbed relationships in the family producing defensive inhibitions and poor anxiety tolerance. Exposure to primal scene (Arlow, 1980) or terror (Cao et al., 2018) can produce disturbance in either social functioning (apparent narcissism) or peculiarities of language usage. Schizophrenia, an apparently neurocognitive illness where the integrative function is damaged, often includes disturbance of language usage (blocking, verbigeration, word salad, and neologisms).

To complicate matters, there is a bewildering variety of treatments recommended for ASD. Psychoanalytic developmentally based treatments (Kliman, 2018; Singletary, 2019) seem to be highly effective and reproducible. On the other hand, the National Institutes of Health (2021) lists 12 other, different

---

3 First described by L. Kanner (1943), who found severe problems in social interactions and connectedness at birth, resistance to change, and insistence on things remaining the same. He also noticed stereotyped movements such as rocking and hand flapping. Hans Asperger (1944) wrote about children with social problems, unusual focused interests, and good verbal ability. [N.B. The syndrome named after Asperger was removed as a separate diagnosis and added to "autism spectrum disorders" in *DSM-5-TR*. Children with these problems, of course, still exist.]

therapies,[4] and does not mention the work of Singletary or Kliman. It is an enormous topic filled with theoretical controversies (Wedge, 2020; The Team at Elemy, 2022).

An Amazon.com book search (May 2022) returned 3,000 results for the terms "autism spectrum disorders."

ADHD

An Amazon book search for "attention deficit hyperactivity disorder" returned 2,000 results, and "attention deficit disorder" another 1,000.

Our Opinions

Regarding ADHD, our opinion is that it is often misdiagnosed. The reason for this is the failure to obtain data regarding the questions we recommend about each stage of the child's development (our "Key Questions" concerning each developmental stage). This book attempts to furnish therapists with questions that can aid them in determining many factors that can, in some cases, cause a child to have trouble concentrating or paying attention. Concentration difficulties can be caused by high affect levels due to conflicts in the family, weaknesses in managing affects due to impediments in secure attachment, and failures in self and object constancy. The concentration function can also become inhibited (Blackman, 2003) as a defense against adolescent conflicts (Blum, 2010) or other anxieties involving guilt and shame about disturbing fantasies or realities (Cao et al., 2018).

Of course, any type of child abuse—neglect, beatings, or sexual overstimulation (from cosleeping beginning at age 2.5 onward)—causes the child disruptions in concentration and many other basic (ego) functions, including social skills. So, a history of "inadvertent" abuse[5] must be considered and ruled out.

Another way of approaching the problem is to consider ADHD as a combination of developmental delays in the concentration/attention and/or psychomotor control functions **when no other conflicts or developmental delays are present.**

In theory, ADHD, as an idiopathic developmental delay syndrome, should be a *rara avis*. The CDC (2021b) admits that 64% of children with a diagnosis of ADHD already have another "mental, emotional, or behavioral disorder." In the reality of 21st-century practice, however, parents, teachers, and

---

4 Those 12 include behavioral management therapy, cognitive behavior therapy, early intervention, educational and school-based therapies, joint attention therapy, medication treatment, nutritional therapy, occupational therapy, parent-mediated therapy, physical therapy, social skills training, speech-language therapy. https://www.nichd.nih.gov/health/topics/autism/conditioninfo/treatments.

5 Blackman and Dring (2016).

physicians commonly refer a child to a therapist with a note that the child should be treated for ADHD. Often, the multiplicity of the diagnostic possibilities when children have trouble concentrating has been overlooked or is unknown to the referring party.[6]

Because fidgeting, daydreaming, social awkwardness, language peculiarities, not listening to directions, and resisting doing homework are usually due to the matters we discuss in this book, we decided not to elaborate on the diagnosis or treatment of *bona fide* ADHD in the main text. Instead, we have added the material in this appendix.

Essay

Diagnostic Psychological Testing for ADHD

ADHD is a neurodevelopmental disorder. Worldwide, ADHD is the third-most-commonly diagnosed mental disorder, after depression and anxiety. ADHD prevalence in the pediatric population has been stable over the past three decades (except in the USA, where it has increased [Bélanger et al., 2018]). The prevalence rate of ADHD in children is estimated between 5% and 10%, with the rate for boys being four times the rate of girls (Biederman et al. 1991; CDC, 2010).

Studies suggest that ADHD is overdiagnosed and overtreated (Bruchmuller et al., 2012; Kazda et al., 2021). One report found that boys are more likely to be overdiagnosed with ADHD (Fresson et al., 2019).

ADHD According to the Diagnostic and Statistical Manual of Mental Disorders 5-TR (DSM-5-TR)-Symptom-Based Diagnosis without Developmental History

The *DSM* lists observable behavioral symptoms in various contexts. Despite extensive research over the past two decades, there are still no neurobiological markers for ADHD leading to a definitive diagnostic method (Dreschler et al., 2020).

DSM indicates that a diagnosis of ADHD should not be made if the symptoms are better explained by another mental disorder (e.g., schizophrenia, psychotic disorder, dissociative disorder, mood or anxiety disorder, personality disorder, substance intoxication, or withdrawal).

The defining symptoms of ADHD are divided into inattention-related vs. hyperactivity/impulsivity related. Of course, one child may have both types.

---

6 The clinical, financial, and political matters involved with these determinations are discussed in Wedge (2020). Another frequently consulted source is *Journal of Autism and Developmental Disorders*.

DSM opines that the symptoms should be present in two or more settings, before age 12, for at least six months.[7]

DSM adds that the symptoms must have impaired the child's social, academic, or occupational functioning.[8] Information is needed from the caretakers about the patient's functioning in all these venues to augment material gleaned from the clinical interview of the child.

Diagnostic Complications

Aside from the information gleaned from multiple informants regarding the child's behavior, the diagnostic evaluation of ADHD is complicated by the frequent need for psychological testing. The many tests include, but are not limited to, self-report, projective tests, continuous performance tests, observational tests, and personality tests. Assessment is further muddied because the results from each of these sources are often contradictory and inconsistent.

ADHD (hyperactivity, impulsivity, and inattention) symptom constellations also get confusing. The presentation of a child with inattention can be very different from that of a hyperactive, impulsive child. One child may be anxious or socially inhibited (internalizing symptoms). Another child ("hyperactive and/or impulsive") may show defiant behaviors (externalizing). Children often manifest emotional problems differently from adults. For example, depressed or angry (sometimes abused) children often exhibit overactivity and sudden impulse discharge (overeating, breaking things, yelling) instead of describing their depressive feelings.

The differential diagnosis is further complicated, as noted earlier, because children who have been diagnosed with ADHD have a high frequency of comorbid psychological disorders (Gilmore, 2002). According to the American Academy of Child and Adolescent Psychiatry (Jensen et al., 1997), comorbidity is present in two-thirds of children who were referred with a diagnosis of ADHD. Fifty-percent of children with those other disturbances suffered with Oppositional Defiant Disorder, 30%–50% with Conduct Disorder, 15%–20% with Mood Disorders, and 20%–25% with Anxiety Disorders (see also Bierdereman et al., 1991; Newcorn & Halperin, 1994).

In adolescents, substance use may be "comorbid" with ADHD (or, of course, may cause the same symptoms). Learning Disorders, in children diagnosed with ADHD, range from 10%–25% (Richters et al., 1995).

The question often becomes (1) is the child suffering from multiple disorders, including ADHD; (2) is the child suffering from non-ADHD psychological disorders that manifest symptoms similar to ADHD; or (3) are the behavioral symptoms of *bona fide* ADHD causing or exacerbating other psychological problems? These differential diagnostic issues often require an

---

7 The reasons for these distinctions are relatively arbitrary, and no explanation is given in the *DSM*.
8 *DSM-5-TR* opines that ADHD may occur in adults.

evaluation that is broad in scope to clarify the specific diagnostic category, as well as the etiology of the problems.

Of some importance, the symptoms associated with ADHD fluctuate, depending upon age, family/academic environment, and any interventions already initiated. Moreover, research indicates that in adolescents referred because of symptoms suggesting ADHD, there is a **high proportion of false positive ratings**. These are likely due to the confounding variables related to other mental disturbances, drug seeking, or current substance use.

The upshot of these complications is that there is no "gold standard" instrument or evaluation procedure for accurately identifying ADHD in any one individual at any given time.

So, what is an evaluator to do? The answer is that the initial stage of any assessment involves a comprehensive interview with the parents, in large part to obtain a **developmental history**—as we have outlined in the text of our book. This should actually be done for any problems for which children are brought to a therapist. The broad-based interview we have suggested, including meeting with the parents and evaluating the child, is preferable to a narrowly focused ADHD interview. Extensive history-taking and clinical child evaluation increase the evaluator's opportunity to ascertain the genesis of the behaviors that have been labeled hyperactive/impulsive or inattentive.

The Following Are Specific Areas of Inquiry for the Parent and Child/Adolescent Where the Symptom Picture Suggests ADHD

Parent Interview

A description of the symptoms that concern the parents and how the symptoms are manifested.

This includes the symptoms observed at home and whether the symptoms appear to be influencing academic and social functioning. Parents can also provide school records that indicate academic and behavior performance issues. The severity and consistency of the symptoms across various contexts, as well as the onset of the symptoms, can also be gathered and placed in the context of the family's history vis-à-vis the child. If problems with inattention, hyperactivity, or impulsivity are discovered, a similar inquiry may be made to a teacher or coach.

Medical Issues May Have Relevance

These include, but are not limited to sleep disturbances; pregnancy complications; health or poor nutrition in infancy; vision or hearing disturbance; medications prescribed for the child/adolescent or over-the-counter medications; fragile X syndrome; seizures, head injury, fetal alcohol syndrome; and phenylketonuria. These data may be provided by medical sources, and may suggest that further medical workup is necessary.

Drug or Alcohol Use by the Patient

This is important in adolescents, as substance abuse may be comorbid with ADHD or, alternatively, be causing the symptoms. Drug seeking, where the teenager is dissembling, must also be ruled out, especially in regard to requests for amphetamines (Adderall and others) and sedatives (Ativan and other benzodiazepines).

It is also useful to know what interventions have been provided by the parents, teachers, medical personnel, and what impact those interventions have had upon the child. If the child has been in psychotherapy, an interview with or information from this therapist is important.

Is There a Family History of ADHD?

Studies have indicated that there may be a genetic contribution to the etiology of ADHD. Adoption studies support this conclusion, and siblings of children with ADHD, statistically, have two to three times the risk of having ADHD compared with siblings of normal controls. Parents of children with ADHD frequently suffer from symptoms that sound like ADHD (Ferone & Biederman, 1994; Nikolas & Burt, 2010). Of course, family environment and the social environment can be overstimulating or produce identifications with certain behaviors; these factors should be sought by the clinician as well.

Developmental History: The Rest of This Book!

Interview with Child or Adolescent

Observations during the clinical interview indicate how well the child/adolescent can pay attention to the interviewer, remain seated, and ignore distractions. How children respond to playroom materials is also a useful barometer: e.g., can they inhibit the impulse to play when they need to respond to questions? Do they jump from one activity to another without deciding on any one play material?

In the adolescent or older child, how do they view the presenting symptoms as revealed by their parents? Do they see the symptoms as interfering with their school or social life? If not, why not? If they do see problems, how do they describe the problems? In what areas do they not see the symptoms as creating a problem or hindering their progress?

If adolescents view their behaviors as problematic, what do they believe might help them, or what has helped them?

What is the child's affect when discussing any issue? Does the child seem indifferent, sad, or anxious?

How long has the adolescent or child felt the symptoms have caused problems? What is their opinion of how their parents and teachers have responded?

Particularly, in adolescents, do they have their own theory about what caused their troubles?

In what activities or settings do the ADHD symptoms seem to be less of a problem?

Is there a history of drug or alcohol use?

What other psychological issues is the child or adolescent concerned about? Do they have low self-esteem, identity issues, anxiety, depression, learning problems?

Ask the child or adolescent about possible victimization by bullying or abuse.

Evaluation Procedures and Specific Tests

The following is a list of commonly used ADHD diagnostic assessment measures. Observation of the child during these individually administered measures is a key factor in an ADHD evaluation. This list is not exhaustive but provides some of the widely used measures and instruments.

Cognitive/Academic Assessments

Most assessments for ADHD involve an evaluation of intellect, cognition, and learning, especially if the child's school performance seems below average or below what would be expected of the child. The specific test used depends on the age of the patient being tested and the specific issues of the child. We have already presented specific information about many of these tests in Chapter 7 (Latency). That information will not be repeated here.

Intellectual Testing/Achievement Testing

- *Wechsler Preschool and Primary Scale of Intelligence–IV* (WPPSI-IV) – (see Latency, Chapter 7).
- *Wechsler Intelligence Scale for Children–Fifth Edition* (WISC-V) – (see Latency, Chapter 7).
- *Wechsler Adult Intelligence Scale–Fourth Edition* (WAIS-IV) – (Wechsler, 2008) – An individually administered test that measures intellectual and cognitive ability. It is appropriate for ages 16–90 years, 11 months. For a review of the WAIS-IV, see Climie and Rostad (2011).
- *Stanford-Binet Intelligence Scale–Fifth Edition* – (see Latency, Chapter 7).

Achievement tests provide information about the child's knowledge and ability in academic areas such as reading, mathematics, spelling, writing, receptive vocabulary, and auditory comprehension. These tests contribute to an assessment of learning disability. Commonly used achievement tests are as follows:

- *Wechsler Individual Achievement Test–Fourth Edition (WIAT-IV)* – (see Latency, Chapter 7)
- *Woodcock-Johnson IV* – (see Latency, Chapter 7)
- *Kaufman Test of Educational Achievement–Third Edition (KTEA-III)* – (see Latency, Chapter 7)

There are other tests of cognitive functioning that are relevant to an ADHD assessment. The choice of which tests to use is based on the particular areas of concern as noted by grades, school testing, observations, and parent/teacher reports. The specific domains (areas of difficulty) often considered in an ADHD assessment include the following: visual and auditory processing, language (especially expressive language), memory (retrieval and organization of information), processing speed (variable rates of work speed), and fine motor skills (problems with handwriting).

Teacher/Parent/Child Rating Scales

These are questionnaires for teachers, parents, and the child/adolescent concerning the child's symptoms. Often, they are used early in the assessment to help the evaluator focus on specific areas of concern. They supplement the information obtained in the clinical interviews. Some of the most widely used are as follows:

- *Conners Third Edition* – (Conners, 2008). This can be administered to both teachers and parents with children ages 6–18 and has a self-report version for children 8–18. It focuses on symptoms suggestive of ADHD but also addresses comorbid disorders such as Oppositional Defiant Disorder and Conduct Disorder. (For a review of the Conners-3, see Grace & Thomas, 2010.)

Achenbach System of Empirically Based Assessment (ASEBA) – (see Latency, Chapter 7). This includes the *Child Behavior Checklist (CBCL)*, *Teacher Report Form (TRF)*, and the *Youth Self-Report (YSR)*. It assesses the DSM-oriented ADHD criteria.

- *Brown Attention-Deficit Disorder Scales* – (Brown, 2001). Measures ADHD across the life span (age 3–adult) and explores the executive and cognitive functioning frequently associated with ADHD.
- *Vanderbilt ADHD Diagnostic Parent/Teacher Rating Scales* – These assess DSM based ADHD criteria, as well as conduct disorder, oppositional disorder, anxiety, and depression. It is appropriate for ages 6–12 years old. (For a review of this assessment measure, see Langberg et al., 2010.)

Personality Tests

These assessment tools are often used if the clinical interview of the parents and child suggests other psychological problems aside from, or concomitant, with ADHD. These tests can be extremely useful in differential diagnosis.

- *Personality Inventory for Children-Second Edition (PIC-2)* – (see Latency, Chapter 7). This is a parent-completed assessment that provides information about a child's personality and emotional functioning.
- *Rorschach Test* is a projective test that can be helpful in elucidating personal motivations, conflicts, prevalent emotions, and severe disturbances in thought. (For a full discussion of the Exner system of interpretation, see Exner & Erdberg, 2005.)
- For younger children (ages 5–15), the *Roberts Apperception Test* is another projective measure that can elicit drives, fantasy material, conflicts, and feelings.
  The Rorschach and the Roberts are useful in assessing areas of disturbance that contribute to the symptoms of inattention, hyperactivity, or impulsivity.
- *The Minnesota Multiphasic Personality Inventory-Adolescent-Restructured Form (MMPI-A-RF)* (Archer et al., 2016) is a personality measure appropriate for adolescents 14–18 years old. It is one of the most widely used personality measures for adolescents.

Continuous Performance Tests (CPTs)

Although used frequently to assist in the diagnosis of ADHD, these tests have been criticized for questions regarding their limited sensitivity, specificity, and ecological validity. For a review of CPT measures of attention, see Roebuck et al., 2016.

Commonly used CPT tests are as follows:

- *Conners Continuous Performance Test-3 (CPT-3)* – This is a task-oriented computerized test to assist with diagnosis of ADHD for individuals 8 years old and older.
- *Test of Variables of Attention Version 9 (TOVA)* – (Leark et al., 2020). This is a computerized measure of attention and inhibitory control. It can be used for anyone between 6 and 80 years old.
- The *Qb Test* is a CPT test that combines measures of attention and impulsivity with motion tracking analysis. (For a critical discussion of the *Qb Test*, see Brunkhorst-Kanaan et al., 2020; Hollis et al., 2018).

Executive Functioning

These tests involve variables such as response inhibition, planning ahead, organization skills, vigilance, and working memory. People with ADHD often have difficulties with finishing homework, remembering material and due dates, planning ahead, and time management due to problems in these areas. Two frequently used measures of executive function are as follows:

- *Barkley Deficits in Executive Functioning Scale-Children and Adolescents (BDEFS-CA)* – (Barkley, 2012). This is a rating scale to evaluate the major components of executive functioning in children and adolescents. It is completed by the parents to measure the daily executive functioning in children ages 6–17 years old.
- *Child Executive Function Scale (CHEXI)* – This is a rating instrument for parents and teachers to measure executive functioning in children 4–12 years old. (For a discussion of the CHEXI, see Camerota et al., 2018.)

Information about executive functioning can also be garnered from a thorough clinical interview of parents and children.

Appendix B
Some Caveats and Disclaimers regarding Culture and Child-Rearing Practices

- The questions to be answered by parents, which we discuss in this book, carry implications regarding child-rearing practices. That is an unavoidable inference but is not completely accurate. It is helpful when a child is showing symptoms (or not adapting) to learn at which stages during prior development there were unresolved problems. These past difficulties are often linkable to later stages of development, and the resultant current problems are explainable. Retrospectively, in other words, the developmental history is very useful. Prospectively, the history is much more limited and prediction much less dependable.
- Child-rearing practices cannot precisely predict the outcome of personality development in any individual. Development is too long and persists into early, middle, and late adulthood. Changes at those stages may have as great an effect as those of the "calamities" of childhood (Brenner, 1982b). The most that can be done by a child therapist is to help any child regain "age-appropriate" functioning when there has been an interference—or to resolve symptomatology through interpretation of symbolic conflicts, when possible.
- At any time, in any century, certain parental behaviors regarding their children are considered normative. That does not necessarily mean such practices are good or bad for children.

  - In the 19th century, for example, beating children was normative in the United States. Today, it is not.
  - Co-sleeping at different stages of development has also achieved cultural acceptance and normalization in much of Asia, and more recently in the United States and other Western countries. This practice can be quite problematic for many children; steps are being taken worldwide to reduce this practice.
  - The outcome of a child's personality cannot be determined by the presence or absence of beatings or co-sleeping, and we are not suggesting a reliable predictive factor for either.

- As exceptions
  - Like the speed of light, sexual abuse of children stands on its own as a factor that is always pathogenic for children, though the exact result, again, is not precisely foreseeable.
  - Torture of children is always emotionally traumatic. Examples include the following:
    - Medically conducted urethral dilatation (without general anesthesia) to "treat" nocturnal enuresis during latency.
    - Ritual clitoridectomy performed by the mother or a female "circumcisor" on 6- to 8-year-old girls in certain African countries (Odukogbe et al., 2017; Kosma, 2021).
  - In both of the aforementioned situations, societal approbation is present, and the procedures are considered culturally normal. Nevertheless, negative consequences of such traumas, to the child, are likely in any culture.
- The culture or subculture in which any child is raised is likely, but not guaranteed, to have marked effect on the child. In evaluating children, cultural normalizations must be considered. On the other hand, if the cultural practice can be shown to affect any individual child in a negative way, child-centered counseling of the parents can be helpful in ameliorating the child or adolescent's painful symptoms, inhibitions, or maladaptive character functioning. (For a philosophical look at the effects of culture, see Jackson, 2007).

References

Achenbach, T. (2011). Child behavior checklist. In: J. Kreutzer, J. DeLuca, & B. Caplan (Eds.), *Encyclopedia of Clinical Neuropsychology*. New York: Springer.

Adatto, C. (1989). Review of C. Sarnoff (1987) *Psychotherapeutic Strategies in Late Latency through Early Adolescence* (Aronson). *Psychoanalytic Quarterly* 58: 478–480.

Adkisson, R., Burdsal, C., Dorr, D., & Morgan, C. (2012). Factor structure of the Millon Adolescent Clinical Inventory scales in psychiatric inpatients. *Personality and Individual Differences* 532: 501–506.

Aichhorn, A. (1935). *Wayward Youth*. New York: Viking Press.

Ainsworth, M. (1967). *Infancy in Uganda: Infant Care and the Growth of Love*. Johns Hopkins Press.

Ainsworth, M., Bell, S., & Stayton, D. (1974). Infant-mother attachment and social development: "Socialization" as a product of reciprocal responsiveness to signals. In: P. Richards (Ed.), *The Integration of a Child into a Social World* (pp. 99–135). Cambridge, UK: Cambridge University Press.

Ainsworth, M., Blehar, M, Waters, E., & Wall, S. (1978). *Patterns of Attachment: A Psychological Study of the Strange Situation*. Hillsdale, NJ: Erlbaum.

Ainsworth, M., Blehar, M., Waters, E., & Wall, S. (2015). *Patterns of Attachment: A Psychological Study of the Strange Situation*. Psychology Press.

Akhtar, S. (1984). The syndrome of identity diffusion. *American Journal of Psychiatry* 141: 1381–1385.

Akhtar, S. (1992). *Broken Structures: Severe Personality Disorders and Their Treatment*. Northvale, NJ: Aronson.

Akhtar, S. (1994). Object constancy and adult psychopathology. *International Journal of Psychoanalysis* 75: 441–455.

Akhtar, S. (2009). *Comprehensive Dictionary of Psychoanalysis*. New York and London: Routledge. Reprinted in 2018.

Akhtar, S. (2014). Psychoanalytic treatment of trauma and the analyst's personality. *Psychoanalytic Inquiry* 34(3): 204–213.

Akhtar, S. (2018). *A Web of Sorrow: Mistrust, Jealousy, Lovelessness, Shamelessness, Regret, Hopelessness*. New York and London: Routledge.

Akhtar, S. (2020). Letting go: Detachment theory & its clinical usefulness.In: *2nd Jerome S Blackman MD Lectureship in Psychoanalysis*. Eastern Virginia Medical School & the Virginia Psychoanalytic Society. Oct. 16, 2020.

Akhtar, S. (Ed.), Blackman, J., & Cantor, J., (contributors). (2011). *The Electrified Mind: Development, Psychopathology, and Treatment in the Era of Cell Phones and the Internet* (Margaret S. Mahler Series). New York: Aronson.

Alfonso, C. A. (2009). Dynamic psychopharmacology and treatment adherence. *Journal of the American Academy of Psychoanalysis* 37: 269–285.

Alpert, A. (1959). Reversibility of pathological fixations associated with maternal deprivation in infancy. *Psychoanalytic Study of the Child* 14: 169–185.

American Academy of Child and Adolescent Psychiatry. (2003). *Research Diagnostic Criteria-Preschool Age (RDC-PA)*.

American Psychological Association. (2015). *Dictionary of Psychology* (2nd ed.). Washington, DC: APA Press.

Ammaniti, M. & Trentini, C. (2009). How new knowledge about parenting reveals the neurobiological implications of intersubjectivity: A conceptual synthesis of recent research. *Psychoanalytic Dialogues* 19(5): 537–555.

Ammaniti, M., Fontana, A., & Nicolais, G. (2015). Borderline personality disorder in adolescence through the lens of the interview of Personality Organization Processes in Adolescence (IPOP-A): Clinical use and implications. *Journal of Infant, Child & Adolescent Psychotherapy* 14: 82–97.

Anders, T. & Dahl, R. (2007). Classifying sleep disorders in infants and toddlers. In: W. Narrow, M. First, P. Sirovatka, & D. Regier (Eds.), *Age and Gender Considerations in Psychiatric Diagnosis: A Research Agenda for DSM-5* (pp. 215–226). American Psychiatric Publishing, Inc.

Anzieu-Premmereur, C. (2017). Using psychoanalytic concepts to inform interpretations and direct interventions with a baby in working with infants and parents. *International Forum of Psychoanalysis* 26: 54–58.

Appelman, E. (2001). Temperament and dyadic contributions to affect regulation: Implications from developmental research for clinical practice. *Psychoanalytic Psychology* 18: 534–559.

Apprey, M. (1987). Projective identification and maternal misconception in disturbed mothers. *British Journal of Psychotherapy* 4(1): 5–22.

Archer, R. (2017). *Assessing Adolescent Psychopathology: MMPI-A/MMPI-A-RF* (4th ed.) New York: Routledge.

Archer, R., Handel, R., Ben-Porath, Y., & Tellegen, A. (2016). *Minnesota Multiphasic Personality Inventory-Adolescent-Restructured Form (MMPI-A-RF): Manual for Administration, Scoring, Interpretation, and Technical Manual*. Minneapolis, MN: University of Minnesota Press.

Arlow, J. (1958). Psychoanalytic Concepts & the Structural Theory. *Journal of the American Psychoanalytic Association* 6: 143–153.

Arlow, J. (1964). *Psychoanalytic Concepts and the Structural Concepts*. New York: International Universities Press.

Arlow, J. (1971). Character perversion. In: I. Marcus (Ed.), *Currents in Psychoanalysis* (pp. 317–336). New York: International Universities Press.

Arlow, J. (1980). The revenge motive in the primal scene. *Journal of the American Psychoanalytic Association* 28: 519–541.

Armstrong, D. & Hutti, M. (1998). Pregnancy after perinatal loss: The relationship between anxiety and prenatal attachment. *Journal of Obstetric, Gynecologic, and Neonatal Nursing* 27(2): 183–189.

Arnett, J. (1999). Adolescent storm and stress, reconsidered. *American Psychologist* 54: 317–326.

Baggio, S., Hasler, R., Giacomini, V., El-Masri, H., Weibel, S., Perroud, N., & Deiber, M. (2020). Does the continuous performance test predict ADHD symptom severity and ADHD presentation in adults? *Journal of Attention Disorders* 24(6): 840–848. DOI: 10.1177/1087054718822060. Epub 2019 Jan 17. PMID: 30654686.

Baranek, G., David, F., Poe, M., Stone, W., & Watson, R. (2006). Sensory experience questionnaire: Discriminating sensory features in young children with autism, developmental delays, and typical development. *Journal of Child Psychology and Psychiatry and Allied Disciplines* 47: 591–601.

Barish, K. (2020). The importance (and limitations) of affective neuroscience of psychotherapy and adolescents: A discussion of Leon Hoffman's article. *Journal of Infant, Child & Adolescent Psychotherapy* 19: 230–238.

Barkley, R. (2012). *Barkley Deficits in Executive Functioning Scale-Children and Adolescents (BDEFS-CA)*. New York: Guilford Press.

Basch, M. (1981). Psychoanalytic interpretation and cognitive transformation. *International Journal of Psychoanalysis* 62: 151–175.

Baum, L., Archer, R., Forbey, J., & Handel, R. (2009). A review of the Minnesota Multiphasic Personality Inventory–Adolescent (MMPI-A) and the Millon Adolescent Clinical Inventory (MACI) with an emphasis on juvenile justice samples. *Assessment* 16(4): 384–400. DOI: 10.1177/1073191109338264

Bayley, N. & Aylward, G. (2019). *Bayley Scales of Infant and Toddler Development– Fourth Edition*. New York: Pearson.

Beaujean, A. & Parkin, J. (2022). Evaluation of the Wechsler Individual Achievement Test–Fourth Edition as a measurement instrument. *Journal of Intelligence* 10(2): 30. DOI: 10.3390/jintelligence10020030.

Becker, T. (1974). On latency. *Psychoanalytic Study of the Child* 29: 3–11.

Beckford, C. & Wallace, B. (2016). Introduction to the special theme issue on health disparities, trauma, disruptive and criminal behaviors, and the adolescent brain: Conference collaborators, major developments in conference planning, and overview of the articles. *Journal of Infant, Child & Adolescent Psychotherapy* 15: 141–154.

Beebe, B. (2000). Co-constructing mother-infant distress. *Psychoanalytic Inquiry* 20: 421–440.

Beebe, B. (2005). Mother-infant research informs mother-infant treatment. *Psychoanalytic Study of the Child* 60: 7–46.

Beebe, B. & Lachmann, F. (2002a). *Infant Research and Adult Treatment: Co-constructing Interactions*. Hillsdale, NJ: The Analytic Press.

Beebe, B. & Lachmann, F. (2002b). Organizing principles of interaction from infant research and the lifespan prediction of attachment: Application to adult treatment. *Journal of Infant, Child, & Adolescent Psychotherapy* 2: 61–89.

Bélanger, S., Andrews, D., Gray, C., & Korczak, D. (2018). ADHD in children and youth: Part 1—etiology, diagnosis, and comorbidity. *Paediatrics & Child Health* 23(7): 447–453. DOI: 10.1093/pch/pxy109

Bell, C. & McBride, D. (2010). Affect regulation and prevention of risky behaviors. *Journal of the American Medical Association* 304: 565–566.

Bellak, L. (1989). *Ego Function Assessment (EFA)*. Larchmont, NY: C.P.S.

Bellak, L. & Bellak, S. (1949). *Children's Apperception Test*. Gracie Station, New York: Consulting Psychologists Press.

Benedek, T. (1959). Parenthood as a developmental phase—a contribution to the libido theory. *Journal of the American Psychoanalytic Association* 7: 389–417.

Bennett, S., Litz, B., Lee, B., & Magnen, S. (2005). The scope and impact of perinatal loss: Current status and future directions. *Professional Psychology Research and Practice* 36: 180–187.

Benoit, D., Parker, K., & Zeanah, C., Jr. (1997). Mother's representations of their infants assessed prenatally: Stability and association with infants' attachment classifications. *Journal of Child Psychology, Psychiatry, and Allied Disciplines* 38: 307–313.

Berens, A. & Nelson, C. (2019). Neurobiology of fetal and infant development. In: Charles H. Zeanah (Eds.), *Handbook of Infant Mental Health–Fourth Edition*. New York: Guilford Press.

Berger, M. (1981). Study group on the problems of adopted children. *Bulletin of the Anna Freud Centre* 4: 292.

Berger, I., Slobodin, O., & Cassuto, H. (2017). Usefulness and validity of continuous performance tests in the diagnosis of attention-deficit hyperactivity disorder children. *Archives of Clinical Neuropsychology* 32(1): 81–93. DOI: 10.1093/arclin/acw101

Bernstein, D. (1983). The female superego: A different perspective. *International Journal of Psychoanalysis* 64: 187–201.

Bibring, G., Huntington, D., & Valenstein, A. (1961). A study of the psychological processes in pregnancy and of the earlier mother-child relationship. *Psychoanalytic Study of the Child* 16: 9–72.

Biederman, J., Newcorn, J., & Sprich, S. (1991). Comorbidity of attention deficit hyperactivity disorder with conduct, depressive, anxiety, and other disorders. *American Journal of Psychiatry* 148: 564–577.

Blackman, J. (1991). Intellectual dysfunction in abused children. *Academy Forum* 35: 7–10.

Blackman, J. (2003a). *101 Defenses: How the Mind Shields Itself*. New York: Routledge.

Blackman, J. (2003b). Bizet's "Carmen" on the couch. In: Jerome S. Blackman (Ed.), *101 Defenses: How the Mind Shields Itself*. New York: Routledge.

Blackman, J. (2006). Olga: The first six months of psychoanalytic treatment of a woman with neurotic conversion symptoms based on unresolved conflicts from the 1st genital phase and latency. *Presented with Sheldon Bach at Annual Meeting of the Virginia Psychoanalytic Society*, Charlottesville, April.

Blackman, J. (2010). *Get the Diagnosis Right: Assessment and Treatment Selection for Mental Disorders*. New York: Routledge.

Blackman, J. (2013). *The Therapist's Answer Book: Solutions to 101 Tricky Problems in Psychotherapy*. New York: Routledge.

Blackman, J. (2016a). Book Review of the following in *Psychoanalytic Psychology* 33: 651–663 of:

    American Psychiatric Association. (2013). *Diagnostic and Statistical Manual of Mental Disorders–5th Edition*. Washington, DC: American Psychiatric Association.

    Barlow, D. (Ed.). (2014). *Clinical Handbook of Psychological Disorders: A Step-by-Step Treatment Manual–5th Edition*. New York: Guilford Press.

    Frances, A. (2013). *Essentials of Psychiatric Diagnosis: Responding to the Challenges of DSM-V*. New York: The Guilford Press.

Blackman, J. (2016b). Laziness and its links to shame. In: S. Akhtar (Ed.), *Shame: Developmental, Cultural, and Clinical Realms* (pp. 115–127). London: Karnac.

Blackman, J. (2018a). Pick up the baby (or dire consequences will ensue)! *International Forum of Psychoanalysis* 26: 33–37.

Blackman, J. (2018b). Defensive arrogance in adult philanderers. In: S. Akhtar & A. Smolen (Eds.), *Arrogance: Developmental, Cultural, and Clinical Realms* London and New York: Routledge.

Blackman, J. (2018c). *Get the Diagnosis Right: Assessment and Treatment Selection for Mental Disorders*. Translated into Mandarin by Zhao Cheng Zhi. Beijing: Beijing Normal University Press.

Blackman, J. (2020). A psychoanalytic view of reactions to the coronavirus pandemic in China. *American Journal of Psychoanalysis* 80: 119–132.

Blackman, J. (2021). *101+ Defenses (Fangyu)*. Translated into Chinese by Wang Jing; Edited by Wu Chunyan. Shanghai: East China Normal University Press.

Blackman, J. & Dring, K. (2016). *Sexual Aggression against Children Pedophiles' & Abuser's Dynamics, Development, Treatability, & the Law*. New York: Routledge.

Blackman, L. & Kaplan, E. (1969). The husband's role in psychiatric illness associated with childbearing. *Psychiatric Quarterly* 43 (1–4). https://pdf.zlibcdn.com/dtoken/e9d4547e2973951b25c06660d56f7299/bf01564257.pdf

Blackmore, E., Côté-Arsenault, D., Tang, W., Glover, V., Evans, J., Golding, J., & O'Connor, T. (2011). Previous prenatal loss as a predictor of perinatal depression and anxiety. *British Journal of Psychiatry* 1985: 373–378. DOI: 10.1192/bjp.bp.110.083105

Blos, P. (1960). *On Adolescence*. New York: International Universities Press.

Blos, P. (1962). *On Adolescence: A Psychoanalytic Interpretation*. Free Press of Glencoe.

Blos, P. (1967). The second individuation process of adolescence. *Psychoanalytic Study of the Child* 22: 162–186.

Blos, P. (1970). *The Young Adolescent*. Free Press.

Blos, P. (1974). The genealogy of the ego ideal. *Psychoanalytic Study of the Child* 29: 43–88.

Blos, P. (1976). How and when does adolescence end? In: S. Feinstein & P. Giovacchini (Eds.), *Adolescent Psychiatry*, vol. 5 (pp. 5–17). New York: Aronson.

Blos, P. (1983). The contribution of psychoanalysis to the psychotherapy of adolescents. *Psychoanalytic Study of the Child* 38: 577–600.

Blum, H. (Ed.). (1977). *Female Psychology*. Madison, CT: International Universities Press.

Blum, H. (1981). The maternal ego-ideals and the regulation of maternal qualities. In: S. Greenspan & G. Pollock (Eds.), *The Course of Life Volume III* (pp. 91–114). Washington, DC: NIMH.

Blum, H. (1983). Adoptive parents: Generative conflict and generational continuity. *Psychoanalytic Study of the Child* 38: 141–163.

Blum, H. (1985). Superego formation, adolescent transformation, and the adult neurosis. *Journal of the American Psychoanalytic Association* 33: 887–909.

Blum, H. (2004). Separation-individuation theory and attachment theory. *Journal of the American Psychoanalytic Association* 52: 535–553.

Blum, H. (2005). Psychoanalytic reconstruction and reintegration. *Psychoanalytic Study of the Child* 60: 295–311.

Blum, L. (2007). Psychodynamics of postpartum depression. *Psychoanalytic Psychology* 24: 45–62.

Blum, H. (2010). Adolescent trauma and the Oedipus complex. *Psychoanalytic Inquiry* 30: 548–556.

Blum, H. (2017). The mother's mental representation of her infant. *International Forum of Psychoanalysis* 26: 64–69.

Blum, E. & Blum, H. (1990). The development of autonomy and superego precursors. *International Journal of Psychoanalysis* 71: 585–595.

Bornstein, B. (1951). On latency. *Psychoanalytic Study of the Child* 6: 279–285.

Bornstein, R. (2010). Psychoanalytic theory as a unifying framework for 21st century personality assessment. *Psychoanalytic Psychology* 27: 133–152.

Bowlby, J. (1944a). Forty-four juvenile thieves: Their characters and home-life. *International Journal of Psychoanalysis* 25: 19–53.

Bowlby, J. (1944b). Forty-four juvenile thieves: Their characters and home-life (II). *International Journal of Psychoanalysis* 25: 107–128.

Bowlby, J. (1958). The nature of the child's tie to his mother. *International Journal of Psycho-Analysis* 39: 350–373.

Bowlby, J. (1969a). Appraising and selecting: Feeling and emotion. In: *Attachment and Loss: Volume I: Attachment*. New York: Basic Books.

Bowlby, J. (1969b). *Attachment and Loss, Vol. 1: Attachment*. New York: Basic Books.

Bowlby, J. (1973). *Attachment and Loss, Volume II: Separation, Anxiety and Anger*. New York: Basic Books.

Bowlby, J. (1980). *Attachment and Loss, Volume III: Loss, Sadness and Depression*. New York: Basic Books.

Brabender, V. & Fallon, A. (2013). *Working with Adoptive Parents: Research, Theory and Therapeutic Interventions*. Hoboken, NJ: Wiley.

Bradley, R., Danielson, I., & Hallahan, D. (2002). *Identification of Learning Disabilities: Research to Practice*. Mahwah, NJ: Erlbaum.

Brakel, L. (1988). A modern "solution" to the oedipal problem; a fantasy of surrogate motherhood. *Psychoanalytic Quarterly* 57: 87–91.

Bram, A. D. & Yalof, J. (2015). Quantifying complexity: Personality assessment and its relationship with psychoanalysis. *Psychoanalytic Inquiry* 35: 74–97.

Bravo, I. (2001). The Impact of early loss on depression: Dynamic origins and empirical findings. *Psychoanalytic Social Work* 8: 47–69.

Brazelton, T. (1973). *Neonatal Behavior Assessment Scale*. Philadelphia: Lippincott.

Brazelton, T. (1980). Neonatal assessment. In: S. Greenspan & G. Pollock (Eds.), *The Course of Life: Psychoanalytic Contributions toward Understanding Personality Development, Vol. 1* (pp. 203–233). Bethesda: National Institute of Mental Health.

Brazelton, T. & Cramer, B. (1990). *The Earliest Relationship: Parents, Infants, and the Drama of Early Attachment*. Addison-Wesley/Addison Wesley Longman.

Brazelton, T., Christophersen, E., Frauman, A., Gorski, P., Poole, J., Stadtler, A., & Wright, C. (1999). Instruction, timeliness, & medical influences affecting toilet training. *Pediatrics* 103(6)(Supplement): 1353–1358.

Brenner, C. (1982a). Meetings of the New York Psychoanalytic Society. *Psychoanalytic Quarterly*.

Brenner, C. (1982b). *The Mind in Conflict*. Madison, CT: International Universities Press.

Brenner, C. (2006). *Psychoanalysis; Mind and Meaning*. Psychoanalytic Quarterly.

Bretherton, I. (1992). The origins of attachment theory: John Bowlby and Mary Ainsworth. *Developmental Psychology* 28(5): 759–775.

Brim, O. G., Jr. & Kagan, J. (1980). *Constancy and Change in Human Development*. Cambridge, MA: Harvard University Press.

Brinich, P. (1990). Adoption from the inside out: A psychoanalytic perspective. In: D. Brodzinsky & M. Schechter (Eds.), *The Psychology of Adoption* (pp. 42–61). New York: Oxford University Press.

Britannica. (2022). *State History of MLDA 21*. https://drinkingage.procon.org/state-history-of-mlda-21/

Bronstein, C. & Flanders, S. (1998). The development of a therapeutic space in a first contact with adolescents. *Journal of Child Psychotherapy* 24: 5–36.

Brown, T. (2001). *Brown Attention-Deficit Disorder Scales: For Children and Adolescents.* San Antonio, TX: The Psychological Corporation.

Brown, S. (2003). *Hello, Darkness.* New York: Simon & Schuster.

Brown, S. (2022). *Overkill.* Grand Central Publishing.

Bruch, H. (1979). *Eating Disorders: Obesity, Anorexia Nervosa, and the Person within.* Basic Books.

Bruchmuller, K., Margraf, J., & Schneider, S. (2012). Overdiagnosis and influence of client gender on diagnosis. *Journal of Consulting and Clinical Psychology* 80(1): 128–138. DOI: 10.1037/a0026582. Epub 2011 Dec 26. https://pubmed.ncbi.nlm.nih.gov/22201328/

Brunkhorst-Kanaan, N., Verdenhalven, M., Kittel-Schneider, S., Vainieri, I., Reif, A., & Grimm, O. (2020). The Quantified Behavioral Test—a confirmatory test in the diagnostic process of Adult ADHD?. *Frontiers in Psychiatry* 11: 216.

Busch, F., Milrod, B., Rudden, M., Shapiro, T., Singer, M., Aronson, A., & Roiphe, J. (1999). Oedipal dynamics in panic disorder. *Journal of the American Psychoanalytic Association* 47: 773–790.

Caccia, O. (2009). Eating difficulties in early infancy and experience of the combined object. *Psychoanalytic Quarterly* 78: 971–976.

Calef, V. & Weinshel, E. (1981). Some clinical consequences of introjection: Gaslighting. *Psychoanalytic Quarterly* 50: 44–66.

Camerota, M., Willoughby, M. T., Kuhn, L. J., & Blair, C. B. (2018). The Childhood Executive Functioning Inventory (CHEXI): Factor structure, measurment invariance, and correlaters in US preschoolers. *Child Neuropsychology* 24(3): 322–337.

Cao, L., Blackman, J., & Guan, E. (2018). Societal change and language change in China: Language-switching during multilingual dynamic psychotherapy. *Psychoanalytic Psychology* 35: 224–230.

Carroll, L. (1865). *The Alice in Wonderland Omnibus Including Alice's Adventures in Wonderland and through the Looking Glass* (with the Original John Tenniel Illustrations). Reader's Library Classics.

Casey, B., & Jones, R.(2010). Neurobiology of the adolescent breain and behavior: Implications for substance use disorders. *Journal of the American Academy of Child & Adolescent Psychiatry* 49: 1189–1201.

Casey, P. (2017). Review of: Discussion: Mothers and fathers of invention: Developing new family narratives by Laura Kleinerman (2007), in *Journal of Infant, Child & Adolescent Psychotherapy* 6: 156–161. *Couple and Family Psychoanalysis* 7: 117–122.

Casey, B. & Caudle, K. (2013). The teenage brain: Self-control. *Current Directions in Psychological Science* 22(2): 82–87. DOI: 10.1177/0963721413480170.

Casey, B., Giedd, J., & Thomas, K. (2000). Structural and functional brain development and its relation to cognitive development. *Biological Psychology* 54: 241–257.

Cassidy, J. & Shaver, P. (2016). *Handbook of Attachment: Theory, Research, and Clinical Applications–3rd Edition.* New York: Guilford Press.

CDC. (2014). Prevalence of ASD among children aged 8 years—Autism and Developmental Disabilities Monitoring Network. *Morbidity and Mortality Weekly Report of Surveillance Summaries* 63(2): 1–21.

CDC. (2017). *Over half of U.S. teens have had sexual intercourse by age 18, new report shows.* CDC, National Center for Health Statistics, Office of Communication. https://www.cdc.gov/nchs/pressroom/nchs_press_releases/2017/201706_NSFG.htm

CDC. (2021a). *Data and Statistics about ADHD.* https://www.cdc.gov/ncbddd/adhd/data.html

CDC. (2021b). Prevalence and characteristics of Autism Spectrum Disorder among children aged 8 years—Autism and Developmental Disabilities Monitoring Network, 11 Sites, United States, 2018. *Surveillance Summaries* 70(11): 1–16.

CDC. (accessed June 2022). Safe Sleep for Babies. *Vital Signs*. https://www.cdc.gov/vitalsigns/safesleep/index.html#anchor_1508427386

Centers for Disease Control and Prevention. (2010). Increasing prevalence of parent-reported attention-deficit/hyperactivity disorder among children—United States, 2003 and 2007. *MMWR Morbidity & Mortality Weekly Report* 59: 1439–1442.

Charles, N., Cowell, W., & Gulledge, L. (2022). Using the personality Assessment inventory-adolescent in legal settings. *Journal of Personality Assessment* 104: 192–202.

Chatoor, I. (1989). Infantile anorexia nervosa: A developmental disorder of separation and individuation. *Journal of the American Academy of Psychoanalysis* 17: 43–64.

Chazan, S. E. & Kuchirko, Y. A. (2017). The Children's Developmental Play Instrument (CDPI): An extended validity study. *Journal of Infant, Child & Adolescent Psychotherapy* 16: 234–244.

Chess, S. & Thomas, A. (1986). *Temperament in Clinical Practice*. New York: Guilford Press.

Chow, C., Nolte, T., Cohen, D., Fearon, M., & Shmueli-Goetz, Y. (2017). Reflective functioning and adolescent psychological adaptation: The validity of the *Reflective Functioning Scale-Adolescent Version*. *Psychoanalytic Psychology* 34: 404–413. https://www.semanticscholar.org/paper/Reflective-Functioning-and-Adolescent-Psychological-Chow-Nolte/40b5e61502be430cee5144533527b86945107e5a

Climie, E. & Rostad, K. (2011). Test review: Wechsler Adult Intelligence Scale. *Journal of Psychoeducational Assessment* 29: 581–586. DOI: 10.1177/0734282911408707

Clower, V. (1976). Theoretical implications in current views of masturbation in latency girls. *Journal of the American Psychoanalytic Association* 24: 109–125.

Clowes, E. (1996). Oedipal themes in latency. *Psychoanalytic Study of the Child* 51: 436–454.

Colarusso, C. (1990). The third individuation—the effect of biological parenthood on separation-individuation processes in adulthood. *Psychoanalytic Study of the Child* 45: 179–194.

Condon, J. & Corklindale, C. (1997). The correlates of antenatal attachment in pregnant women. *British Journal of Medical Psychology* 70: 359–372.

Conners, C. (1997). *Conners' Rating Scales-Revised: Technical Manual*. Multi-Health Systems.

Conners, C. (2008). *Conners–3rd Edition*. Toronto: Multi-Health Systems.

Constantino, J. (accessed June 2022). *(SRS-2) The Social Responsiveness Scale–2nd Edition*. PAR. https://www.parinc.com/Products/Pkey/426

Cooper, P., Whelan, E., Woogar, M., Morrell, J., & Murray, L. (2004). Association between childhood feeding problems and maternal eating disorder: Role of the family environment. *British Journal of Psychiatry* 184: 210–215.

Côté-Arsenault, D. & Mahlangu, N. (1999). Impact of perinatal loss on the subsequent pregnancy and self: Women's experiences. *Journal of Obstetric, Gynecologic, & Neonatal Nursing* 28(3): 274–282. DOI: 10.1111/j.1552-6909.1999.tb01992.x

Côté-Arsenault, D. & O'Leary, J. (2015). Understanding the experience of pregnancy subsequent to perinatal loss. In: P. Wright, R. Limbo, & P. Black (Eds.), *Perinatal and Pediatric Bereavement* (pp. 169–181). New York: Springer Publishing.

Dahl, K. (2002). In her mother's voice. *Psychoanalytic Study of the Child* 57: 3–23.

Dahl, R. (2004). Adolescent brain development: A period of vulnerabilities and opportunities. Keynote address. *Annals of the New York Academy of Sciences* 1021(1): 1–22. DOI: 10.1196/annals.1308.001.

Dalsimer, K. (1982). Adolescent development—a study of the diary of Anne Frank. *Psychoanalytic Study of the Child* 37: 487–522.

DC: 0-5. (2016) *Diagnostic Classification of Mental Health and Developmental Disorders of Infancy and Early Childhood*. Zero to Three, The National Center. https://www.zerotothree.org

Decter, E., Strauss, J., & Farrelly, P. (1998). *There's Something about Mary*. https://www.imdb.com/title/tt0129387/ (accessed June 2022).

DeMijolla-Mellor, S. (2009). *Le Choix de la Sublimation*. Paris: Le Fil Rouge.

DeMijolla-Mellor, S. (2012). *La Sublimation*. Paris: Que Sais Je: PUF Press.

DeMijolla-Mellor, S. (2015). *Le choix de la sublimation*. Paris: Presses Universitaires de France.

Diamond, M. (1998). Fathers with sons: Psychoanalytic perspectives on "good enough" fathering throughout the life cycle. *Gender and Psychoanalysis* 3: 243–299.

DiPietro, J., Novak, M., Costigan, K., Atella, L., & Reusing, S. (2006). Maternal psychological distress during pregnancy in relation to child development at age two. *Child Development* 77: 573–587.

DiStefano, C. & Dombrowski, S. (2006). Investigating the theoretical structure of the Stanford-Binet–Fifth Edition. *Journal of Psychoeducational Assessment* 24: 123–136.

Dorsey, D. (1996). Castration anxiety or feminine genital anxiety? *Journal of the American Psychoanalytic Association* 44: 283–302.

Drechsler, R., Brem, S., Brandeis, D., Grünblatt, E., Berger, G., & Walitza, S. (2020). ADHD: Current concepts and treatments in children and adolescents. *Neuropediatrics* 51(5): 315–335. DOI: 10.1055/s-0040-1701658. Epub 2020 Jun 19. PMID: 32559806; PMCID: PMC7508636.

DSM-5-TR. (2021). *Diagnostic & Statistical Manual of Mental Disorders, 5th Edition—Text Revision*. Washington, DC: American Psychiatric Association.

Dunn, W. (2002). *Infant/Toddler Sensory Profile*. San Antonio, TX: Psychological Corporation.

Emde, R. (1983). The pre-representational self and its affective core. *Psychoanalytic Study of the Child* 38: 165–192.

Emde, R. (1991). Positive emotions for psychoanalytic theory: Surprises from infancy research and new directions. *Journal of the American Psychoanalytic Association* 39: 5–44.

Emde, R., Biringen, Z., Clyman, R., & Oppenheim, D. (1991). The moral self of infancy: Affective core and procedural knowledge. *Developmental Review* 11(3): 251–270.

Erikson, E. (1950a). *Childhood and Society*. New York: Basic Books.

Erikson, E. (1950b). *Growth and Crises of the Healthy Personality in Identity and the Life Cycle*. New York: International Universities Press.

Erikson, E. (1956). The problem of ego identity. In: *Identity and the Life Cycle*. New York: International Universities Press, 1959.

Erikson, E. (1968). *Identity, Youth & Crisis*. W. W. Norton & Company.

Erikson, E. (1980). *Identity and the Life Cycle*. New York: Norton.

Exner, J. & Erdberg, P. (2005). *The Rorschach Advanced Interpretation, Vol. 2, 3rd Edition*. Hoboken, NJ: Wiley.

Fajardo, B. (1987). Neonatal trauma and early development. *Annual of Psychoanalysis* 15: 233–244.

Faust, J. & Burns, W. (1991). Coding therapist and child interaction: Progress and outcome in play therapy. In C. Schaefer, K. Gitlin, & S. Sandgrund (Eds.), *Play Therapy: Diagnosis and Assessment* (pp. 633–689). New York: Wiley.

Feifer, S. (2018). The neuropsychology of reading disorders: How SLD manifests in reading. In: V. Alfonso & D. Flanagan (Eds.), *Essentials of Specific Learning Disability Identification, 2nd Edition.* Wiley.

Feifer, S. & Gerhardstein-Nader, R. (2015). *Feifer Assessment of Reading: Professional Manual.* Lutz, FL: PAR.

Feinstein, L. & Bynner, J. (2004). The importance of cognitive development in middle childhood for adulthood. *Socioeconomics* 75: 1329–1339.

Feldman, R. & Blatt, S. (1996). Precursors of relatedness and self-definition in mother-infant interaction. In: J. Masling & R. Bornstein (Eds.), *Psychoanalytic Perspectives on Developmental Psychology.* Washington, DC: American Psychiatric Publishing.

Ferone, S. & Biederman, J. (1994). Genetics of attention-deficit hyperactivity disorder. *Child and Adolescent Psychiatric Clinic of North America* 48: 112–114.

Field, T. (2010). Postpartum depression effects on early interactions, parenting, and safety practices. *Infant Behavior and Development* 33: 1–6.

Fifer, W. & Moon, C. (1994). The role of mother's voice in the organization of brain function in the newborn. *International Forum of Psychoanalysis* 3: 198.

Finelli, J., Zeanah, C. H., & Smyke, A. (2019). Attachment disorders in early childhood. In: C. H. Zeanah (Ed.), *Handbook of Infant Mental Health–Fourth Edition.* New York: Guilford Press.

Firth, U. (1991). *Asperger Syndrome in Autism* (pp. 7–92). Cambridge: Cambridge University Press. Originally published as 'Die Autistischen Psychopathen' in Kindesalter," Archiv fur Psychiatrie undNervenkrankenheiten 117 (1944): 76–136. Autistic Psychopathy in Childhood by Hans Asperger.

Flanagan, D., Fiorello, C., & Ortiz, O. (2010). Enhancing practice through application of Cattell-Horn-Carroll theory and research: A "third method" approach to specific learning disability identification. *Psychology in the Schools* 47: 739–760.

Fleming, R. (2015). Working with adoptive parents: Research, theory, and therapeutic interventions. *Journal of Child Psychotherapy* 41: 1–5.

Fonagy, P. (1996). The significance of the developmental of metacognitive control over mental representations in parenting and infant development. *Journal of Clinical Psychoanalysis* 5: 67–86.

Fonagy, P. (2000). Attachment and borderline personality disorder. *Journal of the American Psychoanalytic Association* 48: 1129–1146.

Fonagy, P. & Target, M. (1996). Playing with reality 1: Theory of mind and the normal development of psychic reality. *International Journal of Psychoanalysis* 77 (2): 217–233. PMID: 8771375.

Fonagy, P. & Target, M. (1998). Mentalization and the changing aims of child psychoanalysis. *Psychoanalytic Dialogues* 8: 87–114.

Fonagy, P. & Target, M. (2007a). The rooting of the mind in the body: New links between attachment theory and psychoanalytic thought. *Journal of the American Psychoanalytic Association* 55: 411–456.

Fonagy, P. & Target, M. (2007b). In defense of the bridge to attachment theory: Response to commentaries. *Journal of the American Psychoanalytic Association* 55: 493–501.

Fonagy, P., Steele, M., Moran, G., Steele, H., & Higgitt, A. (1991). Measuring the ghost in the nursery: A summary of the main findings of the Anna Freud Centre—University College London Parent-Child Study. *Bulletin of the Anna Freud Centre* 14: 115–131.

Fonagy, P., Gergely, G., Jurist, E., & Target, M. (2002). *Affect Regulation, Mentalization, and the Development of the Self*. New York: Other Press.

Fonagy, P., Gergely, G., Jurist, E., & Target, M. (2005). *Affect Regulation, Mentalization, and the Development of Self*. Other Press.

Fraiberg, S. (1977). *Insights from the Blind: Comparative Studies of Blind and Sighted Infants*. New York, NY: Basic Books.

Fraiberg, S. & Adelson, E. (1973). Self-representation in language and play: Observations of blind children. *Psychoanalytic Quarterly* 42: 539–562.

Fraiberg, S., Adelman, B., & Shapiro, V. (1975). Ghosts in the nursery. *Journal of the American Academy of Child and Adolescent Psychiatry* 14: 387–421.

Frame, L., Vidrine, S. & Hinojosa, R. (2016). Test review: *Kaufman Test of Educational Achievement–Third Edition*. *Journal of Psychoeducational Assessment* 34: 811–818. DOI: 10.1177/0734282905285244.

Frank, A. (1959). *The Diary of Anne Frank*. London: Pan Books.

Frank, M., Tuber, S., Slade, A., & Garrod, E. (1994). Mothers' fantasy representations and infant security of attachment: A Rorschach study of first pregnancy. *Psychoanalytic Psychology* 11(4): 475–490.

Fresson, M., Meulemans, T., Dardenne, B., & Geurten, M. (2019). Overdiagnosis of ADHD in boys: Stereotype impact on neuropsychological assessment, *Applied Neuropsychology: Child* 8(3): 231–245.

Freud, S. (1900). The interpretation of dreams. *Part I. Standard Edition* 4: 1–338 and *Part II. Standard Edition* 5: 339–625.

Freud, S. (1905). Three essays on the theory of sexuality. *Standard Edition* 7: 125–243.

Freud, S. (1914). On narcissism: An introduction. *Standard Edition* 14: 67–102.

Freud, S. (1916). Some character-types met with in psycho-analytic work. *Standard Edition* 14: 309–333.

Freud, S. (1920). *Beyond the Pleasure Principle. Standard Edition* 18: 1–64.

Freud, S. (1921). *Group Psychology and the Analysis of the Ego. Standard Edition* 18: 65–144.

Freud, S. (1923). *The Ego and the Id. Standard Edition* 19: 1–66.

Freud, S. (1924). The dissolution of the oedipus complex. *Standard Edition* 19: 171–180.

Freud, S. (1926). Inhibitions, symptoms, and anxiety. *Standard Edition* 20: 75–176.

Freud, A. (1936). *The Ego and the Mechanisms of Defence*. London: Hogarth Press.

Freud, A. (1956). *Normality and Pathology in Childhood*. New York: International Universities Press.

Freud, A. (1958). Adolescence. *Psychoanalytic Study of the Child* 12: 255–278.

Freud, A. (1963). The concept of developmental lines. *Psychoanalytic Study of the Child* 18: 245–265.

Freud, A. (2018). *Normality and Pathology in Childhood*. New York: Routledge.

Freud, A. & Burlingham, D. (1942). *War and Children*. London: George Allen & Unwin.

Freud, A. & Burlingham, D. (1944). *Infants without Families*. New York: International University Press.

Friday, N. (1997). *My Mother/My Self: The Daughter's Search for Identity*. Delta Press.

Galenson, E. & Roiphe, H. (1980). The preoedipal development of the boy. *Journal of the American Psychoanalytic Association* 28: 805–827.

Garstein, M. & Rothbart, M. (2003). Studying infant temperament via the Revised Infant Behavior Questionnaire. *Infant Behavior and Development* 166: 1–23.

Gaylor, E., Burnham, M., Goodlin-Jones, B., & Anders, T. (2005). A longitudinal follow-up study of young children's sleep patterns using a developmental classification system. *Behavioral Sleep Medicine* 3: 44–61.

George, C., Kaplan, N., & Main, M. (1984). Adult Attachment Interview. Unpublished article, University of California Berkeley–3rd Edition, 1996. http://www.cmap.polytechnique.fr/~jingrebeccali/research/nlp_files/AAI_Scoring.pdf

Gilmore, K. (2002). Diagnosis, dynamics, and development: Considerations in the psychoanalytic assessment of children with AD/HD. *Psychoanalytic Inquiry* 22: 372–390.

Gilmore, K. & Meersand, P. (2014). *Normal Child and Adolescent Development: A Psychodynamic Primer*. Washington, DC: American Psychiatric Publishing.

Goodlin-Jones, B., & Anders, T. (2005). A longitudinal follow-up study of young children's sleep patterns using a developmental classification system. *Behavioral Sleep Medicine* 3: 44–61.

Goodlin-Jones, B., Burnham, M., Gaylor, E., & Anders, T. (2001). Night waking, sleep-wake organization, and self-soothing in the first year of life. *Journal of Developmental and Behavioral Pediatrics* 22: 226–233.

Grace, K. & Thomas, H. (2010). Test review: Conners 3rd Edition. *Journal of Psychoeducational Assessment* 28: 598–602.

Graham, P. (2004). *Hackers and Painters: Big Ideas from the Computer Age*. O'Reilly Media.

Green, V. (2003). *Emotional Development in Psychoanalysis, Attachment Theory and Neuroscience: Creating Connections*. New York: Routledge.

Green, V. & Joyce, A. (2017). Revised Diagnostic Profile 2016: Revisions, rationale, and further thoughts. *Journal of Infant, Child & Adolescent Psychotherapy* 16: 138–148.

Green, M. & Solnit, A. (1964). Reactions to the threatened loss of a child: A vulnerable child syndrome. *Pediatrics* 34: 58–66.

Greenspan, S. (2003). *The Clinical Interview of the Child–Third Edition*. Washington, DC: American Psychiatric Association.

Greenspan, S. (2004). *Greenspan Social-Emotional Growth Chart*. Bulverde, TX: Psychological Corporation.

Greenspan, S. & DeGangi, G. (2001). Research on the FEAS: Test development, reliability, and validity studies. In S. Greenspan, G. DeGangi, & S. Wieder (Eds.), *The Functional Emotional Assessment Scale (FEAS) for Infancy and Early Childhood. Clinical and Research Applications* (pp. 167–247). Bethesda, MD: Interdisciplinary Council on Developmental and Learning Disorders (ICDL). www.icdl.com

Greenspan, S. & Lieberman, A. (1980). Infancy, mothers, and their interaction: A quantitative clinical approach to developmental assessment. In: S. Greenspan & G. Pollock (Eds.), *The Course of Life; Psychoanalytic Contributions toward Understanding Personality Development, Vol. 1* (pp. 271–312). Madison, CT: International Universities Press.

Grout, L. & Romanoff, B. (2000). The myth of the replacement child: Parents' stories and practices after perinatal death. *Death Studies* 24: 93–113.

Halfon, S. (2017). Play profile constructions: An empirical assessment of children's play in psychodynamic play therapy. *Journal of Infant, Child & Adolescent Psychotherapy* 16: 219–233.

Hall, G. (1904). *Adolescence: Its Psychology and Its Relations to Physiology, Anthropology, Sociology, Sex, Crime, Religion, and Education*. New York: D. Appleton.

Asperger, Hans (1991). "Autistic psychopathy in childhood." In: Uta Frith (Ed.), *Autism and Asperger Syndrome* (pp. 37–92). Cambridge: Cambridge University Press. Originally published as 'Die Autistischen Psychopathen' in Kindesalter," Archiv fur Psychiatrie undNervenkrankenheiten 117 (1944): 76–136.

Harrison, A. (2017). Altruism as reparation of mismatch or disruption in the self. *Psychoanalytic Inquiry* 37: 464–473.

Hartmann, H. (1955). Notes on the theory of sublimation. *Psychoanalytic Study of the Child* 10: 9–29.

Hartmann, H. (1964). *Essays in Ego Psychology*. New York: International Universities Press.

Havens, L. (1980). Explorations in the uses of language in psychotherapy: Counterprojective statements. *Contemporary Psychoanalysis* 16: 53–67.

Hesse, E. & Main, M. (2000). Disorganized infant, child, and adult attachment: Collapse in behavioral and attentional strategies. *Journal of the American Psychoanalytic Association* 48: 1097–1127.

Hodges, J. (1989). Aspects of the relationship to self and objects in early maternal deprivation and adoption. *Bulletin of the Anna Freud Centre* 12: 5–27.

Hofer, M. (2014). The emerging synthesis of development and evolution: A new biology for psychoanalysis. *Neuropsychoanalysis* 16: 3–22.

Hoffman, L. (2005). Freud's theories about sex relevant as ever. *Psychiatric News* 40: 18.

Hoffman, L. (2013). Review of reconceptualizing female and male: *Women's Bodies in Psychoanalysis*, by Rosemary M. Balsam. New York: Routledge, 2012. *Journal of the American Psychoanalytic Association* 61: 419–432.

Hollis, C., Hall, C.L., Guo, B., Boadu, J., Groom, M.J., Brown, N, Kaylor-Hughes, C. Moldavsky, M., Valentine, A.Z., Walker, G. M., Daley, D., Sayal, K., & Morriss, R. (April 26, 2018). The impact of computerized test of attention and activity (QbTest) on diagnositc decision-making in children and young people with suspected attention deficit hyperactivity disorder; single-blind randomized controlled trial. *Journal of Child Psychological Psychiatry*. DOI 10.1111/jcpp.12921.

Howe, P. & Silvern, L. (1981). Behavioral observation of children during play therapy: Preliminary development of a research instrument. *Journal of Personality Assessment* 45(6): 168–182.

Huang, X., Wang, H., Zhang, L., & Liu, X., (2010). Co-sleeping and children's sleep in China. *Biological Rhythm Research* 41(3): 169–181. DOI: 10.1080/09291011003687940. https://www.tandfonline.com/action/showCitFormats?doi=10.1080%2F09291011003687940

Hughes, P., Turton, P., Hopper, E., McGaulley, G., & Fonagy, P. (2004). Factors associated with the unresolved classification of the Adult Attachment Interview in women who have suffered stillbirth. *Development and Psychopathology* 16: 215–230.

Huprich, S. (Ed.). (2006). *Rorschach Assessment of the Personality Disorders*. Mahwah, NJ: Lawrence Erlbaum Associates.

Huprich, S., Auerbach, J., Porcerelli, J., & Bupp, L. (2016). Sidney Blatt's object relations inventory: Contributions and future directions. *Journal of Personality Assessment* 98(1): 30–43. DOI: 10.1080/00223891.2015.1099539. Epub 2015 Nov 11. PMID: 26559876.

Huth-Bocks, A., Krause, K., Ahlfs-Dunn, S., Gallagher, E., & Scott, S. (2013). Relational trauma and posttraumatic stress symptoms among pregnant women. *Psychodynamic Psychiatry* 41(2): 277–301.

ICD-10-CM: *International Classification of Diseases, version 10* (2021). American Medical Association.

Individuals with Disabilities Education Improvement Act, (IDEA) (2004). *20 U.S. Code Section 1400.*

IRED. (2022). E. Papiasvili (Chief Global Ed.). *The International Inter-Regional Encyclopedic Dictionary of Psychoanalysis.* https://www.ipa.world/IPA/en/en/ Encyclopedic_Dictionary/English/Home.aspx

Izard, C., Fantauzzo C., Castle, J., Haynes, O. Rayias, M., & Putnam, P. (1995). The ontogeny and significance of infants' facial expressions in the first 9 months of life. *Developmental Psychology* 31(6): 997–1013.

J.C.F. (1927). Review in pep-web.org: *Hymen or the Future of Marriage*, by Norman Haire. London: Kegan.

Jackson, S. (2007). *The Lottery.* Perfect Learning. (Originally published in 1948). https://www.amazon.com/Lottery-Tale-Blazers-Shirley-Jackson/dp/1563127873/ ref=sr_1_3?keywords=shirley+jackson+the+lottery&qid=1654030661&sprefix= jackson+the+lottery%2Caps%2C88&sr=8-3

Jacobson, E. (1961). Adolescent Moods and the Remodeling of Psychic Structures in Adolescence. *Psychoanalytic Study of the Child* 16: 164–183.

Jacobson, E. (1964). *The Self and the Object World.* New York: International Universities Press.

Jacobson, E. (1976). Ways of female superego formation and the female castration conflict. *Journal of the American Psychoanalytic Association* 29: 427–446.

Joffe, W. & Sandler, J. (1968). Comments on the psychoanalytic psychology of adaptation, with special reference to the role of affects and the representational world. *International Journal of Psychoanalysis* 49: 445–454.

Johnson, A. & Szurek, S. (1952). The genesis of antisocial acting out in children and adults. *Psychoanalytic Quarterly* 21: 323–343.

Jones, E. (1922). Notes on Dr. Abraham's article on the female castration complex. *International Journal of Psychoanalysis* 3: 327–328.

Kagan, J. (1994). *Galen's Prophecy: Temperament in Human Nature.* New York: Basic Books.

Kanner, L. (1943). Autistic disturbances of affective contact. *Nervous Child: Journal of Psychopathology, Psychotherapy, Mental Hygiene, and Guidance of the Child* 2: 217–250.

Kaplan, A. (accessed April 2022). How to teach boys to pee standing up. *Potty Genius.* https://pottygenius.com/blogs/blog/how-to-teach-boys-to-pee-standing-up

Karme, L. (1981). A clinical report of penis envy: Its multiple meanings and defensive function. *Journal of the American Psychoanalytic Association* 29: 427–446.

Kaufman, A. & Kaufman, N. (2014). *Kaufman Test of Educational Achievement–Third Edition.* Bloomington, MN: NCS Pearson.

Kaufman, A. & Kaufman, N. (2018). *Kaufman Assessment Battery for Children–Second Edition, Normative Update.* Circle Pines, MN: Pearson (AGS).

Kazda, L., Bell, K., Thomas, R., McGeechan, K., Sims, R., & Barratt, A. (2021). Overdiagnosis of attention-deficit/hyperactivity disorder in children and adolescents: A systematic scoping review. *National Library of Medicine* 4(4): e215335. DOI: 10.1001/jamanetworkopen.2021.5335. https://pubmed.ncbi.nlm.nih.gov/33843998/

Kelly, S., Gryczynski, J., Mitchell, S., Kirk, A., O'Grady, K. & Schwartz, R. (2014). Validity of brief screening instrument for adolescent tobacco, alcohol, and drug use. *Pediatrics* 133: 819–826.

Keren, M. (2019). Eating and feeding disorders in early childhood. In: C. Zeanah (Ed.), *Handbook of Infant Mental Health–Fourth Edition*. New York: Guilford.

Kernberg, O. (1975). *Borderline Conditions and Pathological Narcissism*. New York: Basic Books.

Kernberg, O. (1985). *Borderline Conditions and Pathological Narcissism*. Rowman & Littlefield.

Kernberg, O. (1998). The diagnosis of narcissistic and antisocial pathology in adolescence. *Annals of the American Society of Adolescent Psychiatry* 22: 169–186.

Kernberg, O. (2004). *Borderline Conditions and Pathological Narcissism*. New York: Aronson.

Kernberg, O. (2006). Identity: Recent findings and clinical implications. *Psychoanalytic Quarterly* 75: 969–1003.

Kernberg, P., Chazan, S., & Normandin, L. (1998). The children's play therapy instrument (CPTI): Description, development, and reliability studies. *Journal of Psychotherapy Practice and Research* 7(3): 196–207.

Kernberg, P., Weiner, A., & Bardenstein, K. (2000). *Personality Disorders in Children and Adolescence*. New York: Basic Books.

Kipke, M. (1999). *Forum on Adolescence Research*. Council and Institute of Medicine. http://www.nap.edu/catalog/9634.html

Kleiger, J. (1999). *Disordered Thinking and the Rorschach: Theory, Research, and Differential Diagnosis*. Hillsdale, NJ: The Analytic Press.

Kliman, G. (2018). Reflective network therapy for childhood autism and childhood PTSD. *Neuropsychoanalysis* 20(2): 73–86. DOI: 10.1080/15294145.2018.1535279.

Kliman, G. & Rosenfeld, A. (1980). *Responsible Parenthood: The Child's Psyche Through the Six-Year Pregnancy—A Unique and Comprehensive Psychological Guide to the First Six Years of Life*. New York: Holt, Rinehart & Winston.

Knight, R. (1954). Borderline states. In: M. Stone (Ed.), *Essential Papers on Borderline Disorders: 100 Years at the Border*. New York: NYU Press, 1986.

Knight, R. (2005). The process of attachment and autonomy in latency: A longitudinal study of ten children. *Psychoanalytic Study of the Child* 60: 178–210.

Kohut, H. (1971). *The Analysis of the Self*. New York: International Universities Press.

Kokotos, F. (2009). The vulnerable child syndrome. *Pediatric Review* 30(5): 193–194. DOI: 10.1542/pir.30.5.193

Kosma, M. (2021). What is clitoridectomy? https://rightforeducation.org/2021/03/22/what-is-clitoridectomy/

Kris, E. (1956a). The recovery of childhood memories in psychoanalysis. *Psychoanalytic Study of the Child* 11: 54–88.

Kris, E. (1956b). On some vicissitudes of insight in psychoanalysis. *International Journal of Psychoanalysis* 37: 445.

Krohn, A. (1978a). *Hysteria: The Elusive Neurosis* (p. 244). New York: International Universities Press.

Krohn, A. (1978b). Female oedipal phase development [including chart of Nagera's phases]. In: *Hysteria: The Elusive Neurosis* (p. 244). New York: International Universities Press.

Kubie, L. (2011). The drive to become both sexes. *Psychoanalytic Quarterly* 80: 369–439.

Kuhn, D. (2006). Do cognitive changes accompany developments in the adolescent brain? *Perspectives on Psychological Science* 1: 59–67.

Kumin, I. (1995). *Pre-object Relatedness: Early Attachment and the Psychoanalytic Situation*. New York: Guilford Press.

Lachar, D. & Gruber, C. (1995). *Personality Inventory for Youth (PIY) Manual. Administration and Interpretation Guide—Technical Guide*. Los Angeles: Western Psychological Services.

Lachar, D. & Gruber, C. (2001). *Personality Inventory for Children–Second Edition (PIC-2): Standard Format and Behavioral Summary Manual*. Los Angeles: Western Psychological Services.

Lachmann, F. (2004). Identity and self: Historical antecedents and developmental precursors. *International Forum of Psychoanalysis* 13: 246–253.

Langberg, J., Vaughn, A., Brinkman, W., Froehlich T., & Epstein, J. (2010). Clinical utility of the Vanderbilt ADHD Rating Scale for ruling out comorbid learning disorders. *Pediatrics* 126: 1033–1038.

Laron, Z. (2010). Age at first ejaculation (spermarche)—the overlooked milestone in male development. *Pediatric Endocrinology Review* 7(3): 256–257.

Lax, R. (1997). Boys' envy of mother and the consequences of this narcissistic mortification. *Psychoanalytic Study of the Child* 52: 118–139.

Leark, R., Dupuy, T., Greenberg, C., Kindschi, C., & Hughes, S. (2020). *T.O.V.A. Professional Manual*. Langley and Washington, DC: TOVA Company.

Leon, I. (1996). Revising psychoanalytic understandings of perinatal loss. *Psychoanalytic Psychology* 13: 161–176.

Lerner, H. (1976). Parental mislabeling of female genitals as a determinant of penis envy and learning inhibitions in women. *Journal of the American Psychoanalytic Association* 24(s): 269–283.

Lester, E. & Notman, M. (1986). Pregnancy, developmental crisis, and object relations: Psychoanalytic considerations. *International Journal of Psychoanalysis* 67: 357–365.

Levin, S. (1969). A common type of marital incompatibility. *Journal of the American Psychoanalytic Association* 17: 421–436.

Levin, F. (2002). Attention deficit disorder: A neuropsychoanalytic sketch. *Psychoanalytic Inquiry* 22: 336–354.

Levinson, D. (1986). *The Seasons of a Man's Life*. Ballantine Books.

Levy, K. & Blatt, S. (1999). Attachment theory and psychoanalysis: Further differentiation within insecure attachment patterns. *Psychoanalytic Inquiry* 19: 541–575.

Li, X. (2018). *Keeping Top-Notch Scores—A Kind of Defense Mechanism with Contemporary Chinese Characteristics?* Anhui Province, China. Unpublished.

Lichtenberg, J. (2019). Close encounters in intimacy. *Psychoanalytic Inquiry* 39: 231–233.

Liebman, S. & Abell, S. (2000). The forgotten parent no more. A psychoanalytic reconsideration of fatherhood. *Psychoanalytic Psychology* 17: 88–105.

Lingiardi, V. & McWilliams, N. (Eds.). (2017). *Psychodynamic Diagnostic Manual: PDM-2–2nd Edition*. New York: Guilford Press.

Loewald, H. (1988). *Sublimation: Inquiries into Theoretical Psychoanalysis*. New Haven, CT: Yale University Press.

Lord, C. & Mutter, M. (2012). *Autism Diagnostic Observational Schedule–2nd Edition*. WPS. https://www.wpspublish.com/ados-2-autism-diagnostic-observation-schedule-second-edition

Luna, B., Garver, K., Urban, T., Lazar, N., & Sweeney, J. (2004). Maturation of cognitive processes from late childhood to adulthood. *Child Development* 75: 1357–1372.

Macgregor, J. (1991). Identification with the victim. *Psychoanalytic Quarterly* 60: 53–68.

Mahler, M. (1968). *On Human Symbiosis and the Vicissitudes of Individuation*. New York: International Universities Press.

Mahler, M. (1971). A study of the separation-individuation process and its possible application to borderline phenomena in the psychoanalytic situation. *Psychoanalytic Study of the Child* 26: 403–424.

Mahler, M. (1972). On the first three subphases of the separation-individuation process. *International Journal of Psychoanalysis* 53: 333–338.

Mahler, M. (1974). Symbiosis and individuation—the psychological birth of the human infant. *Psychoanalytic Study of the Child* 29: 89–106.

Mahler, M. (1975). On human symbiosis and the vicissitudes of individuation. *Journal of American Psychoanalytic Association* 23: 740–763.

Mahler, M., Pine, F., & Bergman, A. (1975). *The Psychological Birth of the Human Infant*. New York: Basic Books.

Mahon, E. J. (1991). The "dissolution" of the oedipus complex: A neglected cognitive factor. *Psychoanalytic Quarterly* 60: 628–634.

Main, M. (2000). The organized categories of infant, child, and adult attachment: Flexible vs. inflexible attention under attachment-related stress. *Journal of the American Psychoanalytic Association* 48: 1055–1095.

Main, M., & George, C. (1979). Social interactions of young, abused children: Approach, avoidance, and aggression. *Child Development* 50: 306–318.

Main, M. & Hesse, E. (1990). Parents' unresolved traumatic experiences are related to infant disorganized attachment status: Is frightened and/or frightening parental behavior the linking mechanism? In M. Greenberg, D. Cicchetti, & E. Cummings (Eds.), *Attachment in the Preschool Years: Theory, Research, and Intervention* (pp. 161–182). Chicago, IL: University of Chicago Press.

Main, M., Kaplan, N., & Cassidy, J. (1985). Security in infancy, childhood, and adulthood: A move to the level of representation. *Monographs of the Society for Research in Child Development* 50(1–2): 66–104.

Malberg, N. & Pretorius, I. (2017). Anna Freud's *Diagnostic Profile*: Then and now. *Journal of Infant, Child & Adolescent Psychotherapy* 16: 127–130.

Marcus, I. (1973). The experience of separation-individuation in infancy and its reverberations through the course of life—2. Adolescence and maturity. *Journal of the American Psychoanalytic Association* 21: 155–167.

Marcus, I. & Francis, J. (1975a). Masturbation: A developmental view. In: *Masturbation from Infancy to Senescence* (pp. 22–24). New York: International Universities Press.

Marcus, I. & Francis, J. (1975b). *Masturbation: From Infancy to Senescence*. New York: International Universities Press.

Martinez, G. (2020). Trends and patterns in menarche in the United States: 1995 through 2013–2017. *National Health Statistics Report* 146: 1–12. https://www.cdc.gov/nchs/data/nhsr/nhsr146-508.pdf (accessed June 2020).

Masling, J. & Bornstein, R. (1996). *Psychoanalytic Perspectives on Developmental Psychology: Empirical Studies of Psychoanalytical Theories*. American Psychological Association.

Mather, N. & Wendling, B. (2018). How SLD manifests in writing. In: V. Alfonso & D. Flanagan (Eds.), *Essentials of Specific Learning Disability Identification–2nd Edition*. Wiley.

Mayo Clinic. (2022). Colic. https://www.mayoclinic.org/diseases-conditions/colic/symptoms-causes/syc-20371074 (accessed March 2022).

Mazzocco, M. (2007). Issues in defining mathematical learning disabilities and difficulties. In: D. Berch & M. Mazzocco (Eds.), *Why Is Math So Hard for Some Children: The Nature and Origins of Mathematical Learning Difficulties and Disabilities* (pp. 29–47). Baltimore, MD: Brookes.

McCarthy, J. (1995). Adolescent character formation and psychoanalytic theory. *American Journal of Psychoanalysis* 55: 245–267.

McDevitt, J. (1975). *Separation and individuation.* Presentation to Louisiana State University Department of Psychiatry, New Orleans.

McDevitt, J. (1985). The emergence of hostile aggression and its defensive and adaptive modifications during the separation-individuation process. In: H. Blum (Ed.), *Defense & Resistance* (pp. 273–300). New York: International Universities Press.

McGehee, R. (2021). The effect of marijuana use on personality development in adolescence and young adulthood. *Psychoanalytic Study of the Child* 74: 265–279.

Meers, D. (1973). Psychoanalytic research and intellectual functioning of ghetto-reared, Black children. *Psychoanalytic Study of the Child* 25: 209–230.

Meers, D. (1974). Traumatic and cultural distortions of psychoneurotic symptoms in a Black ghetto. *Annual of Psychoanalysis* 2: 368–386.

Meers, D. (1975). Masturbation and the Ghetto. In: I. Marcus & J. Francis *Masturbation from Infancy to Senescence.* New York: International Universities Press.

Meersand, P. (2011). Psychological testing and the analytically trained child psychologist. *Psychoanalytic Psychologist* 28: 117–131.

Meissner, W. (2009). The genesis of the self I: The self and its parts. *Psychoanalytic Review* 96: 187–217.

Meltzoff, A. (1995). What infant memory tells us about infantile amnesia: Long-term recall and deferred imitation. *Journal of Experimental Child Psychology* 59(3): 497–515. DOI: 10.1006/jecp.1995.1023.

Menninger, K. (1935). A psychoanalytic study of the significance of self-mutilations. *Psychoanalytic Quarterly* 4: 408–466.

Millon, T., Millon, C., Davis, R., & Grossman, S. (2006). *Millon Adolescent Clinical Inventory Manual–2nd Edition.* Minneapolis, MN: National Computer Systems.

Moore, M. (1989). Disturbed attachment in children: A factor in sleep disturbance, altered dream production and immune dysfunction 1: Not safe to sleep—chronic sleep disturbance in anxious attachment. *Journal of Child Psychotherapy* 15: 99–111.

Morey, L. (2007). *Personality Assessment Inventory-Adolescent (PAI-A) Professional Manual.* Psychological Assessment Resources.

Murez, C. (2021). Big Rise in U.S. Teens Identifying as Gay, Bisexual. *Health Day.* https://www.webmd.com/sex-relationships/news/20210615/big-rise-in-us-teens-identifying-as-gay-bisexual (accessed June 2021).

Murray, L., Halligan, S., & Cooper, P. (2019). Postnatal depression and young children's development. In: C. Zeanah (Ed.), *Handbook of Infant Mental Health–Fourth Edition.* New York: Guilford.

Murrie, D. & Cornell, D. (2002). Psychopathy screening of incarcerated juveniles: A comparison of measures. *Psychological Assessment* 14: 390–396.

Nagera, H. (1975). Day-care centers: Red light, green light, or amber light. *International Review of Psychoanalysis* 2: 121–136.

National Institute on Drug Abuse. (2014). NIDA Launches Two Brief Online Validated Adolescent Substance Use Screening Tools. https://nida.nih.gove/nidamed-medical-health-professinals/screening-tools

NCS Pearson. (2020). *Wechsler Individual Achievement Test, 4th Edition.* Bloomington, MN: Pearson.

Newcorn, J., & Halperin, J. (1994). Comorbidity among disruptive behavior disorders: Impact on severity, impairment, and response to treatment. *Child & Adolescent Psychiatric Clinics of North America* 3: 227–252.

NIH (2021). What Are the Treatments for Autism? https://www.nichd.nih.gov/health/topics/autism/conditioninfo/treatments

Nikolas, M. & Burt, S. (2010). Genetic and environmental influences on ADHD symptom dimensions of inattention and hyperactivity: A meta-analysis. *Journal of Abnormal Psychology* 119(1): 1–17.

Novick, J. & Novick, K. (2016). *Freedom to Choose: Two Systems of Self-Regulation.* IpBooks.

Novick, J. & Novick, K. (2022). *Adolescent Casebook.* International Psychoanalytic Books.

Odukogbe, A., Afolabi, B., Oluwasomidoyin, O., & Adeyanju, A. (2017). Female genital mutilation/cutting in Africa. *Translational Andrology and Urology* 6(2): 138–148. DOI: 10.21037/tau.2016.12.01. PMCID: PMC5422681; PMID: 28540220, https://www.ncbi.nlm.nih.gov/pmc/articles/PMC5422681/

Offer, D. & Schonert-Reichl, K. (1992). Debunking the myths of adolescence: Findings from recent research. *Journal of the American Academy of Child and Adolescent Psychiatry* 31: 1003–1014.

Oinffer, D. (1971). Rebellion and anti-social behavior. *American Journal of Psychoanalysis* 31: 13–19.

O'Leary, J. & Gaziano, C. (2011). The experience of adult siblings born after loss. *New Directions in Relational Psychoanalysis and Psychotherapy* 5: 246–272.

O'Leary, J. & Thorwich, C. (2008). Attachment to the unborn child and parental mental representations of pregnancy following perinatal loss. *New Directions in Relational Psychoanalysis and Psychotherapy* 2: 292–320.

Olesker, W. (1984). Sex differences in 2- and 3- year-olds: Mother-child relations, peer relations, and peer play. *Psychoanalytic Psychology* 1: 269–288.

Papiasvili, E. & Mayers, L. (2017). Postpartum depression and attachment: Is anybody here? *International Forum of Psychoanalysis* 26: 22–28.

Parens, H. (1973). Aggression: A reconsideration. *Journal of the American Psychoanalytic Association* 21: 34–60.

Parens, H. (1990). On the girl's psychosexual development: Reconsiderations suggested from direct observation. *Journal of the American Psychoanalytic Association* 38: 743–772.

Parens, H. (1991). A view of the development of hostility in early life. *Journal of the American Psychoanalytic Association* 39: 75–108.

Parens, H., Pollock, M., Stern, J., & Kramer, S. (1976). On the girl's entry into the oedipus complex. *Journal of the American Psychoanalytic Association* 24(S): 79–107.

Parker, K. (2008). *Save the Males: Why Men Matter; Why Women Should Care.* Random House.

Paul, M., Hohman, E., Loken, E., Savage, J., Anzman-Frasca, S., Carper, P., & Marini, M. (2017). Mother-infant room-sharing and sleep outcomes in the INSIGHT Study. *Pediatrics* 140(1): e20170122. https://www.ncbi.nlm.nih.gov/pmc/articles/PMC5495531/

Paus, T. (2005). Mapping brain maturation and cognitive development during adolescence. *Trends in Cognitive Science* 9: 60–68.

Pediatric Endocrine Society. (2020). *Delayed Puberty – Boys.* https://pedsendo.org/patient-resource/delayed-puberty-boys/

Person, E. (1986). Male sexuality and power. *Psychoanalytic Inquiry* 6: 3–25.

Piaget, J. (1952). *The Origins of Intelligence in Children.* New York: International Universities Press.

Piaget, J. (Ed.). (1977). *The Development of Thought: Equilibration of Cognitive Structures.* Viking Press.

Piaget, J. & Inhelder, B. (1969). *The Psychology of the Child.* New York: Basic Books.

Pine, F. (2004). Mahler's concepts of "symbiosis" and separation-individuation: Revisited, reevaluated, refined. *Journal of the American Psychoanalytic Association* 52: 511–533.

Pines, D. (1972). Pregnancy and motherhood: Interaction between fantasy and reality. *British Journal of Medical Psychology* 43: 333–343.

Pines, D. (1982). The relevance of early psychic development to pregnancy and abortion. *International Journal of Psychoanalysis* 63: 311–319.

Pines, D. (1990). Pregnancy, miscarriage, and abortion. A psychoanalytic perspective. *International Journal of Psychoanalysis* 71: 301–307.

Raphling, D. (1989). Fetishism in a woman. *Journal of the American Psychoanalytic Association* 37: 465–491.

Raphling, D. L. (1998). Aggression: Its relation to desire and self-interest. *Journal of the American Psychoanalytic Association* 46: 797–811.

Reinberg, S. (2022). Obesity rates continue to climb among U.S. kids, teens. https://www.webmd.com\diet\obesity\news\20220725\obesity-rates-continue-to-climb-among-us-kids-teens#1

Richters, J., Arnold, L., Jensen, P., Abikoff, H., Conners, C., Greenhill, L., Hechtman, L., Hinshaw, S., Pelham, W., & Swanson, J. (1995). NIMH collaborative multistate multimodal treatment study of children with ADHD: I. Background and rationale. *Journal of the American Academy of Child and Adolescent Psychiatry* 34(8): 987–1000. https://pubmed.ncbi.nlm.nih.gov/7665456/

Ringwalt, S. (2008). *Developmental Screening and Assessment Instruments with an Emphasis on Social and Emotional Development for Young Children Ages Birth through Five.* Chapel Hill, NC: The University of North Carolina FPG Child Development Institute – National Early Childhood Technical Assistance Center.

Roberts, G. (2005). *Roberts Apperception Test for Children-2.* Los Angeles, CA: Western Psychological Services.

Roebuck, H., Freigang, C., & Barry, J. (2016). Continuous performance tasks: Not just about sustaining attention. *Journal of Speech Language and Hearing Research* 59: 501–510.

Roid, G. (2003). *Stanford-Binet Intelligence Scale–Fifth Edition.* Chicago, IL: Riverside.

Roiphe, H. & Galenson, E. (1972). Early genital activity and the castration complex. *Psychoanalytic Quarterly* 41: 334–347.

Rother, E. (2001). Some important contributions of the stepfather to the psychological development of the boy. In: S. Cath & M. Shopper (Eds.), *Stepparenting: Creating and Recreating Families in America Today* (pp. 36–38). Hillsdale, NJ: The Analytic Press.

Sabrina, D. & Burns, T. (2016). Wechsler Intelligence Scale for Children-V: Test review. *Applied Neuropsychology of the Child* 5: 156–160. DOI:10.1080/21622965.2015.1015337.

Saks, E. (2007). *The Center Cannot Hold: My Journey through Madness.* Hachette Books.

Salomonsson, B. (2013). An infant's experience of postnatal depression. Towards a psychoanalytic model. *Journal of Child Psychotherapy* 39: 137–155.

Samish, C. (2006). Alternate pathways to parenthood. *Journal of the American Psychoanalytic Association* 54: 1241–1244.

Samuel, S. & Akhtar, S. (2009). The *Identity Consolidation Inventory (ICI)*: Development and application of a questionnaire for assessing the structurization of individual identity. *American Journal of Psychoanalysis* 69: 53–61.

Sandler, J. (1960). On the concept of superego. *Psychoanalytic Study of the Child* 15: 128–162.

Sandler, J. (2003). On attachment to internal objects. *Psychoanalytic Inquiry* 23: 12–26.

Sandler, J. & Joffe, W. (1966). On skill and sublimation. *Journal of the American Psychoanalytic Association* 14: 335–355.

Sarnoff, C. (1976). *Latency*. New York: Aronson, pp. 4–11, 20–36.

Sarnoff, C. (1989). *Latency*. Northvale, NJ: Aronson.

Schechter, M. D. (1967). Psychoanalytic theory as it relates to adoption. *Journal of the American Psychoanalytic Association* 15: 695–708.

Schechter, D. (2017). On traumatically skewed intersubjectivity. *Psychoanalytic Inquiry* 37: 251–264.

Scheeringa, M. (2003). Research diagnostic criteria for infants and preschool children: The process and empirical support. *Journal of the American Academy of Child & Adolescent Psychiatry* 42: 1504–1512.

Schellinski, K. (2014). Who am I? *Journal of Analytical Psychology* 59: 189–210.

Schmidt, S. & Kenworthy, T. (1986). Cocaine Caused Bias's Death, Autopsy Reveals: Dose Said to Trigger Heart Failure. *Los Angeles Times*. https://www.latimes.com/archives/la-xpm-1986-06-25-sp-20106-story.html

Schrank, F., Mather, N., & McGrew, K. (2014). *Woodcock-Johnson IV Tests of Achievement*. Rolling Meadows, IL: Riverside.

Schriber, R. & Guyer, A. (2016). Adolescent neurobiological susceptibility to social context. *Developmental Cognitive Neuroscience* 19: 1–18.

Schur, M. (1966). *The Id and the Regulatory Principles of Mental Functioning*. New York: International Universities Press.

Settlage, C. (1964). Psychoanalytic theory in relation to the nosology of childhood psychic disorders. *Journal of the American Psychoanalytic Association* 12: 776–801.

Shalin, L. (1983). Phallic integration and male identity development: Aspects of the importance of the father relation to boys in the latency period. *Scandinavian Psychoanalytic Review* 6: 21–42.

Sharma, S. & Fowler, J. (2018). Restoring hope for the future: Mentalization-based therapy in the treatment of a suicidal adolescent. *Psychoanalytic Study of the Child* 71: 55–75.

Sherkow, S., Kamens, S., Megyes, M., & Loewenthal, L. (2009). A clinical study of the intergenerational transmission of eating disorders from mothers to daughters. *Psychoanalytic Study of the Child* 64: 153–189.

Shopper, M. (1989). Toiletry revisited: An integration of developing concepts and the father's role in toilet training. In: S. Cath, A. Gurlitt, & L. Ginsberg (Eds.), *Fathers and Their Families*. Hillsdale, NJ: Analytic Press.

Shopper, M. (2001). Incest: What is it, and how did it come to be? In: S. Cath & M. Shopper (Eds.), *Stepparenting: Creating and Recreating Families in America Today*. Hillsdale, NJ: Analytic Press.

Siddiqui, A. & Hagglof, B. (2000). Does maternal prenatal attachment predict postnatal mother-infant interaction? *Early Human Development* 59: 13–25.

Singletary, W. (2019). Asperger's children: Psychodynamics, aetiology, diagnosis, and treatment. *Psychoanalytic Quarterly* 88: 647–657.

Skerrett, P. (2012). Puberty Starts Earlier in Many American Boys. *Harvard Health Publishing.* https://www.health.harvard.edu/blog/puberty-starts-earlier-in-many-american-boys-201210225437

Slade, A., Cohen, L., Sadler, S., & Miller, M. (2009). The psychology and psychopathology of pregnancy. In C. Zeanah (Ed.), *Handbook of Infant Mental Health* (pp. 22–39). New York: Guilford.

Solms, M. (2021a). *The Hidden Spring: A Journey to the Source of Consciousness.* New York: W.W. Norton & Co.

Solms, S. (2021b). Revision of drive theory. *Journal of the American Psychoanalytic Association* 69: 1033–1091.

Somerville, L. & Casey, B. (2010). Developmental neurobiology of cognitive control and motivation systems. *Current Opinion in Neurobiology* 20: 236–241.

Somerville, L., Hare, T., & Casey, B. (2011). Frontostriatal maturation predicts cognitive control failure in appetitive cues in adolescents. *Journal of Cognitive Neuroscience* 23: 2123–2134.

Sophocles. (n.d. 420 BCE). *Oedipus the King.* https://www.slps.org/site/handlers/filedownload.ashx?FileName=Sophocles-Oedipus.pdf&dataid=25126&moduleinstanceid=22453#:~:text=Oedipus%20the%20King%2C%20also%20called,expression%20of%20Greek%20tragic%20drama

Sotelo-Dinoga, M., Flanagan, D., & Alfonso, V. (2018). Overview of specific learning disabilities. In: Kaufman, A. & Kaufman, L. (Eds.), *Essentials of Specific Learning Disability Identification–2nd Edition.* Hoboken, NJ: Wiley.

Speranza, A., Malberg, N., & Steele, M. (2018). Review of the chapter *Mental Health and Developmental Disorders in Infancy and Early Childhood.* In: N. McWilliams & N. Lingiardi (2017), *PDM-2. Psychoanalytic Psychology* 35: 328–338.

Spitz, R. (1945). Hospitalism: An inquiry into the genesis of psychiatric conditions in early childhood. *Psychoanalytic Study of the Child* 1: 53–74.

Spitz, R. (1951). The psychogenic diseases in infancy—An attempt at their etiologic classification. *Psychoanalytic Study of the Child* 6: 255–275.

Spitz, R. (1957). *No and Yes: On the Genesis of Human Communication.* New York: International Universities Press.

Spitz, R. & Cobliner, G. (1966). *The First Year of Life: A Psychoanalytic Study of Normal and Deviant Development of Object Relations.* New York: International Universities Press.

Spitz, R. & Wolf, K. (1946). Anaclitic depression—An inquiry into the genesis of psychiatric conditions in early childhood. *Psychoanalytic Study of the Child* 2: 313–342.

Sroufe, L. (1989). Relationships, self, and individual adaptation. In: A. Sameroff & R. Emde (Eds.), *Relationship Disturbances in Early Childhood.* New York: Basic Books.

Sroufe, A. (2002). Attachment in developmental perspective. *Journal of Infant, Child & Adolescent Psychotherapy* 2: 19–25.

Stambler, M. (2017). 100 years of adolescence and its prehistory from cave to computer. *Psychoanalytic Study of the Child* 70: 22–39.

Star Trek TV Show. (1966–1969). https://www.imdb.com/title/tt0060028/

Stedman, J., Hatch, J., & Schoenfeld L. (2001). Internship directors' valuation of pre-internship preparation in test-based assessment and psychotherapy. *Professional Psychology: Research and Practice* 32: 421–424.

Steele, M., Steele, H., & Model, E. (1991). Links across generations: Predicting parent-child relationship patterns from structured interviews with expectant parents. *Bulletin of the Anna Freud Centre* 14: 95–113.

Steinberg, L. (2010). A behavioral scientist looks at the science of adolescent brain development. *Brain and Cognition* 72(1): 160–164.

Steinberg, Z. & Patterson, C. (2017). Giving voice to the psychological in the NICU: A relational model. *Journal of Infant, Child & Adolescent Psychotherapy* 16: 25–44.

Stern, D. (1985). *The Interpersonal World of the Infant: A View from Psychoanalysis and Developmental Psychology.* New York: Basic Books.

Stern, D. (1991). Maternal representations: A clinical and subjective phenomenological view. *Infant Mental Health Journal* 12(3): 174–186.

Stern, D. (1995). *The Motherhood Constellation. A Unified View of Parent-Infant Psychotherapy.* New York: Basic Books.

Stokes J., Pogge. D., & Archer, R. (2018). Comparisons between the Minnesota Multiphasic Personality Inventory-Adolescent-Restructured Form (MMPI-A RF) and MMPI-A in adolescent psychiatric inpatients. *Psychological Assessment* 30(3): 370–382. DOI: 10.1037/pas0000488. Epub 2017 Apr 20. PMID: 28425726.

Stoller, R. (1991). A different view of Oedipal conflict. In: S. Greenspan & G. Pollock (Eds.), *The Course of Life, Volume III: Middle and Late Childhood* (pp. 95–114). New York: International Universities Press.

Stortelder, F. & Ploegmakers-Burg, M. (2022). Adolescence and the reorganization of infant development: A neuro-psychoanalytic model. *Journal of the American Academy of Psychoanalysis* 38: 503–531.

Sugarman, A. & Kannur, K. (2000). The contribution of psychoanalytic theory to psychological testing. *Psychoanalytic Psychology* 17: 3023.

Syeda, M. & Climie, E. (2014). Test review: *Wechsler Preschool and Primary Scale of Intelligence–Fourth Edition. Journal of Psychoeducational Assessment* 32: 265–272.

Target, M. & Fonagy, P. (1996). Playing with reality II: The development of psychic reality from a theoretical perspective. *International Journal of Psychoanalysis* 77: 459–479.

Target, M. & Fonagy, P. (1998). Mentalization and changing aims of child psychoanalysis. *Psychoanalytic Dialogues* 8: 87–114.

Tausk, V. (1924). A Contribution to the psychology of child-sexuality. *International Journal of Psychoanalysis* 5: 343–357

The Team at Elemy. (2022). Is autism being overdiagnosed? (The Status in 2022). https://elemy.com/studio/autism-diagnosis/is-it-overdiagnosed/

Thomas, A. & Chess, S. (1977). *Temperament and Development.* New York: Brunner/Mazel.

Toth, S., Rogosch, F., Sturge-Apple, M., & Cicchetti, D. (2009). Maternal depression, children's attachment security, and representational development: An organizational perspective. *Child Development* 80: 192–208.

Trad, P. (1990). On becoming a mother: In the throes of developmental transformations. *Psychoanalytic Psychology* 7: 341–361.

Tuber, S. (2004). Projective testing as a heuristic "snapshot" of themes in child and adult psychoanalysis: The case of Lisa. *Journal of Infant, Child & Adolescent Psychotherapy* 3: 486–508.

Tyson, P. (1990). The adolescent process and adult treatment. In: *Child and Adolescent Analysis: Its Significance for Clinical Work with Adults* (Chapter 7). Classic Books, 75: 95–105.

Tyson, P. & Tyson, R. (1990). *Psychoanalytic Theories of Development: An Integration.* New Haven, CT: Yale University Press.

Volkan, V. (2009). Consequences of societal trauma. In: P. Gobodo-Madikizela & C. van der Merwe (Eds.), *Memory, Narrative, and Forgiveness: Perspectives of the Unfinished Journeys of the Past* (pp. 1–26). Cambridge, UK: Cambridge Scholars Publishing.

Volkan, V. (2014). *Large-Group Identity, Shared Prejudice, Chosen Glories, and Chosen Traumas.* New York: Routledge.

Volkan, V. (2018). *Would-Be Wife-Killer: A Clinical Study of Primitive Mental Functions, Actualized Unconscious Fantasies, Satellite States, and Developmental Steps.* New York: Routledge.

Volkan, K. & Volkan, V. (2022). *Schizophrenia: Science, Psychoanalysis, and Culture.* London: Phoenix.

Waelder, R. (2007). The principle of multiple function: Observations on overdetermination. *Psychoanalytic Quarterly* 76(1): 75–92.

Wallace, B. (2016). The conference morning keynote address of Dr. Laurence Steinberg on the age of opportunity and lessons from the new science of adolescence: With introductory and closing commentary. *Journal of Infant, Child, and Adolescent Psychotherapy* 15(3): 155–170.

Waranch, S. (2022). Personal communication.

Waters, E., Merrick, S., Treboux, D., Crowell, J., & Albers-Heim, L. (2000). Attachment security in infancy and early adulthood: A twenty-year longitudinal study. *Child Development* 71: 684–689.

Wechsler, D. (2008). *Wechsler Adult Intelligence Scale–44th Edition.* San Antonio, TX: Psychological Corporation.

Wechsler, D. (2012). *Wechsler Preschool and Primary Scale of Intelligence–Fourth Edition.* San Antonio, TX: The Psychological Corporation.

Wechsler, D. (2014). *Wechsler Intelligence Scale for Children–Fifth Edition.* Bloomington, MN: The Psychological Corporation.

Wedge, M. (2020). The Politics of ADHD: There Are Two Opposing Schools of Thought regarding ADHD. https://www.psychologytoday.com/us/blog/suffer-the-children/202003/the-politics-adhd

Westen, D., Shedler, J., Durrett, C., Glass, S., & Martens, A. (2003). Personality diagnoses in adolescence: DSM-IV Axis II diagnosis and an empirically derived alternative. *American Journal of Psychiatry* 160: 952–966.

Wieder, S., Jasnow, M., Greenspan, S. I., & Strauss, M. (1987). Antecedent psychosocial factors in mothers in multirisk families: Life histories of the 47 participants in the Clinical Infant Development Program. In S. Greenspan, S. Wieder, R. Nover, A. Lieberman, R. Lourie, & M. Robinson (Eds.), *Infants in Multirisk Families: Case Studies in Preventive Intervention.* Madison, CT: International Universities Press.

Wiener, J. & Schellinski, K. (2020). Individuation for adult replacement children: Ways of coming into being. *Journal of Analytical Psychology* 65: 947–951.

Willoughby, T., Good, M., Adachik P., Hamza, C., & Tavernier, R. (2014). Examining the link between adolescent brain development and risk taking from a social-developmental perspective. *Brain and Cognition* 89: 70–78.

Winnicott, D. (1953). Transitional objects and transitional phenomena. *International Journal of Psychoanalysis* 34: 89–97.

Winnicott, D. (1969). The use of an object. *International Journal of Psychoanalysis* 50: 711–716.

Winnicott, D. (1975). Through paediatrics to psycho-analysis. *International Journal of Psycho-Analysis* 100: 1–325.

Wolfe, T. (2004). *I am Charlotte Simmons: A Novel*. New York: Farrar, Straus, and Giroux.

Wrobel, T., Lachar, D., Wrobel, N., Morgan, S., & Gruber, C. (2000). Performance of the *Personality Inventory for Youth* validity scales. *Assessment* 6: 367–380.

Ysseldyke, J. (2005). Assessment and decision making for students with learning disabilities: What if this is as good as it gets? *Learning Disability Quarterly* 28: 125–128.

Zeanah, C. (1989). Adaptation following perinatal loss: A critical review. *Journal of the American Academy of Child and Adolescent Psychiatry* 28(4): 467–480.

Zeanah, C. & Zeanah, P. (2019). Infant mental health: The clinical science of early experience. In: C. Zeanah (Ed.), *Handbook of Infant Mental Health, Fourth Edition*. New York: Guilford Press.

Zero to Three. (1994). *Diagnostic Classification of Mental Health and Developmental Disorders of Infancy and Early Childhood*. Washington, DC: National Center for Clinical Infant Programs.

Zero to Three. (2005). *Diagnostic Classification of Mental Health and Developmental Disorders of Infancy and Early Childhood* (Review Edition). Washington, DC: National Center for Clinical Infant Programs.

Zero to Three. (2016). *DC: 0-5. Diagnostic Classification of Mental Health and Developmental Disorders of Infancy and Early Childhood*. Washington, DC: National Center for Clinical Infant Programs.

Index

Pages in **bold** refer tables and pages in *italics* refer figures.

For Product Safety Concerns and Information please contact our EU
representative GPSR@taylorandfrancis.com
Taylor & Francis Verlag GmbH, Kaufingerstraße 24, 80331 München, Germany